W9-AGV-814

Precision Journalism

Precision Journalism

A Reporter's Introduction to Social Science Methods

Fourth Edition

Philip Meyer

ROWMAN & LITTLEFIELD PUBLISHERS, INC.
Lanham • Boulder • New York • Oxford

To my grandchildren:

Rachel
Amanda
Jordan
Sophia
Chloe
Olivia
Isabelle

. . . and a future member to be named later.

ROWMAN & LITTLEFIELD PUBLISHERS, INC.

Published in the United States of America
by Rowman & Littlefield Publishers, Inc.
An Imprint of the Rowman & Littlefield Publishing Group
4720 Boston Way, Lanham, Maryland 20706
www.rowmanlittlefield.com

12 Hid's Copse Road, Cumnor Hill, Oxford OX2 9JJ, England

Copyright © 2002 by Philip Meyer

All rights reserved. No part of this publication may be reproduced, stored in a
retrieval system, or transmitted in any form or by any means, electronic, mechanical,
photocopying, recording, or otherwise, without the prior permission of the publisher.

British Library Cataloguing in Publication Information Available

Library of Congress Cataloging-in-Publication Data

Meyer, Philip.
  Precision journalism : a reporter's introduction to social science methods / Philip
Meyer.—4th ed.
    p. cm.
  Includes bibliographical refernces and index.
  ISBN 0-7425-1087-5 (alk. paper) — ISBN 0-7425-1088-3 (pbk. : alk. paper)
    1. Journalism. 2. Social sciences—Statistical methods. I. Title.

PN4775 .M48 2002
070.4'07'23—dc21   2001048802

Printed in the United States of America

∞™ The paper used in this publication meets the minimum requirements of
American National Standard for Information Sciences—Permanence of Paper
for Printed Library Materials, ANSI/NISO Z39.48-1992.

Contents

Preface

Precision journalism is an idea that has been honored more for its applications than for its theory, but, as the publication of this volume demonstrates, neither my new publisher nor I see any reason to stop beating this drum.

When the original edition was issued by Indiana University Press in 1973, the aspect that first impressed its intended audience of journalists was the use of computers. I had been profiled five years earlier in *Newsweek* as a "computer reporter," and since computers were still expensive and mostly hard to use, their adoption by a mere newsperson was a definite novelty.

In the next phase, many newspapers and broadcasters became interested in taking control of public opinion measurement away from politicians and commercial interests. They found *Precision Journalism* a useful how-to book, and so, for them, the concept meant survey research.

But it was never intended to be just about polls or computers, although both are useful tools for many people, including journalists. My intent then, as it is now, was to encourage my colleagues in journalism to apply the principles of scientific method to their tasks of gathering and presenting the news. The idea seemed especially viable when one of my Nieman Fellowship mentors, Professor Thomas Pettigrew, first put me in touch with the Russell Sage Foundation in 1968. The social sciences were enjoying a burst of development as computers made heavy-duty quantification cheaper and easier. It seemed revolutionary at the time. Passing the benefits of this revolution on to those of us who were charged with discovering and imparting the truth on a daily basis was obviously a good idea. So Lee Hills of the Knight Newspapers and Ben Maidenburg, the editor of the *Akron Beacon Journal,* approved my leave, and the Foundation supported me for that purpose.

Now, in the new century, confidence in social science, especially its quantitative side, has ebbed—not just because of the postmodernists who question the existence of universal truth, but also, I believe, because the methods were oversold back when the computer applications were fresh. A backlash of skepticism resulted. But for journalists, these methods still beat the educated guesses, thumb-sucking, and haphazard data collection of the past. Scientific method is still the one good way invented by humankind to cope with its prejudices, wishful thinking, and perceptual blinders. And it is definitely needed in journalism—now more than ever, as the craft struggles to maintain its identity against corruption by entertainment and advertising.

This edition moves the rigor up a notch by suggesting ways to use the power of continuous measurement to tease out the lurking variables in chains of causation. And it restores, at the suggestion of some of my students, the chapter on game theory that was eliminated after the first edition.

So thanks go to my editor Brenda Hadenfeldt, whose encouragement pumped new life into this project; those of my students, especially J. J. Thompson and Shawn McIntosh, who wasted no time in demonstrating that these skills are marketable; and to my colleagues in journalism education. Thanks to Barbara Ellis for giving me her heavily annotated copy to use as a source for revision ideas; to John Bare, Kathy Frankovic, Brant Houston, and Paul Overberg for helping me stay in touch with current practices, and, most important, to Sue Quail Meyer for forty-five years of unwavering support.

1

✦

The Journalism We Need

If you are a journalist or are thinking of becoming one, you may have already noticed this: They are raising the ante on what it takes to be a journalist.

There was a time when all you needed was dedication to truth, plenty of energy, and some talent for writing. You still need those things, but they are no longer sufficient. The world has become so complicated, the growth of available information so explosive, that the journalist needs to be a filter, as well as a transmitter; an organizer and interpreter, as well as one who gathers and delivers facts. In addition to knowing how to get information into print, online, or on the air, he or she also must know how to get it into the receiver's head. In short, a journalist has to be a database manager, a data processor, and a data analyst.

It takes special training. In the good old days, there was serious doubt in professional circles about whether journalism, as a discipline, included any body of knowledge at all. Journalism, in this view, was all procedure, not substance.[1] When James Bryant Conant had to deal with a windfall bequest to Harvard to "improve the standards of journalism," he chose substantive training for midcareer journalists. "Mr. Conant felt that there was not a sufficient knowledge base to justify a journalism school . . . this conclusion led to a remarkably successful program which we have no desire to alter," Harvard president Derek Bok recalled fifty years later.[2]

In a simpler world, journalism programs that ignored journalism might have been justified. In the information society, the needs are more complex. Read any of the popular journals of media criticism and you will find the same complaints about modern journalism. It misses important stories, is

1

too dependent on press releases, is easily manipulated by politicians and special interests, and does not communicate what it does know in an effective manner. All of these complaints are justified. Their cause is not so much a lack of energy, talent, or dedication to truth, as the critics sometimes imply, but a simple lag in the application of information science—a body of knowledge—to the daunting problems of reporting the news in a time of information overload.

Harvard's Nieman program, which gives selected midcareer journalists an academic year to repair whatever educational gaps they perceive, is used by some to broaden their scope as generalists. But the most effective way of using it to adapt to the new demands is to become more specialized. In a world where the amount of information is doubling every five years,[3] it takes a specialist to understand, let alone communicate, very much of it. A good journalist today must still know a little bit about a lot of things, but he or she should also know one subject well.

Today's journalist must also be familiar with the growing journalistic body of knowledge, which, therefore, must include these elements:

1. How to find information.
2. How to evaluate and analyze it.
3. How to communicate it in a way that will pierce the babble of information overload and reach the people who need and want it.
4. How to determine, and then obtain, the amount of precision needed for a particular story.[4]

To the extent that journalists learn how to do these things, they are meeting one of the elements of a profession: access to an esoteric body of knowledge. We are learning, and journalism is becoming more professionalized, but as with any sweeping change, it is proceeding unsteadily and at different rates in different places.

WHERE CRAFT MEETS THEORY

In journalism schools, the concept of precision journalism—the application of social and behavioral science research methods to the practice of journalism—found a ready market. The ready acceptance of this concept in academe was due in part to its contribution to the healing of the breach between the green eyeshade and the chi-square factions. It demonstrated the applicability of social science research methods to the very real problems of newsgathering in an increasingly complex society. It produced work that both the researchers and the craft people could appreciate. The tools of sampling, computer analysis, and statistical inference increased the traditional power of the reporter without changing the nature of his or her mission—to find the facts, to understand them, and to explain them without wasting time.

In the profession, however, the barriers were greater. Precision journalism threatened the twin traditions of journalistic passivity and journalistic innocence. The former tradition holds that media should report news, not make news. Media involvement in public opinion polling has been criticized on the ground that the media should not do polls but should wait passively until other people do them and then report on them.[5] Media polls also violate the innocence rule. A reporter should be a person who casts a fresh eye on everything, something that he or she cannot do if burdened by too much specialized knowledge. Vermont Royster, a fine journalist of the old school, told the 1967 class of Nieman Fellows that a good reporter should strive to be "a professional amateur." The extreme case is a foreign correspondent I once knew who laughed when I asked him if he was learning the language of the country to which he was assigned. In his view it was not necessary, might even be a hindrance. His readers did not know the language, and his job was merely to observe what they would observe if they were there and to report on what he saw. If he learned a foreign language, he might start to think like a foreigner and lose touch with those readers.

The trouble with being a passive and innocent journalist is that like any passive and innocent person, one can be too easily taken advantage of. The underlying theme in most modern criticism of journalism is that the media are too easily dominated by powerful politicians and their skillful spin doctors, whose desires too easily determine what is defined as news and what is not. To defend against being manipulated, the media need more self-confidence, and the best route to self-confidence is through knowledge. Media polls began to proliferate in the 1980s precisely because the editors no longer trusted the polls that politicians tried to give them and armed themselves with their own data-collection operations out of self-defense. Thus polling became not so much a way to make news as an enhanced tool of the newsgathering process itself—provided, of course, that journalists are in charge of the entire process, from conception, through research design, to analysis and interpretation. The precision journalist does not hire a pollster to create a news event; the journalist becomes the pollster. Jim Norman of *USA Today,* Rich Morin of the *Washington Post,* and Warren Mitofsky of CBS were among the prototypes.

BEYOND OBJECTIVITY

The model of the journalist as passive innocent had at least one virtue: It provided a kind of discipline. It was consistent with the tradition of objectivity, a tradition that keeps the journalist from imposing personal viewpoints on the readers. But the objectivity model was designed for a simpler world, one where unadorned facts can speak for themselves. Frustration over the unmet ideal of objectivity led some of the media in the 1960s to embrace something called the "new journalism," which freed journalists from the constraints of objectivity by granting them artistic license to become storytellers. Jimmy Breslin and Tom Wolfe were among the first successful practitioners, and their methods worked until these reached a point where they stopped being journalism. The literary tools of fiction, including exquisite detail, interior monologue (what a newsworthy person is thinking, as well as his or her overt behavior), and short-story structure, with a character, a problem, and a resolution in a short span of words, can yield journalistic products that are a joy to read. Unfortunately, the data-collection process is extremely difficult. To make life appear to be like a short story, one has to be extremely selective, and that requires gathering a very large number of facts from which to select. The constraints of daily journalism will not support that level of effort day after day. Some practitioners of the "new journalism" took to making up their facts in order to keep up with the deadline pressures. Others stopped short of making things up, but combined facts from different cases to write composite portrayals of reality that they passed off as real cases.[6]

Despite the problems, the new nonfiction remains an interesting effort at coping with information complexity and finding a way to communicate essential truth. It pushes journalism toward art. Its problem is that journalism requires discipline, and the discipline of art may not be the most appropriate kind. A better solution is to push journalism toward science, incorporating both the powerful data-gathering and -analysis tools of science and its disciplined search for verifiable truth.

This is not a new idea. Walter Lippmann noted seventy years ago that journalism depends on the availability of objectifiable fact. "The more points, then, at which any happening can be fixed, objectified, measured, named, the more points there are at which news can occur."[7] Scientific method offers a way to make happenings objectified, measured, and named.

JOURNALISM AS SCIENCE

You might think that scientists would object to such an effort as an absurd pretension on the part of journalists. Not so. The first publication of *Precision Journalism* in 1973 was made possible by the Russell Sage Foundation at a time when it was devoted to the support of the social sciences. In 1989, physicist Lawrence Cranberg argued that "journalism itself is a science, and . . . a properly qualified, responsible journalist is a practicing scientist."

Both scientists and journalists, he said, "march to the same orders and serve the common need of mankind for shared knowledge and understanding."[8]

If journalists would only admit that shared responsibility, Cranberg said, it would clear the way for better training in investigative methods, less tolerance for superstition (astrology was a dead issue until newspapers revived it after World War I), and a commitment to a more rational and peaceful social order. Journalists are so steeped in the ideal of objectivity and open-mindedness that any kind of statement of social goals is likely to make us uneasy, even when the goals are as benign as reducing superstition and building a more rational society. But the plea for more powerful tools of investigation appeals to us. Fact-finding ability is, after all, the source of what power we possess.

Yet another benefit of a scientific approach to journalism, not mentioned by Cranberg, ought to sit well with most of us. The information sciences are now sufficiently developed so that we can give some systematic attention to the forms of the messages we prepare and the best ways to compose and send them so that they will be received and understood. This body of knowledge enables us to find out how to get messages into the heads of the audience, not just into their hands. Courses in the processes and effects of mass communication had become standard in the better journalism schools by the 1960s. And by the 1980s, leaders in industry could see the need for getting down to such basics. James K. Batten, chief executive officer of Knight Ridder Inc., told the story of an otherwise promising young journalist who failed to get hired at the prestigious newspaper group after he disdainfully declared in the job interview that he wrote to please himself, not the readers.

"Over the years, we've all hired people like him—and made our newspapers less reader-centered in the process," Batten said. "The time has come to stop. And our allies in the colleges and universities who educate young journalists need to understand that truth—and send us people with an eagerness to reach out to readers."[9]

The new precision journalism is scientific journalism. (In France, the term "precision journalism" has been translated as *le journalisme scientifique*.) It means treating journalism as if it were a science, adopting scientific method, scientific objectivity, and scientific ideals to the entire process of mass communication. If that sounds absurdly pretentious, remember that science itself is restrained about its achievements and its possibilities and has its own sanctions against pretension. "There are always hidden facts, and truths are elusive in every domain of human inquiry," Cranberg the physicist wrote. "What is needed to discover hidden facts and arrive at elusive truths is a skilled determination to get at them, and that is a determination that is as appropriate to a properly trained journalist as to a properly trained physicist."

Starting in the 1970s, journalism began moving toward a more scientific stance along two separate paths. The increasing availability of computers made large bodies of data available to journalists in a way that was not possible before. And in the business office, the failure of newspaper circulation to keep up with the growth in number of households made publishers pay more systematic attention to the marketplace and the factors that motivated readers to spend time and money with the publishers' products. The notion that a newspaper is a product and that a reader is a rational creature who makes a choice about whether to pay the cost of using the product became respectable. And so market forces were pushing journalism as a whole, not just a few isolated players in the field, to a more scientific stance.

Progress always has its detractors and nonbelievers. As recently as 1989, at a summit conference of newspaper people bent on discovering the causes of readership loss, an editor of a metropolitan newspaper publicly denounced the main finding of two decades of readership surveys: that the most frequent reason for not reading the paper is lack of time. "I don't buy it," he said, arguing that if newspapers would just do a better job of providing their fundamental services, like getting the paper delivered on time, things would be better.[10] His was not an isolated view, and a lot of research reports have been written in the effort to explain what "no time to read" really means. Christine Urban, speaking to the American Newspaper Publishers Association in 1986, had the best answer. What the readers are telling us, she said, is "Watch my lips—I don't have the time to read the paper every day."[11] In the hustle and babble of the information age, the cost in time of extracting information from a journalist's report has to be one of the considerations in the preparation of that report. *USA Today's* contribution in the 1980s was that it showed how a newspaper could be positioned as a saver of time. It did this by editing and formatting the newspaper with such care and precision that it could meet the reader's need for surveillance—scanning the world for personal dangers and opportunities—with a minimum commitment of time. It delivered data that had been extensively—and expensively—processed.

WHAT TO DO WITH DATA

Knowing what to do with data is the essence of the new precision journalism. The problem may be thought of as having two phases: the input phase, where data are collected and analyzed, and the output phase, where the data are prepared for entry into the reader's mind. This book is mostly about the first phase, but the two are so intertwined that it will also deal to some degree with the output side.

The main goal of what follows will be to tell you how to do these things with data:

1. *Collect it.* Whether or not you ever try to emulate scientists in their data-collection methods, you can profit from knowing some of their tricks. It is always worth remembering, as Professor H. Douglas Price told me at Harvard in the spring of 1967, that "data do not come from the stork."
2. *Store it.* Old-time journalists stored data on stacks of paper on their desks, in corners of their offices, and, if they were really well organized, in clip-files. Computers are better.
3. *Retrieve it.* The tools of precision journalism can help you retrieve data that you collected and stored yourself, data that someone else stored with a user like you in mind, or data that someone else stored for reasons completely unrelated to your interest, perhaps with no earthly idea that a journalist or public user would ever retrieve it.
4. *Analyze it.* Journalistic analysis often consists of merely sorting to find and list the interesting deviance. But it can also involve searches for implied causation, for patterns that suggest that different phenomena vary together for interesting reasons, or even to evaluate the effectiveness of public policy.
5. *Reduce it.* Data reduction has become as important a skill in journalism as data collection. A good news story is defined by what it leaves out, as well as by what it includes.
6. *Communicate it.* A report unread or not understood is a report wasted. You can make a philosophical case that like the sound of a tree falling in the forest, it does not exist at all.

THEORETICAL MODELS

On a spring morning, running along a misty Chapel Hill street, I topped a low hill and saw in the distance a crouched yellow figure about 18 inches high. It appeared tense, ready to spring, fangs bared, aiming for a point along my path ahead. As I got closer and my eyes were able to resolve the figure more clearly, I saw it for what it really was: an ordinary fireplug. The image of the dog had been the creation of my own brain, imposing an order and a pattern of its own on the ambiguous data relayed by my eyes.

Raw data alone can never be enough. To be useful, to be understood, data have to be processed, abstracted, fit into some kind of structure. You have to put the material into a mental framework that aids in interpretation and understanding. This truism applies equally to the data of everyday perception and to strings of numbers in computers. To think about them at all, you need a perceptual framework. If you don't provide one consciously, then your unconscious mind, perhaps driven by anxiety like that of a jogger in a neighborhood of dog owners, may provide the wrong one for you.

Different writers in different fields have given different names to these perceptual structures. Psychologists sometimes call them "schema." They are also known as constructs, hypotheses, expectations, organizing principles, frames, scripts, plans, prototypes, or even (this one from psychology) "implicational molecules."[12] Walter Lippmann called them "stereotypes."[13] In general, he said, "the way we see things is a combination of what is there and what we expected to find. The heavens are not the same to an astronomer as to a pair of lovers . . . the Tahitian belle is a better looking person to her Tahitian suitor than to the readers of the *National Geographic Magazine*."[14] And whether you see a dog or a fireplug depends on what you expect to see.

In its most sophisticated and conscious form, the schema, construct, or stereotype becomes a theoretical model. A formal model describes the essential parts of a process, natural or man-made, in a way that allows conclusions drawn from the model to be tested by experiment, by observation, or both. But in most cases, our use of models or constructs is not that sophisticated and not that careful. We use them simply because we need them to think at all. The data of everyday life, left unfitted to any model, take too much effort to process and interpret in the raw. Our senses take in too much of them.

TESTING THE MODEL

The problem with theoretical models—both the everyday kind and the formal ones of science—is that we tend to get stuck with them. Two national studies of newspaper credibility published in 1985 and 1986 offer an example. One study (we'll call it Study Y for now) showed that 53 percent of the public believed that news organizations favor one side when presenting news dealing with political and social issues, while only 34 percent thought the media are fair to all sides. And by 73 to 21 percent, most thought news organizations often invade people's privacy.

The other study (Study X) asked about the same issues with a five-point scale, and it showed that by 52 to 10 percent, more people called newspapers fair than unfair. And the public was about evenly split on the privacy issue: 32 percent thought newspapers invade privacy and 30 percent thought they respected privacy. The two studies were conducted only six months apart, between December 1984 and May 1985.

As you might expect, one was presented as a "good news" study full of optimism about public attitudes toward the media. The other resulted in a report full of gloom and foreboding. Now here's the surprise: the sunny report was written by the people who produced Study Y, the one with the unfavorable attitudes cited previously. And the gloomy report was based on the numbers in Study X, the one that found that most people trust newspapers.

Did the wires in the computer get crossed? No. The two research groups were working from different schema. Study X was sponsored by the credibility committee of the American Society of Newspaper Editors. Its chairman, David Lawrence, wanted to use the study as shock therapy to awaken editors to a problem and stir them to action.[15] Study Y was sponsored by Times Mirror, which wanted some corporate visibility and a chance to make some news. Publishing findings "which run counter to the conventional wisdom" is a good way to do that.[16]

Both groups of researchers meant to tell the truth, but whether they saw a dog or a fireplug depended on the schema with which they approached the inquiry. To the journalist trained in objectivity, it may seem that the problem was in starting with any structural framework at all. The journalistic ideal is to be open-minded, to enter an investigation with a clean slate, free of any prejudgment. Having a hypothesis seems a lot like being prejudiced. That view, while well-intentioned, is not practical. You can't begin to think about a problem without some kind of theoretical framework. And you will have one, whether you are conscious of it or not. The process of hypothesis formulation in scientific method forces the framework to the conscious level, where it can be coldly and objectively evaluated.

Now it is true that there is some danger that the evaluation will not be cold and objective enough. The two newspaper studies cited previously are a good illustration. The cure for that problem is not to abandon the process of hypothesis-making but to state your hypothesis and evaluate it in full public view so that other investigators can check on your work. Both the Times Mirror and the ASNE researchers did just that. No long-term harm was done, because both left a paper trail that described their methods, their findings, and the route to their conclusions. Even better, they made their data available for secondary analysis by other scholars. Their publications stimulated much analysis and discussion about the next step in understanding the peculiar relationship between a news medium and its readers, listeners, or viewers. One of the characteristics of science is that it is always subject to such checking and rechecking. That is one of the lessons from the case of the two credibility studies. The other is that it is extremely important to give careful thought to the theoretical structure with which one approaches a problem and to appreciate the consequences of the choice of a schematic model.

REALITY TESTING

Once you choose a model, you may be stuck with it for a long time. A model that works well enough for the purpose at hand soon becomes comfortable, like an old shoe, and is given up reluctantly. Inappropriate models, clung to after their usefulness is gone, are the source of superstition, conventional wisdom, and closed minds. Herbert Butterfield, the historian of modern science, has argued that the development of new models was more important in the creation of modern physics than in the collection of new data. A successful scientist needs "the art of handling the same bundle of data as before, but placing them in a new system of relations with one another by giving them a different framework, all of which virtually means putting on a different kind of thinking-cap for the moment."[17] Modern scientific method provides an incentive to put on that different thinking cap by prompting a continual testing of the old models and a perpetual search for better ones. Aristotle, whose model for the mechanics of motion held that a moving body continued on a given path only so long as something was pushing it, was wrong. And yet his model was the dominant one for centuries, partly because science was not yet conditioned to challenge and to experiment. (One problem encumbering Aristotle and his Greek contemporaries was the sharp distinction between philosophers and working people. To actually conduct an experiment would involve getting one's hands dirty. This disinclination to do more than think persisted even to the time of Galileo, who preferred "thought experiments" to the real thing.)

Modern scientific method provides for aggressive reality testing. Journalists are interested in testing reality, too. The main difference—beyond the obvious one that journalists are in more of a hurry—is that journalists are more passive about it. Instead of testing reality directly with their own observations, deductions, and experiments, they are normally content to do their cross-checking by consulting different authorities with different viewpoints and different interests. The flaw in this methodology is that the journalist may not have any good basis for evaluating the conflicting sources. Journalists' attempts to be objective actually force them into a relativist stance that demands the unlikely assumption that all voices have an equal claim to the truth. Journalists who adapt the tools of scientific method to their own trade can be in a position to make useful evaluations with the more powerful objectivity of science.

Journalists already share some of the characteristics of scientists, often without knowing it. Among them:

1. *Skepticism.* "If your mother says she loves you, check it out," is an aphorism from the culture of journalism, not science, but it fits both equally well. Neither journalists nor scientists are content to rest with what popular opinion or authority claims is true. Truth is always tentative, always has room for sharpening and improvement.

2. *Openness.* The key word is "replicability." A good investigative reporter documents his or her search for truth, making a paper trail that other investigators can follow to reach the same conclusions.

3. *An instinct for operationalization.* To test a model, a scientist thinks about the processes that the model represents and where they lead. Then he or she looks for a place in the observable world where aspects of that process can be measured in a way that will confirm or refute the model. That process of finding the observable and testable piece is called *operationalization.* Both scientists and investigative journalists depend on it. The confirmation of a theory is its power to predict the results of an operational measurement.

4. *A sense of the tentativeness of truth.* In the ancient argument between absolutism and relativism, science is most comfortable with pragmatism. The test of an idea is whether it works. The truths that science discovers are welcomed when they improve our understanding or our technology, but with the recognition that they might be replaced by stronger truths in the future. This concept is not an easy one for journalists, whose quest for simplicity and certainty makes absolutism appealing.

5. *Parsimony.* Given a choice between rival theories, we generally prefer the simpler one. The best theory explains the most with the least. The Copernican theory of the universe prevailed over the older system of Ptolemy because it was simpler. In order to account for the motion of the planets, Ptolemy proposed a system of "epicycles," in which each planet moved in orbits within orbits around the earth. As instrumentation got better, astronomers detected movements that the theory could not explain unless more epicycles within epicycles were postulated. Putting the sun at the center of the system eliminated the need for epicycles.

THE IMPORTANCE OF HUMILITY

It is ironic that journalistic defense of the First Amendment today is often argued from an absolutist position. The eighteenth-century political thought underlying the constitution of the United States, particularly the First Amendment, is based on a rejection of absolutism. In the dawn of the scientific era, the futility of compelling any particular belief was clear because new data or a new interpretation of old data were always arising to challenge the old beliefs. And so it made sense to be tolerant of unorthodox beliefs and to protect them under the basic law of the land. Today's heresy could be tomorrow's wisdom.

So a little bit of humility is good for everyone, but especially for scientists and journalists. Justice Oliver Wendell Holmes noted that what we think of as truths might better be called "can't helps":

> When I say that a thing is true, I mean that I cannot help believing it. . . . But
> . . . I do not venture to assume that my inabilities in the way of thought are

inabilities of the universe. I therefore define truth as the system of my limitations, and leave absolute truth for those who are better equipped. . . . Certitude is not the test of certainty. We have been cock-sure of many things that
were not so.[18]

This unpretentiousness can give the scientist and the journalist a certain
freedom. You do not have to wait to verify that you have found certain, absolute, unassailable truth before sharing the finding. If you have made a mistake and been open about the process that led you to it, someone else will
discover it and publish, and the cause of truth will have been advanced another notch. Democratic pluralism, which lets truth emerge from the com-
bat of many voices, is a good environment for both scientist and journalist.

One of the advantages of adopting a theoretical model for journalistic use
is that it keeps you and your readers focused on the relevant. Much information in public affairs is arcane and complicated. The journalist who becomes an expert in the field being covered can quickly lose the way in irrelevant detail.

My first major investigative story as a newspaper reporter was about
wasteful purchasing of fire and windstorm insurance on school buildings in
Dade County, Florida. Under the plan then in effect, the insurance program
was controlled by an agent whose compensation was a share of the commissions. The more insurance cost, the more money he made. Debates at
school board meetings on the subject were obscure in their detail and impossible to follow. In frustration, the superintendent of schools asked his
board for a $10,000 study to resolve the technical complexities. The request
was tabled and eventually died.

What was needed to understand the situation was a theoretical model
that could be operationalized. Mine was a basic logrolling or mutual back-
scratching model. It led to the following hypotheses:

1. The insurance servicing agent's self-dealing would make insurance
   more costly than for similar bodies without such a conflict of interest.
2. If the board goes along with this cost, its members must be receiving
   something of value: for example, the power to reward their friends in
   the insurance business.
3. If they are rewarding their friends, board members must get something from those friends in return.

Each of those propositions is simple. You don't need a detailed understanding of the insurance business or its regulation to grasp any of them.
And each could be operationalized.

The first proposition was tested by comparing property insurance costs of
the Dade County schools with those of the Metropolitan Government of

Dade County, a separate political unit with the same geographic definition. The Metropolitan Government costs, per dollar of building value, were a third those of the Dade County Schools. Moreover, the loss ratio for school insurance was quite low by industry standards. Over the long history of the program, only 15 percent of the premium money had gone back to the school system in claims.

Direct questioning of the school board members and the benefiting insurance agents verified that the system had the earmarks of political patronage. To keep the other insurance agents in the community happy with the system, the school system's servicing agent shared a portion of his commissions with them. School board members decided how this sharing would be allocated. Now all that was needed was to close the logical loop by showing what the board members got in return.

Florida pioneered in election reporting laws, and each member's campaign contributions were on file at the courthouse. Each entry showed a donor's name, the candidate's name, and a dollar amount. Confirmation of the third hypothesis required a link between the donors and the insurance business. There were 181 agencies participating in the school insurance program. From an industry directory I got the names of their officers and made a card index, one name per card, and alphabetized it. Then I checked each name on the campaign contributor lists against the card index. Bingo! Insurance people were important contributors to all five of the school board members who had run in the previous election. The chairman of the board received 65 percent of his total contributions from insurance people. Two others got more than half from the same sources. The resulting three-part series led the local page.[19] The school board quickly reformed the system and eventually gave teachers a raise with the money that was saved.

A reporter working on such a story today would, of course, use a computer instead of index cards to check out the names. But the mechanics are less important than the concept. A model that points you to the relevant facts and suggests an operationalization is far more important in increasing your power as a reporter than the machine that does the clerical part. The machines do make things possible that could not be done before, but to get the most out of them, we need to think the way that scientists think, building the models that enable us to use the new computing power.

Journalists tend to be practical people, and as such we are sometimes too quick to scorn those who deal in what seems to us to be empty theory lacking in any real-world application. But without theory, we have nothing but unordered raw data, and we suffocate in it. The computer can alphabetize it for us, it can give us lists ordered by any dimension found in the data, but we still have to have a theory to give the list a point.

SOURCES OF THEORIES

Where do theories come from? The range of sources is broad, from folklore
to the products of the most creative and sophisticated minds in science. A
good theory is one that has consequences that can be tested and used as
building blocks for more discoveries and more theories. Science is as dependent on openness as journalism is. Michael Polyani, a chemist who
worked at the dawn of the nuclear age, compared the scientific process to
a group of workers assembling a giant jigsaw puzzle. A group can't do it efficiently unless each member knows what the other members are doing.
"Let them work on putting the puzzle together in the sight of the others, so
that every time a piece of it is fitted in by one, all the others will immediately watch out for the next step that becomes possible in consequence," he
said.[20] The methodology of journalists covering public affairs is exactly the
same, even if the process is less self-conscious. Reporters, like scientists,
are in the business of reality testing, examining the existing theories, thinking through their consequences, developing related hypotheses that can be
operationalized (i.e., tested), and putting them to the test.

THE CASE OF THE DETROIT RIOT

Periods of social upheaval offer especially good opportunities for testing theories. When the race riots of the 1960s began, first in the Watts area of Los Angeles, then in Newark and Detroit, there were several popular theories to explain the cause. One theory, popular with editorial writers, was that the rioters
were the most frustrated and hopeless cases at the bottom of the economic ladder, who rioted because they had no other means of advancement or expression. This theory can be tested with survey research. If you can identify the rioters and compare them with the nonrioters, you will find, if the theory is true,
that the less-educated are more likely to be riot participants. The *Detroit Free
Press* did perform such a survey in 1967 and found that people who had at-
tended college were just as likely to participate in the riot as those who had
failed to finish high school. The theory was not supported by the data.[21]

	Education		
	Dropouts	*High School*	*College*
Rioters (%)	18	15	18
Nonrioters (%)	82	85	82
Total	100	100	100

Another popular theory of the time was that the root cause of the riots
was the difficulty that southern blacks had in being assimilated into north-

ern culture. Forced by southern repression and the effects of slavery into a passive role, they found an outlet for long-suppressed aggression once they left the South. This theory, too, is easily operationalized. If true, rioting should be a more frequent behavior for immigrants from the South than for those blacks raised in the North. The *Free Press* survey produced a different result. Another theory subjected to reality testing and found wanting!

Where Were You Brought Up as a Child?

	South	North
Rioters (%)	8	25
Nonrioters (%)	92	75
Total	100	100

Another opportunity came after the assassination of Martin Luther King in 1968. The immediately popular theory was that his nonviolent movement died with him and that blacks would turn for leadership to the advocates of violence. The *Miami Herald,* which had done an attitude survey among its black population before the assassination, went back to the same respondents and found that King's ideals were stronger than ever.[22]

Sometimes you can get theories just by walking around. When Fred Sherman, the former columnist for the *Miami Herald,* looked around after Hurricane Andrew hit Miami in 1992, he noticed that older houses fared better than newer ones in the same neighborhood. He had been the real estate editor when the Dade County Commission adopted the South Florida Building Code of 1957 to protect houses from 120 mile-per-hour winds. But over the years, the Board of Rules and Appeals, under pressure from developers, gradually weakened the code by allowing cheaper materials. Inspections had also become lax.

An expert's impression from walking around can be enough for a pretty good story. But Stephen K. Doig, a reporter fluent in SAS, turned it into a great story by subjecting the theory of corrupt building codes to a rigorous quantified test. Doig arrived at the theory by a route that was more direct than Sherman's: He noticed that Andrew had removed half the roof from his relatively new home. Doig's verification involved the merging of four databases: the reports of 50,000 storm-damage inspections done by the county; the 1992 property tax roll, with detailed information about housing type, value, and year of construction; the county's Building Master File, with information about the type of construction and materials used for each building; and the county's Building and Zoning database, with more than 7 million records on building permits and inspections in previous years.

The *Herald* published a map and chart listing 420 subdivisions, comparing the percentage of homes judged uninhabitable and the average year of construction. A summary graph controlled for wind speed and showed, for example, that in the areas of milder winds, 85 to 127 miles per hour, houses built after 1979 were more than three times as likely to be rendered uninhabitable as those built earlier.[23]

Readers love maps because they can find themselves in them. And the statistical tables made the building-code corruption theory virtually impossible to refute, although the reporters did not, of course, stop there. With good old shoe-leather reporting they found more direct evidence, including inspectors logging more reports on a single day than they could reasonably have accomplished.

The lesson for future precision journalists: generating piles of description is not enough. Just as storytellers need plots to hold their descriptions together, social scientists and precision journalists need theories to give their data its fullest meaning. There are times when we are so proud of the data spewing out of our computers that we'd like to just print it unaltered in the paper or online. But we can't! We have to have theoretical justification, and that is where the old style of narrative journalism and the new precision journalism come together.

NOTES

1. For example, Ron Lovell, *The Quill* (October 1987): 22–24: "There is no substantive body of knowledge for the field."

2. Derek Bok, personal communication, February 27, 1990.

3. "Soon it will be doubling every four." Richard Saul Wurman, *Information Anxiety* (New York: Doubleday, 1989), 32.

4. For help in putting this problem in historical perspective, see James Franklin, *The Science of Conjecture: Evidence and Probability before Pascal* (Baltimore, Md.: Johns Hopkins University Press, 2001).

5. See, for example, Nicholas Von Hoffman, "Public Opinion Polls: Newspapers Making Their Own News?" *Public Opinion Quarterly* 44, no. 4 (Winter 1980): 572.

6. For some examples, see the discussion of "the new nonfiction" in Philip Meyer, *Ethical Journalism: A Guide for Students, Practitioners, and Consumers* (New York: Longman, 1987).

7. Walter Lippmann, *Public Opinion* (New York: Free Press, Paperback Edition, 1965; first publication, 1922), 216.

8. Lawrence Cranberg, "Plea for Recognition of Scientific Character of Journalism," *Journalism Educator* (Winter 1989): 46–49.

9. James K. Batten, Press-Enterprise Lecture, Riverside, California. April 3, 1989. Miami, Fla.: Knight-Ridder, Inc.

10. Michael J. Davies, quoted in *Keys to Success: Strategies for Newspaper Marketing in the '90s* (Reston, Va.: American Newspaper Publishers Association, 1989), 5.

11. Christine D. Urban, "Reader Expectations—What They Think of Us," address to American Newspaper Publishers Association, San Francisco, Calif., April 1986.

12. Reid Hastie, "Schematic Principles in Human Memory," in N. Cantor and J. F. Kihlstrom, eds., *Personality, Cognition and Social Interactions* (Hillsdale, N.J.: Erlbaum, 1981), 39–40.

13. Lippman, *Public Opinion,* 53–68.

14. Lippman, *Public Opinion,* 76.

15. "Newspaper Credibility: Building Reader Trust" (Reston, Va.: American Society of Newspaper Editors, 1985).

16. "The People & the Press: A Times Mirror Investigation of Public Attitudes toward the News Media Conducted by the Gallup Organization" (Los Angeles: Times Mirror, 1986), 4.

17. Herbert Butterfield, *The Origins of Modern Science,* Revised Edition (New York: Free Press, Paperback Edition, 1965; first publication, 1957), 13.

18. Oliver Wendell Holmes. Quoted by Arthur Schlesinger, Jr., "The Opening of the American Mind," *New York Times Book Review,* July 23, 1959, 27.

19. "Freeloading Insurors Get Your $59,000," *Miami Herald,* September 27, 1959, 1B.

20. Quoted in Richard Rhodes, *The Making of the Atomic Bomb* (New York: Simon & Schuster, 1986), 34.

21. Philip Meyer, "The People beyond 12th Street: A Survey of Attitudes of Detroit Negroes after the Riot of 1967," *Detroit Free Press* reprint, 1967.

22. Philip Meyer, "The Aftermath of Martyrdom: Negro Militancy and the Death of Martin Luther King," *Public Opinion Quarterly* (Summer 1969).

23. "What Went Wrong," *The Miami Herald,* Special Report, December 20, 1992.

2

+

Using Numbers Rationally

Numbers are like fire. They can be used for good or for ill. When misused, they can create illusions of certitude and importance that render us irrational. As David Boyle has noted, some things are easier to quantify than others, and our attention is often drawn to those aspects of a problem that have numbers attached to them. The numbers make them seem more important than they sometimes are.[1] On the other hand, when well used, numbers can draw attention to the relevant conditions among all the noisy buzz and glare of the Information Age. In a world where not much is certain beyond death and taxes, we are sometimes tempted to give up on quantification, preferring instead to rely on intuition and story-telling. But the advantage of numbers, used properly, is that their strength can itself be quantified. Much of modern science is based on probability theory, not because we believe that God plays dice with the world (to borrow Einstein's famous phrase), but because it is a way of codifying and organizing our ignorance. And so anyone in the information business, whether as journalist or propagandist, must use and understand numbers in the business of counting, measuring, and evaluating the things that happen and the things we do. To the layman, as well as to the old-fashioned journalist, it sometimes seems unlikely that so slippery a thing as human behavior can be reduced to elements that will yield to counting and measuring. We are used to counting things that hold still.

To help you convince yourself that it can be done, this chapter takes a bold step. We are going to jump directly into one of the most esoteric and

---

In its original form, this chapter appeared as "Playing for the Upper Hand" in *Playboy* (April 1969), p. 111.

sophisticated uses of numbers yet invented: the theory of games and economic behavior. But we'll do it with everyday examples.

The first case study was supplied to me long ago by Daniel Ellsberg, several years before he made the cost-benefit calculation that led to his fame as the conduit for the Pentagon Papers. His action has been credited with helping turn public opinion against the war in Vietnam. The example I choose here is more trivial. In 1964, Ellsberg toiled obscurely for the Rand Corporation and lived in Beverly Hills, California. It was a year of a big brush fire. Ellsberg was there, watching the flames sweep north of Sunset Boulevard. He lived south of Sunset, and he and his neighbors, standing in front of their homes a half mile from the fire, were trying to decide what to do. All that was needed to send the fire in their direction was a shift in the wind. Would it shift? Should they evacuate and risk doing a lot of work for nothing? Or should they stay and risk having their possessions burned?

"Everyone was very reluctant to evacuate," recalled Ellsberg. "They stood there and kept saying it wouldn't come across Sunset, as though the street were some sort of firebreak. The talk had a spiritual premise, really. It was as though God was destroying the people north of Sunset, and it wouldn't be consistent to wipe out our side, too."

It was an interesting philosophical point. Ellsberg didn't waste time on it. First, he estimated the probability that wind would shift, based on his own knowledge of the fickleness of the weather in that location. Then he calculated the value of his goods and the cost of moving them various distances. It was a two-person game, with Ellsberg on one side and nature rolling the dice on the other, and his equation demonstrated that moving his household goods completely out of the danger zone would not be worth the trouble. However, it would be worthwhile to move them a short distance away. So he did.

The fire did not reach his house, and the work of moving turned out to be wasted. But Ellsberg went to sleep that night as he would have no matter which way the fire went, with the comforting knowledge that he had not made an *avoidable* mistake.

"A neighbor down the street made an even nicer calculation," Ellsberg recalled. "They had a bomb shelter in the back yard, and the governess told the butler to never mind the mink, just get the sable down."

Ellsberg's method in this case was to measure an expected cost against an expected return. The idea of mathematical expectancy is simple enough. When you bet at the race track in Florida, the state and the track take 15 percent off the top of all bets. In the parimutuel system, you are betting against all the other participants with the remaining 85 percent. If everyone bets at random or if all bettors are equally skilled, your expected return is 85 cents for each dollar you bet. In game theory, it simplifies matters to assume that an expected return is always equal in usefulness to a fixed return—as, indeed, it is in real life when you play the game often enough to even out the deviations. But it is important to keep in mind that there can be cases where the relevant expectancy cannot be expressed so straightforwardly. Suppose you have borrowed $1,000 from a loan shark and don't have the money to repay him. In fact, you are flat broke, and if you do not pay, he will, under the terms of the loan, break your leg. An eccentric student of human nature appears and offers you two choices: a 90 percent chance of winning $1,000 or a 50 percent chance of winning $3,000. If the numbers stand by themselves, the second choice is better: a mathematical expectancy of $1,500 versus an expectancy of $900. But with the loan shark about to call at any moment and no likelihood of your ever playing this game more than once, you'd clearly do better to take the first option. The relevant expectancy in this case is not the number of dollars you might gain but the chance of having a whole leg at the end of the day. (Unless, of course, you decide that an unbroken leg is worth less than the difference between $1,500 and $900—that is, $600. If you value your limbs that little, then you are justified in trying for the bigger money gain.)

Properly applied, mathematical expectancy is a handy concept in making decisions, even when the decisions must take into account the actions of other people. This was brought home to me quite clearly one winter day when the former Sue Quail and I were driving on U.S. 128 west of Boston, and we spotted a stranded motorist with his hood up and a red sign displaying the plea, SEND HELP.

"We'll stop at the next phone booth and call the highway patrol," I said.

"Never mind," said Sue. "Somebody else will stop."

"No," I replied. "Everyone will say somebody else will stop, and therefore no one will stop, and so we must stop."

"Don't be a nut," Sue said. "Everyone will say somebody else will stop, and therefore no one will stop, and so they will stop, and why should we? In fact, if we do stop, we will just add to the confusion. The highway patrol switchboard might even get jammed, and we, by contributing to the jamming, would delay the sending of help."

I am pretty good at mental gymnastics of this sort, and if I had counted on my fingers, I could have carried this argument through one more reversal without losing it. But I needed my hands to drive, and Sue did have a point. If everyone who had an impulse to call did call, it would be both wasteful and inefficient. We had an obligation here too, but it lay at some point on a continuum between calling and not calling—between zero calls and one call. How to calculate it? Easy.

A check of the visible traffic around us led to the estimate that 300 cars an hour had an opportunity to observe the stranded motorist. I am an optimist about human nature and figured that 80 percent of these drivers would feel some concern. They would follow the same reasoning we did, and about half would come out on the side of calling and half in favor of not calling.

Of those who still felt an obligation to call, half might find an excuse not to. This left a net expectancy of 60 calls.

Sixty calls is clearly an inefficient number to rescue one stranded motorist. That many calls could tie up the switchboard and keep the line busy so that other emergency calls might not get through. We would not want that on our consciences, any more than we would want the stranded motorist to go unattended. Six calls, instead of 60, would be better—enough to ensure that the message got through but not enough to cause unnecessary confusion. (I know that the danger of confusion is real. Once when I reported an accident on the highway, I had a long, frustrating conversation with the police dispatcher while we tried to decide whether the accident I had seen was a new one or the one to which he had already dispatched a patrol car.)

From society's viewpoint, the problem was one of reducing the 60 calls to 6. If there were perfect communication, the drivers passing by could count off by 50s, with every 50th driver stopping. Or the motorist could take his sign down and display it only to every 10th car passing by.

These solutions require more direction than is available in a free society. Each of the individual actors must make an independent calculation of his or her responsibility. What I needed was a way to carry out my exact share of society's obligation. My share was one-tenth of a phone call.

There is, of course, no such thing as one-tenth of a phone call. Phone calls are not divisible. But there can be such a thing as a mathematical expectancy of one-tenth of a phone call.

"No problem," I said to Sue. "When you say, 'Veritas,' I shall peek at the second hand of my watch. If it is between zero and six, we call. Otherwise, we don't."

"Veritas," she said.

It was 17 seconds after the minute. We did not call.

Later, I asked Thomas Schelling, who taught Harvard's undergraduate course in game theory in my Nieman year, whether we had acted properly.

"Exactly," he said, "given two requirements: that Sue wouldn't feel resentful if you did stop; and that you don't feel guilty because you didn't stop."

This requirement, as Schelling pointed out, is exactly what held up the idea of a Vietnam draft lottery for so long. Before the lottery, everyone who has a number in the fishbowl has an equal expectancy of military service. Nothing could be fairer. But after the drawing, those who are not drafted may feel guilty and those who are might be resentful. Both feelings, while understandable, represent a lack of appreciation for the beautiful, numerical fairness of the solution. It is a common failing. At faculty teas, when I tell the story of the stranded motorist, people insist on trying to make me feel guilty for not stopping and calling the highway patrol. They fail. I contributed my precise obligation to society on that occasion. Over a lifetime of equivalent incidents, I shall make, on the average, every tenth call.

Whether I call or not in any given case, whether the motorist is aided or not, I shall go to bed that night in the comfort of knowing that I did not make an avoidable mistake.

These cases show how to use chance to weigh gains and losses, and they approach the problem of taking into account the actions of other people. Now we shall introduce the most interesting element of game theory: conflict. Let us assume for the moment a case in which conflict is total: two adversaries whose interests are in complete opposition. One's gains are the other's losses. Because subtracting one's losses from the other's gains yields a sum of zero, this is called a *zero-sum game*.

Consider now the plight of a city council member who has positioned himself as a vocal opponent of gambling. His secret is that he likes to gamble himself and hates to pass up a chance to spend an evening at the dog track or a veteran's association bingo game, the only honest gambling institutions in town.

Here's the conflict: An investigative reporter has built a case of misappropriation of funds against the mayor, and the apparent motive is to support his gambling habit. The story is ready to run, but at the last minute, the editor asks the reporter to try to give it some sizzle by catching the mayor in the act of gambling. The reporter knows the mayor will go to the track if he thinks no one is watching. If he does expect to be watched, he'll go to the politically correct but boring bingo game instead. To which event should the reporter go? To decide, she assigns a numerical value to each of the possible outcomes, on a scale of 1 to 10. Then she constructs a game matrix.

		Reporter	
		Track	Bingo
Mayor	Track	4	10
	Bingo	0	8

The numbers in each cell represent payoffs to the mayor. The same numbers, to the reporter, represent losses. Observe their logic. The mayor gets his highest payoff, valued at 10, if he goes to the track unobserved because the reporter is looking for him at the bingo game. And he can bet as much of his ill-gotten gains as he wants.

The second-best combination occurs if the mayor goes to the veterans' bingo game, and the reporter does, too. There is political gain in being seen supporting the veterans. Score it 8. Should he and the reporter both go to the track, the evening will not be a total loss because he will at least be among friends even if he can't place a bet: 4 points. And the worst possibility of all, assigned the value of zero, is that he will have a dull time at bingo and have it wasted by not being observed by the media.

At this point you may wish to challenge the neatness by which complex attitudes have been assigned simple numbers. Later, I shall demonstrate that there are valid ways to order almost any set of preferences into exact numerical ranking. But for this example, all you need accept is the order of the priorities, and that is easy. For the hero of this problem, going to the track unobserved is clearly the best outcome and going to the veteran's game unobserved is the worst. And if he is observed, it is better to be observed with the veterans than at the track.

If you look at the table and reflect a bit, the solution becomes obvious. No matter what the reporter does, the mayor will score at least 4 and possibly as much as 10 if he goes to the track. From the reporter's point of view, the best strategy is equally clear: She loses the least if she goes to the track. Each chooses the option that will assure him or her of the least of the worst possible outcomes. Their two strategies converge at the dog track in the upper left-hand cell.

So the game has a natural outcome. The place where strategies converge like this is called a *saddle point*. According to Anatol Rapoport, the term is derived from the analogy with the point where the center of a saddle touches the horse's back. If you look at the horse from the side, it is the lowest point on his back. If you sit in the saddle and slide from side to side, it is the highest point. A game with a saddle point requires no further effort at solution, and there is a quick way to spot this condition. Look for a number that is both the lowest in its row and highest in its column. If no number meets these conditions, there is no saddle point. There will be no one strategy that will enable you to maximize your own security and seek the best available gain with a straightforward choice. And on that dismal note, matters might stand except for what we now know about using probability theory.

First we refresh ourselves on two simple rules of probability:

1. To find the probability that both of two separate independent events will occur, multiply their separate probabilities: The probability of flipping heads once is .50. The probability of doing it twice is .50 * .50 or .25.
2. To find the probability that either of two mutually exclusive events will occur, add their separate probabilities: The probability of getting heads or tails on one flip of the coin is .50 plus .50 = 1 or certainty.

Now for our next case study. This time, picture an affluent, lovesick undergraduate as the hero. On a double date, he has met an attractive history major who shares his passion for skiing. Unfortunately, she was the other guy's date. He calls the next day and invites her for a weekend of winter sport. She accepts, provided the trip is either to Snow Village, New Hampshire, or Aspen, Colorado, the only places she skis.

That is fine. But unfortunately her boyfriend finds out. The boyfriend is insecure about women, and so our hero is concerned, though not surprised, when he hears that his rival has resolved to track him down and create an unpleasant scene. Although the rival knows that they will be in Aspen or Snow Village, he will have time to search in only one place.

Assigning payoffs for the matrix is easy. The opponent wants to catch our college boy with his woman. The boy doesn't want to get caught. So he expresses each payoff in terms of the probability of not getting caught at each location. That takes some judgment, of course. He has been to Aspen and knows that it is big and tends to be crowded, and he'd have a 60 percent chance of getting lost in the crowd. Snow Village is more intimate. If he took the history major there and the rival also looked there, the chance of ducking him would be only 40 percent.

		Rival	
		Snow Village	Aspen
Hero	Snow Village	40	100
	Aspen	100	60

The numbers, remember, are payoffs to our hero. Two of the cells are worth 100 because his chance of success reaches certainty if he skis in one location while his rival is looking in the other.

First, he looks for a saddle point and notes that the game has none. No number is both smallest in its row and largest in its column. That being the case, the impulse may be to take the historian to Aspen, where the odds of not being found are the most favorable. But before deciding, he might have the same sort of conversation with himself that I had with Sue on Route 128:

First thought: Why don't I take her to Aspen? A 60 percent chance of not getting caught beats a 40 percent chance.

Second thought: Don't be simpleminded. He'll expect me to go to Aspen for that reason. Therefore, I should go to Snow Village.

Third thought: But he'll figure that I expect him to expect me to go to Aspen and that I would therefore go to Snow Village. So that's where he'd look, and so I should go to Aspen.

Fourth thought: No. He'll expect me to expect him to expect me to . . . arrrrgh.

There is a way out of all this. Ancient Chinese warriors used it to decide their routes of attack. If you don't want the enemy to figure out what you are thinking, don't think. Flip a coin. If you reach a decision through a random device, no one will be able to read your intentions because you won't know them yourself. Primitive hunters unconsciously followed the same principle when they cracked bones and studied patterns in the cracks to decide where to look for game. While they thought the gods were telling them what to do, the effect was to randomize their search so that the animals would never be able to sense a pattern and stay out of the way. A fleeing rabbit is another example. Its zigs and zags, leaps and bounds, are governed by unconscious nerve centers. The hunter can't solve the pattern and predict the right place to aim his rifle because the rabbit itself doesn't know which way it will jump.

So flipping a coin is one way to decide where to ski. But it's not quite the best way. If the skier is equally likely to be in Snow Village or Aspen, the prudent pursuer will look in Snow Village, where the hunting is easier. The trick is to mix the two strategies and mix them so that the pursuer has no such straightforward choice; mix them, in fact, so that it doesn't make any difference where he looks. You don't need to be a mathematical genius. Just take the difference between the two possible Snow Village payoffs and use that value as the weight assigned to the Aspen odds. And take the difference between the Aspen payoffs and make that number the weight for the Snow Village odds. Thus:

$$\begin{aligned} \text{Snow Village:} \quad & 100 - 60 = 40 \\ \text{Aspen:} \quad & 100 - 40 = \underline{60} \\ \text{Total of both weights} \quad & 100 \end{aligned}$$

That the total adds to the round sum of 100 in this case is merely a convenient coincidence. Different games will produce different totals. What the numbers mean is that our hero wants to arrange things so that he has 40 chances out of 100 of going to Snow Village and 60 chances out of 100 of going to Aspen. How? He can put 40 black marbles and 60 white marbles in a hat, close his eyes, and draw one. Or he can make it 4 black and 6 white and use a mason jar. He goes to Snow Village if he draws black and Aspen if he draws white.

Pause now, and appreciate the beauty of this way of mixing strategies. He has trimmed the chances of being caught with the history major from a nerve-wracking 40 percent—which would have been the result had he and the rival both done the obvious and gone to Aspen—to a more relaxing 24 percent. And the rival is limited to this 24 percent chance of finding the hero, no matter what he does:

1. Rival goes to Snow Village. Odds that hero will be there are 40 percent. Chance of being found if he is there is 60 percent. Forty percent of a 60 percent chance is a 24 percent chance.
2. Rival goes to Aspen. There is a 60 percent chance the hero will be there and a 40 percent chance he'll be caught if he is. Sixty percent of a 40 percent chance is a 24 percent chance. Indifference! Even if he is caught and has his eye blackened, he'll know he didn't make an avoidable mistake.

Now, suppose the rival knows these tricks, too? He can do this much: He can assure himself that no matter what the hero does, he will have at least a 24 percent chance, which, after all, is better than the zero he would get by guessing wrong. And he does it, of course, by getting a mason jar and putting in four black marbles and six white marbles . . .

If you have followed the chapter this far, you are to be congratulated because you now understand some of the basic logic behind game theory, as set forth in 1944 when John von Neumann and Oskar Morgenstern published their *Theory of Games and Economic Behavior.*[2] It has real-life applications. Economists use some of the techniques to aid decision making in the marketplace. Military planners use it. The City of New York applied some of the techniques to calculate the most efficient deployment of fire-fighting equipment.

When the late Edward G. Bennion was consulting economist for Standard Oil of New Jersey, he demonstrated how it could be used in making capital budgeting decisions. In Bennion's example, described in *Harvard Business Review,*[3] the businessman assumes that nature is his enemy. However, he does not assume a malevolent nature consciously trying to outwit him. That makes an important difference.

Bennion's illustration involves a company with some extra cash on hand and two alternatives for investment: plant expansion or securities. Nature also has two moves: The business cycle can move toward prosperity or toward recession. The numbers in the matrix assume that in recession, investment in the plant will yield 1 percent, while securities will yield 4 percent. In prosperity, the plant will yield 17 percent and securities will produce 5 percent.

		Company	
		Plant	Securities
Nature	Prosperity	17	5
	Recession	1	4

When nature is the enemy, we can ignore the saddle point, for we have the advantage of being able to calculate the probability of its various moves, based on past experience, just as Dan Ellsberg estimated the probability of the wind's shifting the fire toward his home. In this business case, the company economist figures there is a 60 percent chance of recession and a 40 percent chance of prosperity. How? "We are not concerned," says Bennion, "with what kind of crystal ball he gazes into, but rather with how top management uses his findings."

The unsophisticated manager might decide that since recession is more probable, he ought to put the company money in securities, thus assuring a minimum 4 percent return rather than 1 percent. But applying what we have already learned about mathematical expectancy, we can see that this move would be bad judgment. The expected return from investment in securities is 60 percent of 4 plus 40 percent of 5, or 4.4 percent. The expected

return from the plant is 60 percent of 1 plus 40 percent of 17, or 7.4 percent. (Probabilities are added because recession and prosperity are mutually exclusive—one will happen, but not both.)

Bennion suggests a nicer judgment. The company ought to calculate, he
says, the level of probabilities for recession and prosperity, which will leave
the company indifferent to nature's move. High school algebra is all that is
required. Call the probability of recession R and the probability of prosperity P. The expected return of securities is $4R + 5P$ and the expected return
of plant is $1R + 17P$. The expected returns are equal when $4R + 5P = 1R +
17P$. Solving for R in terms of P, we find that $R = 4P$. Since the sum of the
probabilities of recession and prosperity is always one, R is the same as $1 -
P$; therefore $1 - P = 4P$. Solving this, we find that $P = .2$ and $R = .8$. These
are the indifference probabilities, and they mean that when the odds in favor of recession reach 80-20, it makes no difference where the company
puts its money. The moment recession is judged to have higher than 80 percent probability, the company should shift its investment from the plant to
securities. The smart businessman has a figure to paste on the wall while
he thinks ahead of possible changes in the economic trend. It also tells him
exactly how accurate his economist's forecasting needs to be to keep the
company out of trouble. If the economist predicts a 60 percent chance of
recession and the indifference point is 80 percent, then top management
can relax as long as it trusts its economist to keep his forecasting within a
20 percent error tolerance.

A problem of finding the optimum mix cannot always be figured with
such straightforward algebra. Irving Adler has described the search for
the most efficient way to check the blood samples of armed forces inductees for syphilis. The disease is sufficiently rare and the test sufficiently expensive that running a separate test on each individual blood
sample is clearly inefficient. It is better to pool blood samples for testing.
If the test is negative, all of the owners of the blood in the pool may be
presumed to be free of syphilis. If it is positive, members of the pool must
be retested. Assuming that experience shows that the probability of a
positive reaction in any one person is 5 percent (again, we can peek at
nature's cards), what is the optimum pool size? There is no direct alge-
braic solution. But the expected return can be calculated for any given
pool size. The optimum point is found by starting with a small pool size—
say, a combined sample from two individuals—figuring the expected saving in reduced number of tests, repeating the procedure for three, and so
on, until the expected saving ceases to increase and begins to decline.
This repetitive procedure is called an algorithm, and computers are very
good at it. No computer is needed in this case, because Adler finds the
solution quickly. The advantages of pooling taper off after the number in
the pool reaches five. So, as long as the incidence of syphilis among pre-

inductees remains at 5 percent, the blood samples should be batched in groups of five.[4]

Such applications of quantitative techniques also extend to bargaining theory, an area that, at first glance, might seem to depend wholly on human intuition. Bargaining problems can be quantified, although the mathematics often go far beyond the basic two-person, two-strategy case.[5] The going gets murky when you deal with the possibility of mutual gain for the players, as well as conflict. Such non-zero-sum games are more readily found in life, and von Neumann and Morgenstern did not shrink from considering them. But at this point their mathematics becomes too difficult for most of us to follow. Indeed, it reaches the outer limits of modern math. This does not mean, however, that theory involving non-zero-sum games is wasted on us. Fortunately, game theory has opened up new ideas and novel ways of thinking about problems that can be considered on a nonmathematical level.

Bargaining with a used car dealer is a game in which there are elements of both conflict and mutual interest. Somewhere between the highest price you are willing to pay and the lowest price for which the dealer is willing to sell there is an overlapping zone in which both of you would rather settle than call off the deal. To the extent that you both want to find a point within this zone to make a deal, you are in harmony. To the extent that you want to keep this point low and he wants it to be high, you are in conflict.

Sometimes the area of mutual interest is much more important than the area of conflict. You and your company may both place more importance on your continuing employment there than on the issue of a $50 raise. Paradoxically, the winner in the contest over the raise may be the side that can seem to care the least about the larger area of mutual concern. In dealing with these non-zero-sum situations, you must learn to manipulate two critical elements: commitment and communication. Neither is as simple as it sounds. To illustrate them, I can offer a real-life case study: my own negotiations with the used car sales manager of Loving Chevrolet Co. of Silver Spring, Maryland, over a Pontiac station wagon. It was a classic case, because both of us quickly realized that somewhere below the original asking price there was a range in which we would each prefer to close the deal than call it off. The problem was to find the equilibrium point within that range at which we could converge.

I entered the contest well prepared with a strategy I always employ in buying secondhand cars. I shop only for cars priced at a figure that I cannot possibly afford to pay. It is the only way I know to convince the dealer that I will not, indeed, cannot, pay his asking price. Truth, as Thomas Schelling has noted, is always easier to demonstrate than falsehood. "The sophisticated negotiator," he warns us in *The Strategy of Conflict,* "may find it difficult to seem as obstinate as a truly obstinate man. If a man knocks at a door and says that he will stab himself on the porch unless given $10, he is more likely to get the $10 if his eyes are bloodshot."[6]

In buying a car, financial constraint can make one truly obstinate, an illustration of the paradox that there is strength in having your options closed. I offered the sales manager a sum of $195 below the asking price. The next step was to try to confirm that this sum did lie within the range where he would rather sell than not and, equally important, whether I could convince him that this was to be my only offer. Why $195 instead of $200? Car dealers invariably price their merchandise $5 below a round number, knowing that the ordinary mind considers only the first digits on a price tag and ignores the rest. The buyer, by expressing the price he wishes to pay in round numbers, transfers to the seller the mental burden of keeping track of the odd digits.

The sales manager reacted to the offer by reciting the car's history, explaining the slimness of the profit margin, and suggesting that the company's prices weren't at all flexible. However, because they did like to keep the inventory moving, he might let it go for $95 below the asking price. I registered indifference and explained that I, too, was counting dollars with care. He then made a standard but effective probe for the equilibrium point: "Let's split the difference," he said.

Splitting the difference is one of the many folkways that provide cues in games of coordination. Such cues lack intrinsic logic, but they are recognized as distinctive, and so players seeking coordination can use them as landmarks. Schelling has demonstrated their existence in a fascinating series of experiments. In one case, he posed this problem to a sample of forty-one persons in New Haven: You are to meet someone in New York City. You both know the date of the meeting, but not the hour or the place. Where would you go and at what hour? A majority of his sample chose the information booth at Grand Central Station. Virtually all picked the same time, 12 noon.

When large groups of people are involved, tacit coordination is still possible, but the landmarks become harder to find. In 1958, when the first black family moved into my former neighborhood of Shepherd Park, D.C., there were two schools of opposing opinion among the white residents. One faction wanted to buy the blacks out. The other faction wanted to pack up and leave. Eventually, a third group became the dominant neighborhood force. Composed of white liberals and black newcomers, it sought to stabilize a mixed racial balance by promoting open housing and fighting a real estate industry pact to close the area to white buyers. The organization stopped short of setting a fixed ratio of whites to blacks. A quota system was too close to discrimination for liberal consciences to accept. So while their efforts slowed the process, the neighborhood steadily tipped over the years

from white to black. Whites were reluctant to move in because they expected it to become all black and this expectation can be self-fulfilling.
Conversely, blacks can be reluctant to move into all-white areas, despite the
open-housing laws, unless they expect other blacks to move there. This, too,
can be a self-fulfilling expectation. The problem was that there were no
cues, no equilibrium points between virtually zero blacks and 100 percent
blacks.

Many years later, as integration became more accepted, the neighborhood did stabilize. In the 1980 census, Shepherd Park was 66 percent
black. In 1990, it was 67 percent.[7]

The international arms race can be interpreted as a close parallel.
Equilibrium points between total disarmament and total war exist, but
they are fragile and hard to find. The world has rested at such a point in
recent years, with each of the two major powers having the capacity for
annihilating the other and each deterred from using this capacity by the
lack of a good defense against retaliation. This is not the most comforting kind of equilibrium imaginable, but it is better than none. And the
chief disadvantage of building an antiballistic missile system is that it
might move the international balance of power off this tested equilibrium point without any guarantee that we shall ever find another, short
of war.

So the sales manager knew what he was doing when he offered to split
the difference. Indeed, like Schelling's subjects converging at noon, we had
been thinking of the same thing. I was deterred only by my previous, self-
imposed commitment, although even this was beginning to lose its credibility. I had calculated my financial means carefully, but even with the best
of calculating it is hard to convince oneself that another $50 can't be
squeezed out of the grocery money. I searched for a way out of the commitment.

A way out must always be found, for to go back coldly on a commitment
is to signal that the commitment was a lie and that your next commitment
may be a lie also. (This fact can in itself contribute to the credibility of a
commitment. A labor union says to Company A, if we back down for you,
we'll have to do it for Company B and all the others.) So before backing
down, it is necessary to find a rationalization, something to differentiate the
case at hand from all others.

"I might be able to get the extra $50," I admitted, "but I would have to
adjust my repair budget. How about this: I'll pay it if you will agree to fix
that funny thumping noise in the rear wheels?"

It was a nice move, if I do say so. The sales manager did not want to fix
that funny thumping noise. No used car dealer wants to fix a funny thumping noise. But this offer gave him the needed excuse to abandon his own
commitment.

"No," he said, "I guess I'd rather you kept the $50 and had it fixed your-self." And so I drove away in the new lifestyle that owning one's first station wagon implies.

Sometimes a commitment and communication can be combined in a single act. When an advancing army burns the bridges behind it, the flames that bar its retreat signal the foe that the invaders have no choice but to advance.

At Harvard Square, pedestrians and motorists are continually challenging each other's commitment. Both want to occupy the territory in the middle of the street, but neither want it so badly they would purposely cause a bloody accident. Most pedestrians try to fix the oncoming drivers with hope-fully hypnotic stares while taking tentative steps toward the street. But the driver knows that the pedestrian will hold back at the last minute. Harvard students who have studied game theory use a more successful tactic. Instead of looking at the oncoming traffic, they turn their heads the other way and step out. This signals commitment. Oncoming drivers, seeing that they are not seen, are deprived of the expectation that the pedestrian will leap out of the way, and so they stop. They lose.

You can build matrices for non-zero-sum games, those where it is possible for you and the other player to both come out ahead. They are more complicated, because each cell must contain two numbers—one representing your payoff and the other representing the payoff of the opponent. This is worth doing, even without trying to probe the murky mathematics involved, because it helps to clarify the situation. Generally, you will be able to spot the strategies where both you and the opponent come out ahead. Then the problem becomes one of fair division of the gain, and you can develop a bargaining strategy.

It is therefore helpful to have a method for quantifying preferences. Von Neumann and Morgenstern figured out a way. To adapt an example used by Hayward Alker, suppose you were a delegate to the Republican national convention in 2000, and your most preferred candidate was John McCain and your least preferred was Pat Buchanan. You anchor your scale by assigning McCain a value of 100 and Buchanan a value of zero. That is simple enough, but what about your in-between preferences, such as George W. Bush or Elizabeth Dole? You find their values on the scale by asking yourself such questions as, "Which would I prefer between an 80 percent chance of getting my favorite, McCain, and a 100 percent chance of landing my second choice, Bush? You do this until you find the point at which you are *indifferent* to the hypothetical probability (P) of the favorite and a sure thing for the lower-ranked choice. Bush's value (or *utility*, in economic terminology) is equal to $100 * P$ at the point where you would be equally satisfied with the certainty of the second choice and the probability (P) of the first choice.

This provides an interval ranking of the candidates, which means that the delegate knows the degree to which he prefers one to the other instead of just a simple rank ordering. Therefore, as he wheels and deals on the convention floor, he can decide how much trouble and risk he ought to take for each person.

What makes this system of scaling preferences workable is, of course, the ability of the scaler to find his indifference level. It need not be difficult. Children dividing cake can do it. One cuts and the other chooses, the cutter realizing that he must make the pieces as equal as possible so that he will be indifferent to the decision of the chooser. Most of us make such judgments unconsciously every day.

For some, there is a basically offensive quality about assigning cold numbers to human factors. But legends of the practice go all the way back to Babylon. Students in Schelling's course were asked to ponder the game-theory aspects of a Babylonian custom of assembling each village's marriageable women in the central square once a year. An auctioneer would begin with the prettiest and most desirable woman and auction her off to the highest bidder. At some point in the scale, there would be no more pretty women or rich men willing to pay for the privilege of marrying them. At that tipping point, the rules would be reversed. The money collected for the desirable mates would be used to pay poorer men as an incentive to take the less desirable choices.

Whether or not the legend is true, it demonstrates that a life governed by caprice and chance can be made to make sense through the use of numbers. Even so, there are always situations that resist solution. One in particular has a haunting effect on game theorists, who keep bringing it up just because it is so difficult. It is known as the prisoner's dilemma:

You and a friend have been busted in a marijuana raid. Before the district attorney can gain a conviction, he must get one of you to confess, and he is willing to make some concessions as an inducement. However, if you both talk, he has no incentive to make concessions, and both of you are likely to get heavy sentences. You are in separate cells and cannot communicate.

The payoffs can be put in a matrix. But briefly, they add up like this: If both of you confess, you both get stiff sentences. If neither confesses, you both get off. If one confesses and the other doesn't, the talker goes free and gets a cash reward to boot; the nontalker gets the heaviest possible sentence.

There is no best strategy. At first glance, the safe thing seems to be to talk, because you are then assured of avoiding the worst fate, the heaviest possible sentence, and you might get by with a light sentence. But your friend will see it that way, too, in which case both of you will talk and both will get heavy sentences. Clearly, the best outcome is for both of you to keep quiet.

But if you do, you run the risk that your friend will play it safe and talk, thus giving you the worst of the possible outcomes.[8]

Game theorists have dreamed up even more brutal examples of cases where victory goes to the person who is most successful at winning and betraying confidence. Martin Shubik of Yale has postulated this agonizing situation:

Imagine a prison that consists of an outer concrete wall one mile square. In the center of the walled space is a small blockhouse.

The blockhouse is surrounded by a steel barrier. There are no guards.

Next to the barrier is a row of buttons—one for each prisoner. If all the buttons are pressed at the same time, the steel barrier will fall, so that all can reach the blockhouse.

The blockhouse is large enough to hold only one man. Inside are two buttons that operate only when the door is shut and are wired so that pressing one permanently inactivates the other. One button will open the gate in the outer wall for 10 seconds. The other button will activate an ejection device to fly the blockhouse over the wall, leaving the gate closed.

Neat. The prisoners cannot afford to lower the steel barrier until they have decided who will enter the blockhouse. And the only person they could afford to choose would be whoever was successful at persuading his fellow inmates that he would sacrifice his own freedom by pressing the gate button instead of the ejection button. Once chosen and once alone with his thoughts in the security of the blockhouse, he might, of course, reconsider.[9]

Not content to leave such an intriguing situation to idle theory, Shubik and two colleagues devised a parlor game that reproduces a parallel in real life. Appropriately, the game is called "So Long, Sucker." It can be played with cards or chips. When Shubik tried it out in the parlor with dinner guests, the guests, a husband and wife, went home in separate cabs. "One of them double-crossed the other," he explains. "I think it was the wife."

The feature of the game, of course, is that you must enter into a temporary, unenforceable agreement with another player. But that is not a sufficient condition to win. You must also betray your partner in this coalition.

"A psychiatrist acquaintance of mine," recalls Shubik, "tried to use this in therapeutic sessions on disturbed individuals. He hoped it could be controlled, but he found it to be so vicious that he abandoned it."

That this game is as painful as predicted by theory and that it grew from a line of once obscure mathematical thought begun by von Neumann and Morgenstern a half century ago is comforting evidence that everyday-life applications of game theory do, indeed, exist. If you believe in a capricious universe, if you think of yourself as the product of a random wandering of atoms, it still applies. Game theory tells us not only how to bring order to randomness, but how to use randomness to order our lives.

One can, of course, get too cute about this. Once you develop the habit of breaking down a problem into a two-by-two matrix with your preferences ordered and quantified, you may get a heady sense of fate control that leaves you dangerously exposed. Schelling tells the story of a colleague who loaned his office to a friend but lacked an extra key. It was therefore necessary to hide the key somewhere, and not under the mat, which as everyone knows, is the first place a burglar looks. Being a game theorist, the key owner felt he could cope with the problem. He analyzed all the possible hiding places and all the possible actions and judgments that a burglar might make. He then arrived at the hiding place that was the least likely place for a burglar to look. It was agreed that the key would be left there. At the end of his day's work, he locked his office door, went to the agreed-upon hiding place, and found his sense of personal efficacy brutally shattered. Someone else's key was already there. But it was an unavoidable mistake, and he at least had the comfort of knowing he had rolled his own dice.

With any luck, this chapter has convinced you that numbers dealing with human behavior can be manipulated with profit—once you get the numbers. Finding the numbers is part of a process that social sciences call operationalization: reducing the complexities of human behavior to their essential elements in order to create a simpler model that preserves the essence of the original in a form subject to quantification. Before manipulating any more numbers, we shall consider that problem.

NOTES

1. David Boyle, *The Sum of Our Discontent: Why Numbers Make Us Irrational* (New York: Texere, 2001).

2. John von Neumann and Oskar Morgenstern, *Theory of Games and Economic Behavior* (Princeton, N.J.: Princeton University Press, 1944).

3. Edward G. Bennion, "Capital Budgeting and Game Theory," *Harvard Business Review* (November–December 1956).

4. Irving Adler, *Probability and Statistics for Everyman* (New York: New American Library, 1963).

5. For the rules for solving *n*-strategy games, see J. D. Williams, *The Compleat Strategyst: Being a Primer on the Theory of Games of Strategy* (New York: Dover Publications, 1986).

6. Thomas Schelling, *The Strategy of Conflict* (New York: Oxford University Press, 1963).

7. The story of Shepherd Park and associated neighborhoods that organized to maintain integration in northwest Washington is told by Marvin Caplan in *Farther Along: A Civil Rights Memoir* (Baton Rouge: Louisiana State University Press, 1999).

8. An excellent explanation of the Prisoner's Dilemma, plus an account of experimental efforts to solve the problem of coordination, is found in Douglas R. Hofstadter, *Metamagical Themas: Questing for the Essence of Mind and Pattern* (New York: Basic Books, 1985), 715–34. See also M. Mitchell Waldrop, *Complexity: The Emerging Science at the Edge of Order and Chaos* (New York: Simon & Schuster, 1992), 262–65.

9. Martin Shubik, *Game Theory and Related Approaches to Social Behavior* (New York: Wiley, 1964).

3

+

Some Elements
of Data Analysis

It doesn't take many numbers to make a story quantitative. When the
United States Supreme Court ordered a halt to the Florida ballot recount
after the 2000 election, the relevant number was 5.

If you already knew the background of the case, knew that the Court has
nine justices, the fact that the number voting to overrule the Florida
Supreme Court was five would have given you all the additional information you needed. Such one-number quantitative stories are quite common
in the news business.

Usually, however, a number standing alone does not convey a lot of meaning. It has to be compared with another number or even a string of numbers before much sense can be made of it. When comparisons are made,
care must be taken that the numbers are being compared on an apples-to-
apples basis. In journalism, many mistakes are made in trying to do that
simple thing, and so this chapter is going to get very basic in its explanation
of how to compare numbers.

Strategies for analysis vary, depending on whether you are dealing with
continuous data or categorical data. Continuous data place, for practical
purposes, no limits on values, and so they preserve fine differences—for example, the difference between an annual income of $32,456 and one of
$32,460. Categorical data sort things into bins. Public opinion surveys, for
example, usually use only four or five categories to represent all possible incomes. These ordered categories can be more convenient to handle, but the
convenience comes at the cost of losing some of the information.

To start, we will assume the richness of continuous data, commonly found
in government reports, such as the census, and in economic statistics. Later

chapters will cover categorical data, such as those found in public opinion surveys.

FIGURING A RATE

One way to build a comparison into a number is to convert it into a rate. That procedure automatically provides a comparison against some easily recognized baseline. The number of deaths from AIDS for each nation is not as meaningful as the number of deaths per 100,000 population. By converting the raw number to a rate, you assess the impact on the population, and you provide a way to compare relative impact from one country to another, regardless of differences in their size.

Journalists need to remember two important things about rates.

1. They are proportions, not absolute values.
2. In many situations, they are more meaningful than their underlying absolute values.

The most commonly used rate is the rate per hundred (*per centum,* in Latin) or percentage. A percentage is the decimal equivalent of a fraction, but with the decimal point moved two places to the right. Thus:

$$\frac{1}{2} = .5 = 50\%$$

The first rule of percentages is this:

No percentage makes sense unless you know its base.

The way to figure a percentage without losing track of the base is to think about the fraction first. If 11 members of the 42-man football squad graduate in four years, the squad's four-year graduation rate is 11/42 or 26 percent. The 11 in the fraction is the number who graduated, and the 42 is the base to which the number who graduated is being compared. The base is the bottom of the fraction. I know, that sounds elementary, but you would be surprised at how many students have trouble remembering that. (When I explain this to students, I ask them to visualize a statue on campus: for example, Silent Sam at Carolina or Tommy Trojan at Southern California. The base is at the bottom. That seems to help.)

Being able to identify the base is important, because of the next rule:

When you compare two percentages, you need to make certain that they have the same base.

Some news writers evidently think it is boring to hold the base constant when making percentage comparisons. I have seen newspaper stories where the base was shifted in midsentence: "Ninety percent of the blacks in Baxter County voted for Gore, but 95 percent of Bush supporters were white." In one case, the base is blacks; in the other, it is Bush supporters. That comparison makes no sense at all, although you could puzzle something meaningful out of it if you knew the percentage black in the electorate. How much better to say, "Gore got 90 percent of the black vote and 40 percent of the white vote."

When you have the base firmly in mind, you can convert the fraction to a decimal by division. Don't forget the two-place move of the decimal point implied in the concept of percentage:

$$.5 = \text{five-tenths} = .50 = 50 \text{ hundredths}$$

Fifty percent is another and easier way of saying 50 hundredths. If we left the decimal where it was and said .50 hundredths or .5 percent, we would have more than a redundancy, we would have an entirely different number (one-half of 1 percent). Sometimes you will see in print expressions like .50 percent where the writer really means 50 percent. The decimal point was evidently thrown in just for emphasis. So here is another rule of life:

Decimal points are for meaning, not for emphasis.

Sometimes the rate you are describing will be so small that it needs to be expressed in fractions of a percentage point. In that case, consider expressing it as a rate per 1,000 or rate per 100,000, whatever leaves you with whole numbers to compare. That will reduce the chance of typographical error, as well as of misunderstanding.

PERCENTAGE DIFFERENCE

Maybe you thought that using the image of a statue to reinforce the concept of a percentage base was silly. But when you try to figure a percentage difference, you will really appreciate the importance of keeping the base identified.

On August 3, 1998, the Dow Jones Industrial Average closed at 8786.74. On the following day, Tuesday, August 4, 1998, it closed at 8487.31. Question: What was the percentage drop?

Percentage difference means just what it says: the difference between two values taken as a percentage of whichever value you are using as the base.

If you want the percentage change from *Time 1* to *Time 2*, then the *Time 1* value is the base.

So first obtain the absolute value of the difference. Subtract 8487.31 from 8786.74, and you find that the Dow dropped 299.43 points. Now you can set up the fraction. (Be sure you use the right base.) The percentage decline is:

$$299.43 / 8786.74 = .034077 = 3.41\%$$

Notice that to get from the decimal to the percentage, we moved the decimal two places to the right and added a percent sign. We also rounded to two decimal places, which is probably more precision than we need, but I bow to *Wall Street Journal* style.

Notice also that rounding is not the same as truncating. If we truncated, we would come out with 3.40 percent. But since the dropped value is more than half, we round up to 3.41. To evaluate the dropped digits, put an imaginary decimal in front of them. In this case, .77 is greater than .5, and so you round up. If it were less than .5, you would truncate (i.e., drop the surplus digits). What if it were exactly .5? It doesn't make much difference, but, for consistency's sake, I round up—unless I have enough information to carry out the division to enough decimal places to tell me which way it should go.

So the market fell 3.41 percent on August 4.

When they reported that decline, newspapers everywhere fell into an apples-and-oranges trap. On August 5, 1998, the *St. Louis Post-Dispatch* led with the headline "Dow Takes Third-Biggest Drop." And the lead said, "Stocks went into a tailspin Tuesday and the Dow Jones Industrial Average dropped 299.43 points—its third biggest point loss ever."

Making historical comparisons is good, but using the absolute drop for an index that goes back to 1896 is absurd. The index has increased enormously over the years, both from inflation and from real increases in the value of the nation's industrial capacity. For all but a brief moment in its first fifty years, a 299-point drop would have taken it into negative territory—a logical impossibility.

What was the 299.43-point drop rank in percentage terms? It was the 215th greatest. Not one for the record books, and certainly not like the disaster the page-one headlines implied. And yet news media almost invariably focus on the absolute change when making historical comparisons, as though there were no difference in a Dow of 100 and one of 10,000. That pattern, hyping the story by focusing on the point decline and then backpedaling to tell what really happened in percentage terms, is still a common pattern. Writers prefer to give priority to the less important point comparison simply because it yields a bigger number. That it is a misleading number does not seem to matter to them.

The reasons for the Dow being so much higher now than it was in the 1930s are straightforward. The economy has grown and companies are worth more. Part of the growth is real and part is inflation. These are *secular* trends, meaning that they affect just about everything in society. If you are going to make comparisons across time, you have to filter out that secular effect in order to see what is going on specifically with the phenomenon you are investigating. In other words, you need to detrend the numbers, to use a term favored by Cook and Campbell.[1] Expressing change in percentage terms is one way to *detrend*, but it is not the only way. Adjusting the Dow Jones for inflation would be another. Financial analysts and accountants do not routinely do that, but if they did, the effect on the Dow Jones Industrial Average would be eye-opening. Its long-term growth, though still real enough, would not be nearly as impressive.

One other point about percentage change. When you reverse the direction of the change, the base changes. It your favorite stock falls from $100 a share to $10, the drop is 90 percent. If, on the next day, it gains 90 percent, you might rejoice, but you will not have been made whole. A 90 percent gain from $10 is only $19. To get back to $100, it has to gain 900 percent.

"TIMES MORE" VERSUS "TIMES AS"

Before leaving the problem of figuring a percentage difference, we need to consider a simple shortcut.

In newsrooms, I have heard people use the rule "Divide the little number by the big number." That's the wrong rule. It only works if the percentage difference is going to be less than 100. In our hypothetical stock recovery, from $10 to $100, the base is 10, the change is 90, and the percentage change is 90/10 or 900 percent.

Here is a shortcut derived from high school algebra: Percentage difference $= (N/O) - 1$, where N is the new value and O is the old value. It works for both percentage increase and decrease, regardless of whether the change is greater or less than 100 percent.

In the previous example of a stock gain from 10 to 100, the steps would be:

$$N/O = 100/10 = 10.$$
$$10 - 1 = 9.$$
$$9 * 100 \text{ (to convert to a percentage)} = 900.$$

Now let's think about how to put that change into words.

It would be accurate to say the new value of the stock is "nine times greater than the old." That's another way of saying "900 percent greater." But I don't recommend using that language because "times greater" is commonly used to mean "times as great." And the number nine times as great as 10 is, of course, 90, not 100.

There is a simple explanation for this confusion. "Times greater" compares the base value to the difference (the amount "greater"). And "times as great" compares the base value to the new value.

That is clear enough once you think about it. Unfortunately, many news writers do not think about it and use "times greater" and "times as" interchangeably, as if they meant the same thing. They don't! The problem will continue until the AP decides to ban "times greater" in its style book. (I actually proposed this several years ago. AP's leadership defended "times greater" as a harmless "mathematical colloquialism.") But it's not harmless if the reader thinks it means what it says.

The mistake does not matter much when you are talking about large, order-of-magnitude changes. It gets you into more trouble when you are talking about smaller, two- or threefold changes. If you are 25 years old, and I am *three times as old* as you, I must be 75. But if I am *three times older* than you, then I am 100. Try to keep it straight for my sake.

ADJUSTING FOR INFLATION

When dollar amounts are compared across time, it is usually a good idea to detrend the figures by taking out the effect of inflation. One barrier to doing this is the lack of a good statistical indicator of inflation. The most common one is the Consumer Price Index of the Bureau of Labor Statistics. It was created during World War I when runaway prices, especially in ship-building centers, made it necessary to make frequent cost-of-living adjustments in wages. The CPI shows the relative value of a dollar's purchasing power from year to year. It does this by checking the price of a "market basket" of goods and services that is held relatively constant over time. The market basket includes food, clothing, shelter, fuels, transportation, medical services, and other things that people buy for daily living. The problem comes in trying to define a market basket that means the same thing in 1990 as in, say, 1952. Some goods and services that were relevant and considered necessary in 1990 did not exist in 1952: antipollution equipment for cars, for example. The bureau tries to solve this problem by redefining the market basket from time to time to keep it abreast of changing lifestyles and technology.[2]

Even so, it is not possible to create one market basket that applies equally to all groups. For example, retirees who own their homes are not affected by changes in rental or mortgage rates. For home-owning federal government retirees, whose pensions are indexed to the CPI, the indexing creates a windfall. Their incomes automatically go up more than their own normal living costs.

Such indexing is, of course, a form of detrending, squeezing out the secular trend of inflation so that you can see the real meaning. Doing it only approximately is better than not doing it at all, as the millions of retirees living on non-indexed private pensions, whose real value shrinks year by year, will agree.

And yet accountants don't like to index or detrend because of the element of uncertainty that it introduces into their work. Corporate balance sheets seldom show the effect of inflation. Press releases boasting of record profits sometimes show profits that would be below historic levels if constant dollar comparisons were made. Labor leaders have made the same idle boasts, taking credit for gains that are really losses when they are detrended for inflation.

The procedure for detrending for inflation is simple. When you compare dollar amounts across time, express them in the constant dollars of one of your comparison years. When one of the years being compared is the current year, the usual practice is to convert the older amounts into their current equivalents or constant dollars. But it can just as easily be done the other way.

Here is an example chosen because it involves a historical period of raging inflation. David H. Weaver and G. Cleveland Wilhoit reported in 1986 that the median income of journalists had increased from \$11,133 in 1970 to \$19,000 in 1981. That was bad news for journalists, they pointed out, because journalists actually lost about \$7,000 a year in purchasing power.[3] To verify their calculation, you need the CPI for 1970 and for 1981. According to the *Statistical Abstract of the United States,* published annually by the U.S. Government Printing Office, it was 38.8 and 90.9, respectively (the index uses the prices for the 1982–84 period as a base of 100). Then convert the median journalistic income for 1970 into constant 1981 dollars. Use the formula for fraction equivalents that you learned in high school:

$$\frac{38.8}{11,133} = \frac{90.9}{X}$$

Perhaps you are more comfortable with an English sentence than an equation: 38.8 is to \$11,133 as 90.9 is to the unknown quantity (1970's income expressed in 1981 constant dollars). Following the cross-multiplication rule from your high school algebra, you find that

$$38.8 * X = 11,133 * 90.9$$

Dividing each side of the equation by 38.8 yields

$$X = (11,133 * 90.9) / 38.8$$

(Formulas in this book use computer notation: The "times" sign is an asterisk, "*," instead of the old-fashioned "X." That frees "X" to represent an unknown. A slash, "/," means "divided by.")

Punch it into your calculator, and 1970's $11,133 turns out to be equal to $26,082.21 in constant 1981 dollars. So the wages of journalism actually fell by 27 percent over that period. How come? Two things happened. The performance of two young *Washington Post* reporters in the Watergate scandal motivated many young people to become journalists. In the same time, barriers to women in the profession were lowered. Both events greatly increased the pool of available workers in journalism. This windfall of idealistic, motivated youth gave the owners of the media a wonderful choice. Option 1: Raise the standards of journalism by tapping the best of the enlarged pool and welcoming the best and the brightest into journalism. Option 2: Choose the next generation of journalists by selecting those who would work for the least amount of money and carry the savings to the bottom line. We know how that one came out.

The Bureau of Labor Statistics Web site includes the current CPI and historical comparisons. It also has an online calculator that will perform the high school math for you.[4] If you want to go back further than 1913, see a beautiful set of volumes called *Historical Statistics of the United States*.[5] It gives all the BLS numbers back to their World War I beginning and then uses estimates from other historical sources to produce yearly CPIs back to 1800.

The monthly figures come in two categories, the CPI-U and the CPI-W. The CPI-U is for all urban consumers and covers about 80 percent of the population. The CPI-W is for urban wage earners and clerical workers. They are collected separately so that the different effects on inflation can be tracked for the two groups (although they overlap considerably). For most public policy purposes, the broader-based CIP-U is used to make inflation adjustments.

ADJUSTING FOR POPULATION GROWTH

Trends make news, either because they have been going on quietly and not many have noticed or because of a sudden interruption in a trend. To focus on the newsworthy trend, you have to separate it from all the parallel trends in the background. Population growth is one secular trend that, like inflation, can make other trends be more or less than they seem.

The Newspaper Association of America every year issues a booklet of statistical trends in the news business. It shows that newspaper circulation fades a little bit every year in the United States. But the situation is much worse than the absolute numbers reveal because the population and the number of households are growing. Circulation penetration, defined as circulation divided by households, has been dropping for a longer time and at a steeper rate, and that is the number the newspaper

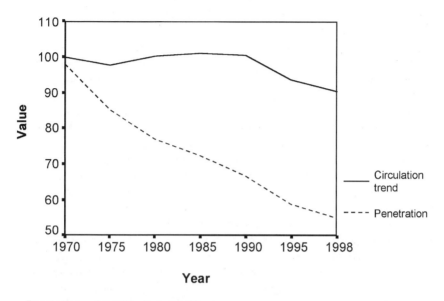

Penetration = circulation / households
Circulation indexed: 1970 = 100

Figure 3.1   Newspaper Circulation and Penetration

association really cares about, even though it does not publish the number in the booklet.

It is a number that is easy to understand at the intuitive level. When penetration was at 100 percent in a given market, one newspaper was sold for every household. When it was above 100 percent, more newspapers were sold than there were households—common in the 1950s. Today the number is much smaller and still falling, with some metropolitan newspapers experiencing household penetration of less than 50 percent. Expressing newspaper circulation as a ratio to households (because home-delivered circulation is sold to households rather than to individuals) makes the real trend easier to see.

Where do you get population numbers to use in detrending? The U.S. census is collected only every ten years, but its Current Population Survey updates basic demographics every March. Lots of organizations produce interim estimates of population characteristics. Standard Rate and Data Service produces media audience studies and population estimates, and its reports are available in larger libraries and in the marketing departments of media organizations. The Audit Bureau of Circulations has county-level household estimates year by year. Most newspapers and many journalism schools are ABC members and have access to its data, both in print form and on diskette.

CURVE FITTING

Sometimes interesting trends are confused by a variety of factors, including random error. Survey research based on sample data is subject to random error, particularly when small subgroups are examined. One way to get a clearer picture of a trend is to try to fit it to a smooth line.

A straight-line fit works for many kinds of trend data. You can use your calculator or a statistical program, such as SPSS (Statistical Package for the Social Sciences), to do a regression and scatterplot with time as the independent or X variable. The correlation coefficient (chapter 4) will tell you how well your data fit the straight-line model. If it is a good fit, you can even try to predict the future by drawing in the best-fitting straight line and extending it with a straightedge. Such a linear projection tells you what will happen if present trends continue unchanged, which, of course, they might not do.

Nature, unfortunately, is not fond of straight lines. Not to worry. You can use the same regression program to fit a curved line. First, examine the scatterplot and use your imagination to see what kind of a line might fit. If it is a simple curve, one that does not twist in a new direction at some point along its length, you can sometimes straighten it out by reexpressing one of the variables in terms of some nonlinear function such as its square or its square root.

SMOOTHING

If nature does not like straight lines, she is not too fond of smooth logarithmic curves, either. The most interesting trends are often those that twist and turn the most exotically. Tukey has a procedure for dealing with such convoluted data that he calls "smoothing." The theory behind smoothing is that measurement error is itself a secular trend and can be taken out by using each point as a check on the neighboring points. A rolling average is a fairly familiar method of smoothing. If you have monthly data that need smoothing, express January as the mean of December, January, and February. Then for February, use the mean of January, February, and March. Pre-election tracking polls sometimes show the candidate standings as rolling three-day averages.

Tukey's recommendation is to use rolling medians of three, rather than means. Here's how to do that: Compare each data point with those on either side and then replace it with the middle one of the three. For example, in the series 324, the 2 would be changed to a 3 because 3 is the median of the set. That way, wildly out-of-range points will be buried. That's good, says Tukey, because those oddball points catch the eye and make it difficult to see what is really going on. "The value of smoothing," he says, "is the clearer view of the general, once it is unencumbered by detail."[6] In other words, it is exactly what a journalist needs. And if one smooth of running medians of three leaves some jagged places, Tukey recommends doing it again—and again—until smoothing no longer changes things. There are more complicated ways to smooth, and one of them is found in the SPSS procedure for creating a time series (under the menu choice "Transform"). A good place to try it out is with the General Social Survey data on newspaper readership. Editors have known for decades that younger people are harder to coax into reading newspapers. Figure 3.2 uses aggregate date for all the GSS surveys in the 1990s.

Figure 3.3 is the same chart after readership has been smoothed using one of Tukey's more complicated procedures.

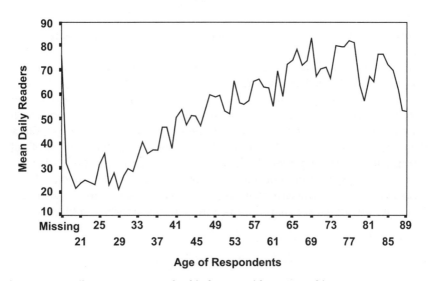

Figure 3.2   Daily Newspaper Readership by Age without Smoothing

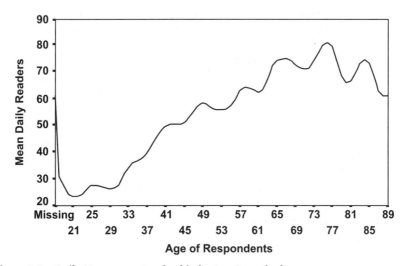

Figure 3.3   Daily Newspaper Readership by Age Smoothed

The main cause for the jagged nature of the line in the first chart is the small samples for each year of age. There are other ways to deal with that problem. One is to collapse the age groupings into larger categories. Another is to try fitting the data points to a curve specified by some prior theory. We'll deal with both of those strategies in later chapters.

INDEX NUMBERS

Another way to achieve clarity for analysis and communication is to use index numbers. The CPI is a good example of an index number. With 1982–84 set at 100, it was easy for everyone to see when it reached 175 in January 2001 that prices had increased 75 percent.

Newspaper advertising salespeople sometimes use index numbers to compare a newspaper's audience with its market. If 35 percent of the adults in the market have college degrees and 47 percent of the readers have college degrees, the index is 134. This is another way of saying that the rate of college graduation is 34 percent higher among readers than in the market as a whole. By applying this indexing to a variety of competing media, the ad salesman can make the case that his paper's readership is more upscale and has more buying power than the raw circulation numbers would indicate.

SEASONAL ADJUSTMENT

Yet another form of detrending is seasonal adjustment. When the Bureau of Labor Statistics (BLS) issues its monthly unemployment figures, it gives us numbers that can be directly compared from one month to the next so that we can see at a glance whether things are getting better or worse.

But unemployment is seasonal. School openings and closings and climate conditions can affect the number of people looking for work at different times of the year. To assess the health of the economy, we are interested in the month-to-month changes that cannot be ascribed to the seasonal variation. The BLS statisticians perform this detrending by looking at past seasonal changes and assuming that the current year will not be very different. Then they subtract the portion attributable to the change in season and report the rest. There is some risk in this, of course, because the seasonal variations are not uniform from year to year. But it is better than not doing it at all. If the White House puts out unemployment numbers in the fall of an election year that show a dramatic drop in unemployment, careful reporters will check to be sure that the seasonal adjustment has not been omitted. If it has, the decline can be merely the result of much of the teenage labor force going back to school.

REGRESSION RESIDUALS

Another statistical technique for detrending comes in handy when you need to control for some overpowering continuous variable that conceals most of what you are looking for. Andrew Brack was studying the editorial quality of newspapers in North Carolina, but he was handicapped by the fact that circulation size explains most of the variance. Bigger papers have more resources, and so they give their readers more for their money. Brack nevertheless assembled a sample of large and small papers, measured them on a number of indicators of editorial quality, combined the indicators into an index, and plotted them on a chart. See figure 3.4 for the result. The vertical axis represents quality and the horizontal axis represents circulation. When each paper is plotted on the chart, their distribution approximates a straight line.

Using the general linear model (GLM) to plot the best-fitting straight line for describing the effect of circulation on quality, Brack then turned his attention to the deviations from that line. Some papers were much higher in quality than would be predicted by their circulation size, and others were much lower. By measuring those deviations from what circulation would predict, he obtained a detrended measure of quality that eliminated the effect of circulation size. The technical term for this technique is *residual analysis*, because it looks at the residual variance, or the variance that is left over after circulation size explains what it can. (More about this later.)

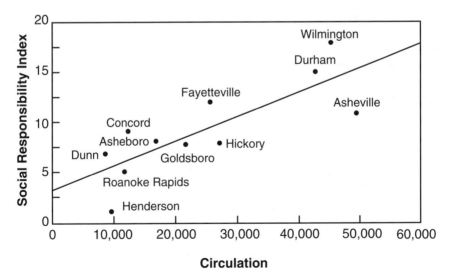

Figure 3.4   Social Responsibility and Newspaper Circulation

STANDARDIZED SCORES

Another way to put apples and oranges on a comparable basis is to use standardized or *z-scores*, which reexpress each measurement in terms of how much it deviates from a group average. Consider the case of a quarterback who is a master strategist on the football field but can't run very fast. Sports writers might say he is "smarter than he is fast." Because intelligence and speed are different dimensions, the comparison does not seem to make sense. But if you interpret that short description to mean that he deviates in a positive direction from the norm in intelligence more than he does in speed, it make pretty good sense.

This way of making comparisons is useful if you have a number of measures to combine into an index but can't use simple addition because each measure is on a different scale. A z-score is a measure of relative peculiarity. Calculating it requires some knowledge of statistics, and it, too, will be covered in a later chapter.

NOTES

1. Thomas D. Cook and Donald T. Campbell, *Quasi-Experimentation: Design and Analysis Issues for Field Settings* (Boston: Houghton Mifflin, 1979), 323.

2. *BLS Handbook of Methods: Vol. II, The Consumer Price Index* (Washington, D.C.: U.S. Government Printing Office, 1984).

3. David H. Weaver and G. Cleveland Wilhoit, *The American Journalist: A Portrait of U.S. News People and Their Work* (Bloomington: Indiana University Press, 1986), 82.

4. In 2001, the Web address for the online CPI calculator was http://stats.bls.gov/cpihome.htm.

5. *Historical Statistics of the United States: Colonial Times to 1970*, Bicentennial Edition (Washington, D.C.: U.S. Government Printing Office, 1975), 211.

6. John W. Tukey, *Exploratory Data Analysis* (Boston: Addison-Wesley, 1977), 205. See also the Help function in SPSS for Windows for details of the procedure.

4

✛

Harnessing the Power of Statistics

It is the things that vary that interest us. Things that do not vary are inherently boring. Winter weather in Miami, Florida, may be more pleasant than winter weather in Clay Center, Kansas, but it is not as much fun to talk about. Clay Center, with its variations in wind, precipitation, and temperature, has a lot more going on in its atmosphere. Or take an extreme case of low variation. You would not get much readership for a story about the number of heads on the typical human being. Since we are all one-headed and there is no variance to ponder, explain, or analyze, the quantitative analysis of number of heads per human gets dull rather quickly. Only if someone were to notice an unexpected number of two-headed persons in the population would it be interesting. Number of heads would then become a *variable*.

On the other hand, consider human intelligence as measured by, say, the Stanford-Binet IQ test. It varies a lot, and the sources of the variation are of endless fascination. News writers and policy makers alike are always wondering how much of the variation is caused by heredity and how much by environment, whether it can be changed, and whether it correlates with such things as athletic ability, ethnic category, birth order, and other interesting variables.

Variance, then, makes news. And in any statistical analysis, the first thing we generally want to know is whether the phenomenon we are studying is a variable, and, if so, how much and in what way it varies. Once we have that figured out, we are usually interested in finding the sources of the variance. Ideally, we would hope to find what causes the variance. But causation is difficult to prove, and we often must settle for discovering what correlates or covaries

51

with the variable in which we are interested. Because causation is so tricky to establish, statisticians use some weasel words that mean almost—but not quite—the same thing. If two interesting phenomena covary (meaning that they vary together), they say that one *depends* on the other or that one *explains* the other. These are concepts that come close to the idea of causation but stop short of it, and rightly so. For example, how well you perform in college may depend on your entrance test scores. But the test scores are not the cause of that performance. They merely help explain it by indicating the level of underlying ability that is the cause of both test scores and college performance.

Statistical applications in both journalism and science are aimed at finding causes, but so much caution is required in making claims of causation that the more modest concepts are used much more freely. Modesty is becoming, so think of statistics as a quest for the unexplained variance. It is a concept that you will become more comfortable with, and, in time, it may even seem romantic.

MEASURING VARIANCE

There are two ways to use statistics. You can cookbook your way through, applying formulas without fully understanding why or how they work. Or you can develop an intuitive sense for what is going on. The cookbook route can be easy and fast, but like most things in life that are fast and easy, it is full of risks. To protect yourself, you will have to get some concepts at the intuitive level. Because the concept of variance is so basic to statistics, it is worth spending some time to get it at the intuitive level. If you see the difference between low variance (number of human heads) and high variance (human intelligence), your intuitive understanding is well started. Now let's think of some ways to measure variance.

A measure works best if it starts with a baseline. (Remember the comedian who is asked, "How is your wife?" His reply: "Compared to what?")

In measuring variance, one logical "compared to what" is the central tendency, and the convenient measure of central tendency is the arithmetic average or mean. Or you could think in terms of probabilities, like a poker player, and use the *expected* value.

Start with the simplest possible variable, one that varies across only two conditions: zero or one, white or black, present or absent, dead or alive, boy or girl. Such variables are encountered often enough in real life that statisticians have a term for them. They are called *dichotomous* variables. Another descriptive word for them is *binary*. Everything in the population being considered is either one or the other. There are two possibilities, no more.

An interesting dichotomous variable in present-day American society is minority status. Policies aimed at improving the status of minorities require that each citizen be first classified as either a minority or a nonminority. (We'll skip for now the possible complications of doing that.) Now picture two towns, one in the rural Midwest and one in the rural South. The former is 2 percent minority and the latter is 40 percent minority. Which population has the greater variance?

With just a little bit of reflection, you will see that the midwestern town does not have much variance in its racial makeup. It is 98 percent nonminority. The southern town has a lot more variety, and so it is relatively high in racial variance.

Here is another way to think about the difference. If you knew the racial distribution in the midwestern town and had to guess the category of a random person, you would guess that the person is a nonminority, and you would have a 98 percent chance of being right. In the southern town, you would make the same guess, but would be much less certain of being right. Variance, then, is related to the concept of uncertainty. This will prove to be important later on when we consider the arithmetic of sampling.

For now, what you need to know is that:

1. Variance is interesting.
2. Variance is different for different variables and in different populations.
3. The amount of variance is easily quantified. (We'll soon see how.)

A CONTINUOUS VARIABLE

Now to leap beyond the dichotomous case. Let's make it a big leap and consider a variable that can have an unlimited number of divisions. Instead of just 0 or 1, it can go from 0 to infinity. Or from 0 to some finite number but with an infinite number of divisions within the finite range. Making this stuff up is too hard, so let's use real data: the frequency of misspelling "minuscule" as "miniscule" in nine large and prestigious news organizations. To assure some variance, we'll go back to the dawn of the spell checker, 1989.

Miami Herald	2.5%
Los Angeles Times	2.9
Philadelphia Inquirer	4.0
Washington Post	4.5
Boston Globe	4.8
New York Times	11.0
Chicago Tribune	19.6
Newsday	25.0
Detroit Free Press	30.0

Just by eyeballing the list, you can see a lot of variance there. The worst-spelling paper on the list has more than ten times the rate of misspelling as the best-spelling paper. And that method of measuring variance, taking the ratio of the extremes, is an intuitively satisfying one. But it is a rough measure because it does not use all of the information in the list. So let's measure variance the way statisticians do. First they find a reference point (a compared-to-what) by calculating the mean, which is the sum of the values divided by the number of cases. The mean for these nine cases is 11.6. In other words, the average newspaper on this list gets "minuscule" wrong 11.6 percent of the time. When we talk about variance, we are really talking about variance around (or variance from) the mean. Next, do the following:

1. Take the value of each case and subtract the mean to get the difference.
2. Square that difference for each case.
3. Add to get the sum of all those squared differences.
4. Divide the result by the number of cases.

That is quite a long and detailed list. If this were a statistics text, you would get an equation instead. You would like the equation even less than the previous list. Trust me.

So do all of the previous steps, and the result is the variance in this case. It works out to about 100, give or take a point. (Approximations are appropriate because the values in the table have been rounded.) But 100 what? How do we give this number some intuitive usefulness? Well, the first thing to remember is that variance is an absolute, not a relative, concept. For it to make intuitive sense, you need to be able to relate it to something, and we are getting close to a way to do that. If we take the square root of the variance (reasonable enough, because it is derived from a listing of squared differences), we get a wonderfully useful statistic called the *standard deviation of the mean*. Or just standard deviation for short. And the number you compare it to is the mean.

In this case, the mean is 11.6 and the standard deviation is 10, which means that there is a lot of variation around that mean. In a large population whose values follow the classic bell-shaped normal distribution, two-thirds of all the cases will fall within one standard deviation of the mean. So if the standard deviation is a small value relative to the value of the mean, it means that variance is small—that is, most of the cases are clumped tightly around the mean. If the standard deviation is a large value relative to the mean, then the variance is relatively large.

In the case at hand, variation in the rate of misspelling of "minuscule," the variance is quite large, with only one case anywhere close to the mean. The cases on either side of it are at half the mean and double the mean. Now that's variance!

For contrast, let us consider the circulation size of each of these same newspapers at the time their spelling was tested.[1]

Miami Herald	416,196
Los Angeles Times	1,116,334
Philadelphia Inquirer	502,756
Washington Post	769,318
Boston Globe	509,060
New York Times	1,038,829
Chicago Tribune	715,618
Newsday	680,926
Detroit Free Press	629,065

The mean circulation for this group of nine is 708,678 and the standard deviation around that mean is 238,174. So here we have relatively less variance. In a large number of normally distributed cases like these, two-thirds would lie fairly close to the mean—within a third of the mean's value.

One way to get a good picture of the shape of a distribution, including the amount of variance, is with a picture called a *histogram*. Let's start with a mental picture. Intelligence, as measured with standard IQ tests, has a mean of 100 and a standard deviation of 16. So imagine a Kansas wheat field with the stubble burned off, ready for plowing, on which thousands of IQ-tested Kansans have assembled. Each of these Kansans knows his or her IQ score, and there is a straight line on the field marked with numbers at one-meter intervals from 0 to 200. At the blast of a trumpet, each Kansan obligingly lines up facing the marker indicating his or her IQ. Look at figure 4.1. A living histogram! Because IQ is normally distributed, the longest line will be at the 100 marker, and the length of the lines will taper gradually toward the extremes.

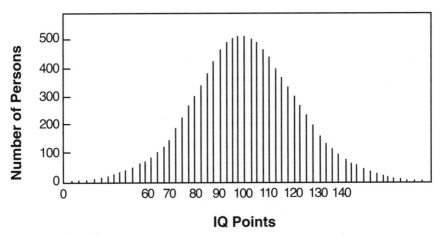

Figure 4.1   IQ Histogram

Some of the lines have been left out to make the histogram easier to draw. If you were to fly over that field in a blimp at high altitude, you might not notice the lines at all. You would just see a curved shape as in figure 4.2. This curve is defined by a series of distinct lines, but statisticians prefer to think of it as a smooth curve, which is okay with us. We don't notice the little steps from one line of people to the next, just as we don't notice the dots in a halftone engraving. This is the familiar bell shape known as the normal curve.

But now you see the logic of the standard deviation. By measuring outward in both directions from the mean, with the standard deviation as your unit of measurement, you can define a specific area of the space under the curve. Just draw two perpendiculars from the baseline to the curve. If those perpendiculars are each one standard deviation—16 IQ points—from the mean, you will have counted off two-thirds of the people in the wheat field. Two-thirds of the population has an IQ between 84 and 116.

For that matter, you could go out about two standard deviations (1.96 if you want to be precise) and know that you had included 95 percent of the people, for 95 percent of the population has an IQ between 68 and 132.

When you are looking at a variable for the first time, the first thing you are going to want is a general picture in your head of its distribution. Does it look like the normal curve? Or does it have two bumps instead of one—meaning that it is *bimodal?* Is the bump about in the center, or does it lean in one direction with a long tail running off in the other direction? The tail indicates *skewness* and suggests that using the mean to summarize that particular set of data carries the risk of being overly influenced by those extreme cases in the tail. Figures 4.3 and 4.4 are histograms illustrating these two departures from normality.

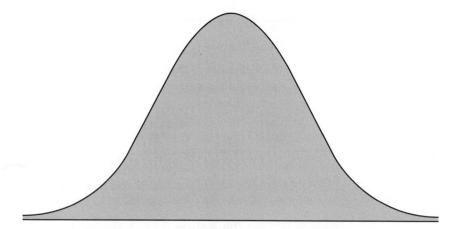

Figure 4.2   Normal Curve

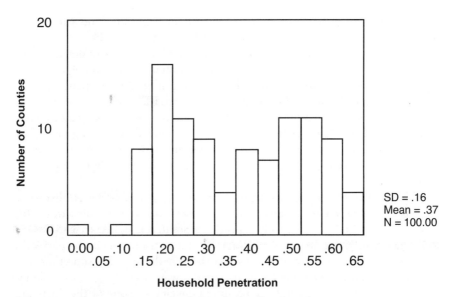

SD = .16
Mean = .37
N = 100.00

Household Penetration

Figure 4.3   Newspaper Penetration in North Carolina Counties

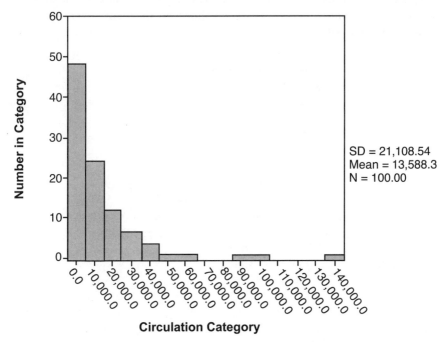

SD = 21,108.54
Mean = 13,588.3
N = 100.00

Circulation Category

Figure 4.4   Raw Newspaper Penetration in North Carolina Counties

The first, Fig. 4.3, shows a two-humped distribution. The variable is household penetration of Audit Bureau of Circulation member newspapers in the one hundred counties of North Carolina. The ticks under the bars represent the midpoints of each range represented by the bars. The height of the bar represents the number of counties in that range of penetration.

Another word for a two-humped distribution is bimodal.

Figure 4.4 is a histogram for the same hundred counties using a different variable, total ABC newspaper circulation. This one shows a long tail off to the right, caused by a small number of counties with very large newspaper circulation. These are, of course, the counties with relatively large populations.

This chart is skewed to the right or positively skewed—that is, distorted by a few relatively high values. If the tail went in the other direction, the distribution would be negatively skewed. In popular use, "skewed" is sometimes taken to mean distorted or invalid. But a distribution can be perfectly accurate and still be skewed. That's just the way the world is sometimes.

Statistical innovator John Tukey invented a way of sizing up a variable by hand.[2] You can do it on the back of an old envelope in one of the dusty attics where interesting records are sometimes kept. Or you can ask SPSS to do it. Here is an example, using quarterly averages of the Gallup approval rating for U.S. presidents since World War II. Tukey calls his organizing scheme a *stem-and-leaf chart*. The stem shows, in shorthand form, the data categories arranged along a vertical line.

Quarterly Average for Presidential Approval

Frequency	Stem & Leaf
2.00	2 . 34
7.00	2 . 6666689
8.00	3 . 00112224
13.00	3 . 5567788889999
20.00	4 . 11111111223334444444
31.00	4 . 5556666666666777777778899999999
23.00	5 . 00000011223333333344444
39.00	5 . 555556666677777778888888888889999999999
34.00	6 . 0000011111112222222333333444444444
19.00	6 . 55556677888889999
14.00	7 . 00000112333444
8.00	7 . 56666688
2.00	8 . 22
1.00	8 . 7

Stem width: 10.0000
Each leaf: 1 case(s)

Approval ratings are two-digit numbers showing the percentage who respond "approve" to the question, "Do you approve or disapprove of the way (name) is handling his job as president?"[3] The column headed "stem" gives the first or tens place in the two-digit number. The second digits, or units places, appear as leaves. Thus each leaf represents one quarterly average.

The leaves in the first line represent values from 20 to 24, the second from 25 to 29, and so on. The stem-and-leaf chart is really a histogram that preserves the original values, rounded here to the nearest full percentage point. It tells us something that would not be obvious from eyeballing an unsorted list. Most of the public, most of the time, approves presidential performance. The low points, 23 and 24 percent respectively, came toward the start of Harry Truman's final year and shortly before Richard Nixon's resignation. The high of 87 was awarded Truman right after he succeeded Franklin D. Roosevelt.

Whenever Gallup announces a new presidential approval rating, it is made more meaningful if placed in context. Having the stem-and-leaf chart in your hand is one way of getting context, but you need something simpler for the typical media audience. You need a typical value.

The most common measure of central tendency is the mean. Its popular name is "average." It is the value that would yield the same overall total if every case or observation had the same value. The mean presidential approval rating for the 221 quarters from 1945 to the first quarter of 2001 is 54.6 percent. The mean is an intuitively satisfying measure of central tendency because of its "all-things-being-equal" quality. If every quarter were the same but the total across all 221 cases remained unchanged, every value would be 54.6.

There are, however, situations where the mean can be misleading: situations where a few cases or even one case is wildly different from the rest. When *USA Today* interviewed all 51 finalists in the 1989 Miss America competition, its researchers asked the candidates how many other pageants they had been involved in on the road to Atlantic City. The mean was a surprisingly high 9.7, but it was affected by one extreme case. One beauty had spent a good portion of her adult life in the pageant business and guessed she had participated in about 150 of them. So the median was a more typical value for this collection of observations. It turned out to be 5.[4]

Median is frequently used for the typical value when reporting on income trends. Income in almost any large population tends to be severely skewed to the high side because a billionaire or two can make the mean wildly unrepresentative. The same is true of many other things measured in money, including home values. The median is defined as the value of the middle case. If you have an even number of cases, as in our 38-newspaper example, the usual convention is to take the point midway between the two middle cases. And the usual way of describing the median is to say that it is the point at which half the cases fall above and half are below. If you have ties—some cases with the same value as the middle case—then that statement is not literally true, but it is close enough.

The stem-and-leaf chart, when you are in a situation where you have to scratch one down by hand, makes it easy to spot the median. In the one above, you need to find the 111th case. There are 110 cases below it and 110 above it. Accumulating with the aid of the column labeled "frequency," you find it in the 8th row, and its value is 56.

The other typical value is the mode or most frequent value. In the stem-and-leaf chart, we can see with the naked eye that 58 is the most frequent, occurring 12 times. Watch your language when referring to the mode. While 58 is the most common value, it is not accurate to say that most of the values are 58. "Most frequent" should not be abbreviated to "most" because the latter implies a majority. The mode denotes only a plurality.

To recapitulate: The interesting things in life are those that vary. When we have a series of observations of something that interests us, we care about the following questions:

1. Is it a variable? (Constants are boring.)
2. If it is a variable, how much does it vary? (Range, variance, standard deviation.)
3. What is the shape of the distribution? (Normal, bimodal, or skewed.)
4. What are the typical values? (Mean, median, mode.)

RELATING TWO VARIABLES

Now we get to the fun part. The examples of hypothesis testing in the previous chapter all involved the relationship of one variable to another. If two things vary together—that is, if one changes whenever the other changes—then something is connecting them. That something is usually causation. Either one variable is the cause of changes in the other, or the two are both affected by some third variable. Many issues in social policy turn on assumptions about causation. If something in society is wrong or not working, it helps to know the cause before you try to fix it.

The first step in proving causation is to show a relationship or a covariance. We have already seen how a histogram can give you a picture of the distribution of a single variable. There is also a graphic display that shows how two continuous variables are related. It is called a scatterplot. Each data point is graphed on two dimensions. If they are not related, you will see a blob. If they are related, you will see something else.

Figure 4.5 is a simple example with U.S. government data on the engine size of certain makes of compact cars and their highway gasoline mileage.

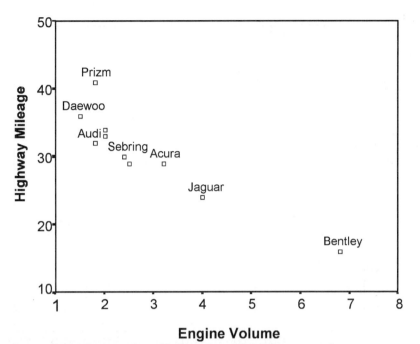

Figure 4.5 Highway Gasoline Mileage and Engine Displacement (Litres)

Engine size, expressed in litres, is on the horizontal or *X*-axis, while gasoline mileage is on the vertical or *Y*-axis. You can see at a glance that as engines get larger, mileage decreases.

Another use of the scatterplot is to discover deviant cases. Figure 4.6 is one from the 2000 presidential election in Florida, showing the vote in each of the sixty-seven counties. The horizontal or *X* scale is the total number of votes for president. The vertical scale is the vote for Pat Buchanan. It should be no surprise that Buchanan's vote tends to increase as the total increases. But look at the outlier!

Palm Beach was the site of the infamous "butterfly ballot," where voters could not clearly determine which punch location was for Al Gore and which was for Pat Buchanan. Without Palm Beach, the counties form a good approximation to a straight line, with some falloff for the two large metropolitan counties in South Florida, where Miami and Ft. Lauderdale, both Democrat strongholds, are located.

Some basic rules for interpreting scatterplots:

1. For consistency's sake, always put the independent variable on the vertical (*X*) scale and the dependent variable on the horizontal (*Y*) scale.

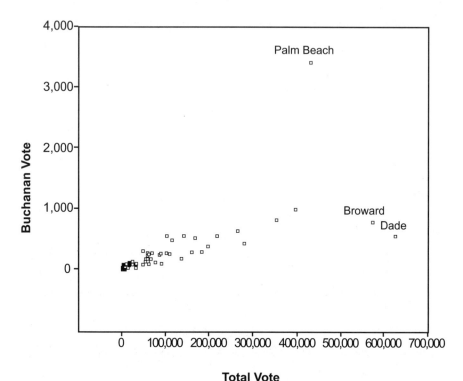

Total Vote

Figure 4.6   Vote for President in Florida Counties, 2000

2. Look for patterns than resemble straight lines or uniform curves.
3. Remember that the news is often in the outliers.

You don't see very many scatterplots in newspapers. Let's take another look at the figure (Fig. 4.5) that shows the effect of engine size on gasoline mileage and consider ways to describe it. Three things make it interesting.

1. The data points fit very closely to a straight line.
2. The line slants quite steeply.
3. The relationship between X and Y is probably not a coincidence.

Each of these observations can be quantified. First we'll look at the plot again, this time with the best-fitting straight line drawn in (Fig. 4.7).

This line is called the "least squares line" because it is the straight line that minimizes the squared distance on the vertical scale between the data points and the regression line (the slanted one). If you want to know how to work it out by hand, get a statistics text. I produced this one with SPSS.

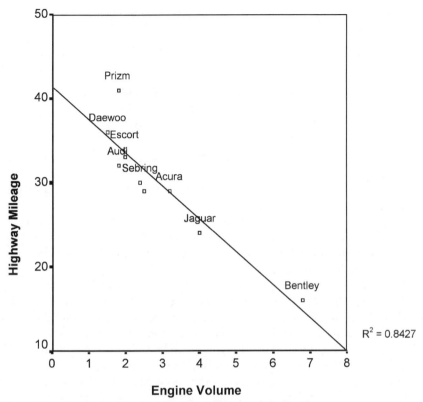

Figure 4.7   **Regression Line for Gasoline Mileage and Engine Size**

The correlation coefficient (r) is a number between 1 and minus 1 that includes three important pieces of information: how tightly the data points fit the line, which way it slopes, and the steepness of the slope. For this line r is −.918, indicating a very close fit and a negative relationship—that is, as X increases, Y decreases.

The best thing about r is that its square can be interpreted as variance explained. In this case, the value of r^2 is .843, meaning that engine size accounts for 84.3 percent of the variation in highway gasoline mileage. (If engine size accounted for all of the variance in gasoline mileage, all of the data points would be exactly on the line and . r^2 would be 1.)

The unexplained variance is represented by each data point's vertical distance from the regression line. The Chevrolet Prizm deviates the most, getting about 6 more miles per gallon than its engine size would predict. Why? Chances are that it is a bit lighter than the other cars. Or it might have a more fuel-efficient engine design. Once we have adjusted for the effect of engine displacement, we can go after the other variables.

Adjusting is easy, because the formula for a straight line is simple. The general formula is

$$Y = C + (b * X)$$

For this particular line, the values make the formula:

$$\text{Highway mileage} = 41.4 - (3.93 * X)$$

where X represents engine displacement in litres. Now let's try a simple declarative sentence: The expected gasoline mileage for cars in this class is 41.4 miles per gallon minus 3.93 miles for each litre of engine displacement.

That's the formula converted to words. To verify it, look at the chart again. The line crosses Y above the zero point of X at 41.4. For that reason, the C in the equation is also called the Y intercept. (The C stands for "constant.") It anchors the sloping line.

And, by inspecting the line, you can verify that it slopes from left to right with a drop of 3.93 miles for each additional litre of engine displacement.

The other quantifiable piece of this picture is how far this correlation is removed from something that would have happened by chance alone. Given the variance in engine sizes and in gasoline mileage scores, how likely would they have fit this closely to a straight line by chance alone?

The answer is $p < .001$. In words, there is less than one chance in a thousand that this relationship is nothing more than an accident. That's worth knowing when you are dealing with sample data and want to know how strong a lead to write, whether or not you ever include a p-value in a story.

Where do these numbers come from? They all came from the following SPSS table (Table 4.4).

The unstandardized coefficients are the components for the straight-line equation. The standard error lets you make an allowance for sampling error. The standardized coefficient (also the correlation coefficient) tells you what the slope would be if you were using standardized scores instead of

Table 4.4 Coefficients[a]

Model	Unstandardized Coefficients		Standardized Coefficients		
	B	Std. Error	Beta	t	Sig.
1 (constant)	41.406	1.910		21.676	.000
Engine volume	−3.931	.600	−.918	−6.547	.000

[a]Dependent variable: highway mileage

raw values. The *t* is an intermediate step in figuring statistical significance, but the number you really want is in the column headed "Sig." It gives the *p*-value or the probability that mere chance produced the appearance of a relationship where there was none. SPSS stops at three zeros, so all you can say is that it is less than one chance in a thousand.

Now let's loop back to the notion of variance explained. We love variance because it's what makes news. We love even more being able to explain it. To appreciate the importance of explaining variance, consider what we would do if we were driving one of these cars across the desert and desperately needed to know its gasoline mileage. If we had no information except that the mean highway mileage for this class of compact automobiles is 30.4, our most prudent guess would be the mean. But if we also knew that the range was from 16 to 41, we would be painfully aware that there was a pretty good chance of serious error.

Now suppose that we had the regression formula and knew the engine displacement of the car we were driving. Now we can produce an estimate that much less prone to error than the mean. Variance explained is the reduction in error we get compared to the errors we would have made by pegging each car's estimate at the mean. In this case, that's 84 percent, which could mean a lot if the desert is vast.

Now a confession. To make this example simple and compelling, I deliberately chose compact cars that are close to one another in weight. In the language of experimental science, I held weight constant, or at least fairly constant. That's good if you want to isolate the effect of engine size, but if you really want to predict gasoline mileage, you should know a car's weight, as well as the size of its engine.

Fortunately, regression works with more than one independent variable. Or you can take the residuals from the previous regression and use them as the dependent variable in a new regression that has weight as the independent variable. What's a residual? Look at the scatterplot again. The residual is the vertical distance from each data point to the regression line. It represents leftover variance that engine displacement did not explain.

And here's a warning: God did not make the world in straight lines. But there are models other than straight-line models that can use the same theory and the same math.

Another warning. In neither social science nor journalism do we always have the luxury of continuous variables. A lot of the variables that make news are measurable only on a categorical level. The table from the previous chapter on the riot participation of southerners and northerners in Detroit is an example. We are still looking for covariance. But instead of seeing it in the form of a linear pattern, we simply compare the incidence of riot participation between the two groups.

Where Were You Brought Up as a Child?

	South	North
Rioters (%)	8	25
Nonrioters (%)	92	75
Total	100	100

It does not take a lot of statistical sophistication to see that there is an association between being brought up in the North and participation in the riot. The table does not tell all that is worth knowing about riot behavior, but it provides some grounding in data for whatever possibilities you might choose to explore.

Let us examine some of the characteristics of this table that make it so easy to understand. Its most important characteristic is that the percentages are based on the variable that most closely resembles a potential cause of the other. The things that happen to you where you are brought up might cause riot behavior. But your riot behavior, since it occurs later in time, can't be the cause of where you were brought up. To demonstrate what an advantage this way of percentaging is, here is the same table with the percentages based on row totals instead of column totals:

Where Were You Brought Up as a Child?

	South	North	Total
Rioters (%)	27	73	100
Nonrioters (%)	59	41	100

This table has as much information as the previous one, but your eye has to hunt around for the relevant comparison. It is found across the rows of either column. Try the first column. Fifty-nine percent of the nonrioters, but only 27 percent of the rioters, were raised in the South. If you stare at the table long enough and think about it earnestly enough, it will be just as convincing as the first table. But thinking about it is harder work because the percentage comparisons are based on the presumed effect, not the cause. Your thought process has to wiggle a little bit to get the drift. So remember the First Law of Cross-Tabulation:

Always base the percentages in a cross-tabulation on the totals for the independent variable.

And what is the independent variable? *Independent* is one of those slippery words discussed earlier that helps us avoid leaping to an assumption about causation. If one of these variables is a cause of the other, it is the *independent* variable. The presumed effect is the *dependent* variable. You can make all of this easy for yourself if you always construct your tables—whether it is on the back of an envelope or with a computer program—so that the independent variable is in the columns (the parts of the table that go up and down) and the dependent variable is in the rows (the parts of the table that go from side to side).

If you can do that, and if you can remember to always make the percentages add up to 100 in the columns, your ability to deal with numbers will take a great leap forward. Just make your comparisons across the rows of the table. My years in the classroom have taught me that journalism students who have mastered this simple concept of statistics understand covariance much better. So it is worth dwelling on. For practice, look at the now-familiar Detroit riot table.

Where Were You Brought Up as a Child?

	South	North
Rioters (%)	8	25
Nonrioters (%)	92	75
Total	100	100

If we want to know what might cause rioting—and we do—the relevant comparison is between the numbers that show the rioting rates for the two categories of the independent variable, the northerners and southerners. The latter's rate is 8 percent and the former's is 25 percent, a threefold difference. Just looking at those two numbers and seeing that one is a lot bigger than the other tells you much of what you need to know.

Here are some comparisons *not* to make (and I have seen their like often, in student papers and in the print media):

Bad comparison no. 1: "Eight percent of the southerners rioted, compared to 92 percent who did not." That's redundant. If 8 percent did and there are only two categories, then you are wasting your publication's ink and your reader's time by spelling out the fact that 92 percent did not riot.

Bad comparison no. 2: "Eight percent of the southerners rioted, compared to 75 percent of the northerners who did not riot." Talk about apples and oranges! Some writers think that numbers are so boring that they have to jump around a table to liven things up, hence the comparison across the diagonal. That it makes no sense at all is something they seem not to notice.

Finally, pay attention to and note in your verbal description of the table the exact nature of the percentage base. Some people who write about percentages appear to think that the base doesn't matter. Such writers assume that saying that 8 percent of the southerners rioted is the same as saying 8 percent of the rioters were from the South. It isn't! If you are not convinced of this, look at the table with the raw numbers that follows in the next section.

But first, one more example to nail the point down. Victor Cohn, in an excellent book on statistics for journalists, cited a report from a county in California that widows were 15 percent of all their suicides and widowers only 5 percent. This difference led someone to conclude that males tolerate loss of marital partners better than females do. The conclusion was wrong. Widows did more of everything, just because there were so many of them. What we really want to know is the *rate* of suicide among the two groups, and that requires basing the percentage on the gender of the surviving spouse, not on all suicides. It turns out that females were the hardier survivors, because 0.4 percent of the widows and 0.6 percent of the widowers were suicides.[5]

DRAWING INFERENCES

When an interesting relationship is found, the first question is "What hypothesis does it support?" If it turns out to support an interesting hypothesis, the next question is "What are the rival hypotheses?" The obvious and ever-present rival hypothesis is that the difference that fascinates us and bears out our hunch is nothing but a coincidence, a statistical accident, the laws of chance playing games with us. The northerners in our sample were three times as likely to riot as the southerners? So what? Maybe if we took another sample, the relationship would be reversed.

There is a way to answer this question. You will never get an absolute answer, but you can get a relative answer that is pretty good. The way to do it is to measure just how big a coincidence it would have to be if indeed coincidence is what it is. In other words, how likely is it that we would get such a preponderance of northern rioting over southern rioting by chance alone, if in fact the two groups were equal in their riot propensity?

And the exact probability of getting a difference that peculiar can be calculated. Usually, however, it is estimated through something called the chi-square distribution, discovered by an Englishman named Carl Fisher who applied it to experiments in agriculture. To understand its logic, we are going to look at the Detroit table one more time. This time, instead of percentages, we shall put the actual number of cases in each cell.

Where Were You Brought Up as a Child?

	South	North	Total
Rioters (%)	19	51	70
Nonrioters (%)	218	149	367
Total	237	200	437

The two sets of totals, for the columns and the rows, are called *marginals,* because that's where you find them. The question posed by Fisher's chi-square test is this: Given the marginal values, how many different ways can the distributions in the four cells vary, and what proportion of those variations is at least as unbalanced as the one we found?

That is one way to ask the question. Here is another that might be easier to understand. If the marginals are given and the cell values are random variations, we can calculate the probable or mathematically *expected* value for each of the cells. Just multiply the row total for each cell by its column total and divide the result by the total number of cases. For the southern rioters, for example, in the upper left corner, the expected value is (200 * 70) / 437 = 32. That expected value is considerably different from the observed value of 51.

By finding the differences between your observed values and the expected values derived from the chi-square test, you can figure out just how goofy and unexpected your table is. You need two things: the formula for calculating the chi-square value and Fisher's table that gives the probability of getting a value that high. (If you have a computer and a good statistical package, you don't need either, but that's another chapter.) It is good to be able to calculate a chi-square by hand. Here is the short formula for doing it with a two-by-two table with cells A, B, C, and D:

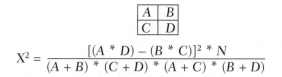

$$X^2 = \frac{[(A * D) - (B * C)]^2 * N}{(A + B) * (C + D) * (A + C) * (B + D)}$$

The formula is not as difficult as it looks. All it says is that you multiply the diagonals of the table, subtract one result from the other, square the outcome, and multiply by the total number of cases in the table. Then divide by each of the values in the margins of the table.

Here's what happens when you apply it to the previous Detroit table: 19 times 149 is 2,831 and 51 times 218 is 11,118. Subtract one product from the other, and you get 8,287.

The square of 8,287 is 68,674,369. Multiplying that by the total number of cases in the table, 437, produces a big, hairy number: 30,010,699,253. That number is so big that your standard four-function calculator can't handle it. A better calculator that uses scientific notation might show it as 3.0011 10, meaning that the decimal point belongs ten places to the right and that precision in the last few digits is not available in your calculator's display. No problem. The next step in your formula makes the number smaller.

Just divide that number by each of the marginals in turn. First divide by 237, divide the result by 200, that result by 367 and so on. The end result rounds off to a chi-square value of 24.6.

In a two-by-two table, the chi-square values needed for different levels of probability are as follows:

Chi-square	Probability
2.706	.10
3.841	.05
5.412	.02
6.635	.01
10.827	.001

Since the chi-square in the Detroit table is greater than 10.827, the likelihood that the difference between northern and southern riot behavior was a chance aberration is less than one in a thousand. It now becomes a case of which you find easier to believe: that something about being from the North makes a person more likely to participate in the riot, or that a greater than a thousand-to-one long-shot coincidence occurred.

That is really all chi-square is good for: comparing what you have to what pure chance would have produced. If coincidence is a viable explanation, and it often will be, then in evaluating that explanation it helps to know how big a coincidence it takes to produce the sort of thing you found. The chi-square test is that evaluation tool.

In the statistical literature, there has been a debate over whether chi-square applies to all situations where coincidence is an alternative explanation or just to those where sample data are involved. Some social scientists say the test measures nothing but sampling error, the random deviation of a sample from the population out of which it was drawn. If your study covers every case in an entire population, you don't need a chi-square or similar test, they argue. But in both journalistic and social science applications there will be situations where you will look at an entire population and still be concerned about the chance factor as one way to account for the peculiar things you find.

For example, you might examine the academic records of all the NCAA Division I basketball players for a given year and compare the graduation rates of these athletes at different schools. If some schools have higher or lower graduation rates, one explanation is that there is a lot of variation in graduation rates and the differences are just due to the random patterns of that particular year. The chi-square test lets you compare the distribution you found to a chance distribution. Of course, even this case involves a sample of sorts, because when you look at the record for a year, you are probably going to draw inferences about the way different schools manage their basketball programs and you are projecting to past years and maybe even to future years. You might even think of your one-year data set as a sample of an infinite universe of all possible years and all possible Division I schools.

The bottom line for journalistic applications: Whenever you have a situation where someone is likely to challenge your results by claiming coincidence, use chi-square or a related test to find out how big a coincidence it takes to explain what you have.

Chi-square belongs to a large family of statistical tests called *significance tests*. All yield a *significance level*, which is just the probability of getting, by chance alone, a difference of the magnitude you found. Therefore, the lower the probability, the greater the significance level. If $p = .05$, it means the distribution is the sort that chance could produce in 5 cases out of 100. If you are planning to base a lead on your hypothesis and want to find significance, then the smaller the probability number, the better. (A big coincidence is an event with a low probability of happening.)

In addition to chi-square, there is one other significance test you are likely to need sooner or later. It is a test for comparing the differences between two means. It is called *Student's t*, or the t-test for short. There are two basic forms: one for comparing the means of two groups (*independent samples*) and one for comparing the means of two variables in the same group (*paired samples*). This test is not as easy to calculate by hand as chi-square. If you want to learn how, consult a statistics text. All the good statistical packages for computers have t-tests as standard offerings.

One final point about significance tests:

Low probability (i.e., high significance) is not always the same thing as important. Low probability events are, paradoxically, quite commonplace, especially if you define them after the fact. Here is a thought experiment. Make a list of the first five people you passed on the street, on the campus, or at the most recent public place where you walked. Now think back to where you were one year ago today. Projecting ahead a year, what would have been the probability that all the random events in the lives of those five people would have brought them into your line of vision in that particular order on this particular day? Quite remote, of course. But it doesn't mean anything, because there was nothing to predict it. Now suppose you had met a psychic with a crystal ball, and she had written the names of those five people on a piece of paper, sealed it in an envelope, and given you the envelope to open one year later. If you did and her prediction proved to be true, that would have led you to search for explanations other than coincidence. That's what statistical significance does for you.

When unusual events happen, it is not their unusualness alone that makes them important. It is how they fit into a larger picture as part of a theoretical model that gives them importance. Remember Rick (played by Humphrey Bogart) in the film *Casablanca* when he pounds the table? "Of all the gin joints in all the towns in all the world, she walks into mine," he says. The coincidence is important only because he and the woman who walked in had a history with unresolved conflict. Her appearance fit into a larger pattern. Most improbable events are meaningless because they don't fit into a larger pattern. One way to test for the fit of an unusual event in a larger pattern is by using it to test a theory's predictive power. In science and in journalism, one looks for the fit.

CONTINUOUS VARIABLES

You have noticed by now that we have been dealing with two different ways of measuring variables. In the Detroit riot table, we measured by classifying

people into discrete categories: northerner or southerner, rioter or nonri-
oter. But when we measured highway mileage and engine displacement for
compact cars, both measures were continuous. Most statistics textbooks
suggest four or five kinds of measurement, but the basic distinction is between categorical and continuous.

One kind of measurement is a hybrid of the two. It is called *ordinal* measurement. If you can put the things you are measuring in some kind of rank
order without knowing the exact value of the continuous variable on which
you are ordering them, you have something that gives more information
than a categorical measure but less than a continuous one. In fact, you can
order the ways of measuring things by the amount of information they involve. From lowest to highest, they are

Categorical (also called *nominal*);
Ordinal (ranking); and
Continuous (also called *interval,* unless it has a zero point to anchor it,
  in which case it is called *ratio*).

Categorical measures are the most convenient for journalism because
they are easiest to explain. But the others are often useful because of the
additional information about relative magnitude that they contain. When
collecting data, it is often a good idea to try for the most information that
you can reasonably get. You can always downgrade it in the analysis.

In the Detroit case, we used categorical measures to show how two conditions, northernness and rioting, occur together more often than can readily be explained by chance. If the rioters in Detroit had been measured by
how many hours and minutes they spent rioting, a nice continuous measure
of intensity would have resulted. And that measure could easily have been
converted to an ordinal or categorical measure just by setting cutting points
for classification purposes. The Detroit data collection did not do that, however, and there is no way to move in the other direction and convert a categorical measure to a continuous one because that would require additional
information that the categorical measure does not pick up.

SAMPLING

Everybody samples. Your editor looks out the window, sees a lot of women
in short skirts, and commissions the style section to do a piece on the return of the miniskirt. You buy a Toyota and suddenly you notice when you
drive down the street that every other car you pass is a Toyota. Their ubiq-
uity had escaped your notice before, and you hadn't realized what a con-
formist you were turning out to be. All of us extrapolate from what we see

to what is unseen. Such sampling might be termed *accidental sampling*. If the results are generalizable, it is an accident.

Scientific method needs something better. Unfortunately, there is no known way to produce a sample with certainty that the sample is just like the real world. But there is a way to sample with a known risk of error of a given magnitude. It is based on probability theory, and it is called *probability sampling*.

Try an experiment. It requires ten pennies. You can do it as a thought experiment or you can actually get ten pennies, find a cup to shake them in, and toss them onto a flat surface so that each penny has an even chance of landing with the head facing up.

That is a sample. Of what? It is a sample of all of the possible coin flips in the universe through all of recorded and unrecorded time, both past and future. In that theoretical universe of theoretical flips of unbiased coins, what is the ratio of heads to tails? Of course: 50-50. When you flip just ten coins, you are testing to see how much and how often a sample of ten will deviate from that true ratio of 50-50. The "right" answer is five heads and five tails. (That's redundant. For the rest of this discussion, we'll refer only to the number of heads because the number of tails has to be, by the definition of the experiment, equal to ten minus the number of heads.)

So go ahead, try it. Are you going to get exactly five heads on the first throw? Probably not. While that outcome is more likely than any other definite number of heads, it is not more probable than all the other possibilities put together.

Probability theory can tell us what to expect. There are exactly 1,024 ways to flip ten coins. (To understand why, you'll have to find a basic statistics text. But here is a hint: The first coin has two possibilities, heads and tails. For each of those, the second coin creates two more possible patterns. And so it goes until you have multiplied two times itself ten times. Two to the tenth power is 1,024.) Of those finite possibilities or permutations, only one contains ten heads and only one contains zero heads. So those two probabilities are each 1/1024 or, in decimals, .00098. The other outcomes are more probable because there are more ways to get them. A total of one head can happen in ten different ways (first toss, second toss, etc.). A total of two can happen in 45 different ways. Here is chart to show the expected outcome of 1,024 flips of ten coins (figure 4.8 provides a histogram to help you visualize it):

Heads:	10	9	8	7	6	5	4	3	2	1	0
Frequency:	1	10	45	120	210	252	210	120	45	10	1

If you think of each toss of ten coins as a sample, you can see how sampling works. The chances of your being badly misled by a sample of only ten are not too great. But the best part is that the risk is knowable.

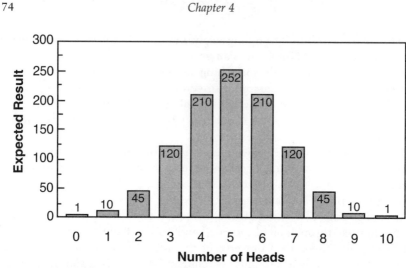

Figure 4.8   Flipping 10 Coins: 1,024 Trials

Figure this out: What is the risk that your sample of ten would be more than 20 percentage points off the "true" value? The true value in our imaginary universe of all coin flips is 50 percent heads. Allowing for a 20-point deviation in either direction gives us a range of 30 to 70 either way. And if you add up the expected outcomes in the 1,024 possible, you find that only 112 of them (56 in each *tail* of the distribution) are outside the 30-to-70 range. So you can be 90 percent certain that your first toss—or any given toss—will yield from 3 to 7 heads. In other words, it will be within 20 percentage points of being exactly representative of the total universe.

That is a pretty important concept, and to let it soak in, you might want to flip ten coins a few times and try it. Or if you are using this book in a class, get the whole class to do it and track a hundred or so tries on the blackboard. The distribution will gradually start to look like the histogram in figure 4.8, and it will help you convince yourself that there is some reality to these hypothetical probabilities.

Now consider what we can do with it. Two important tools have just been handed to you:

1. When you sample, you can deal with a known error margin.
2. You can know the probability that your sample will fall within that error margin.

The first is called *sampling error.*
The second is called *confidence level.*

Here's the good part: You can choose whatever sampling error you want to work with and calculate its confidence level. We did that with the coin flips: We set the sampling error at 20 percentage points and found out by looking at the sampling distribution that the confidence level was 90 percent.

Alternatively—and this happens more often in everyday life—you can set the confidence level you are comfortable with and then calculate an error margin to fit it.

To do that, you have to have an equation. Here is the equation for calculating the error margin at the 68 percent level of confidence:

$$E = \text{sqrt}\ (.25\ /\ n)$$

The n in the formula is the sample size. That .25 in the parentheses represents the variance in the coin-flipping case or, for that matter, in any case where the real-world distribution is 50-50—a close election with two candidates, for example. The shortcut formula for variance in any situation where there are just two possible outcomes (heads or tails, Republican or Democrat, boy or girl) is

$$p\ ^*\ q$$

where p is the probability of getting one outcome and q is the probability of the other. The sum of p and q has to be 1, so q is defined as $1 - p$. The formula for sampling error uses .25 to be conservative. That's the maximum variance in the two-outcome situation. If the split were 60-40 instead of 50-50, the variance would be .24. If it were 90-10, the variance would be .09.

To see that the formula makes intuitive sense, try it out for a sample of one. Sound crazy? Sure. If you tried to generalize to the universe of all possible coin flips from just one trial, you couldn't possibly get it right. And the formula lets you know that. Work it out. It gives you a sampling error of .5, or plus or minus 50 percentage points, which pretty much covers the ballpark. Now try it for a sample of 100. Sampling error is now plus or minus 5 percentage points, which is a lot better.

In most sampling situations, we are not content with a confidence level of 68 percent. The formula gives the sampling error for that confidence level because it covers one standard error around the true value. Standard error is like the concept of standard deviation around the mean in a population. When dealing with a sample, it makes sense to call it standard error because the reference point is an exact (although often unknown) real-world value, rather than the foggier concept of central tendency. Remember the example of the Kansans in the wheat field? And how one standard deviation in each direction from the mean of a population covers two-thirds of the cases in a normal distribution? In a sample distribution, something similar happens. One standard error in each direction covers two-thirds of the expected samples. If you flipped coins in groups of 100, two-thirds of the groups would yield an error of no more than 5 percentage points: that is, they would turn up between 45 and 55 heads. In real life, one usually deals with one sample at a time, and so it is easier to think in terms of probabilities. In a sample of 100, the probability is 68 percent that the error is within plus or minus 5 percentage points.

Suppose 68 percent isn't enough confidence? If you kept that as your life-long standard, you would be embarrassed one time out of three. If you did a dozen polls a year, four of them would turn out wrong. In both journalistic and social science applications, most practitioners prefer a higher level of confidence. How do you get it? By covering more of the space under the sampling distribution curve. Covering two standard errors, for example, includes slightly more than 95 percent of the possibilities. Of course, the error margin goes up when you do that, because those added possibilities all involve greater error than the 5 percent that falls within the one standard error range. Life is a trade-off.

Because of a fondness for round numbers, most people who work with samples set the 95 percent confidence level as their standard. That means being right 19 times out of 20, which is pretty good over the course of a career. The exact number of standard errors it takes to attain that is 1.96 in either direction. And cranking it into the formula is simple enough:

$$E = 1.96 * \text{sqrt} (.25 / n)$$

And you can modify the formula to change the confidence level whenever you want. The standard textbook designation for the term we just added to the formula for sampling error is z. When $z = 1$, the confidence level is 68 percent, and when $z = 1.96$, the confidence level is 95 percent. Here are some other confidence levels for different values of z.

z	Confidence
.95	65.0%
1.04	70.0
1.17	75.0
1.28	80.0
1.44	85.0
1.65	90.0
1.96	95.0
2.58	99.0
3.29	99.9

Remember that you can have a high confidence level or you can have a small margin for sampling error, but you usually can't have both unless your sample is very large. To get a feel for the trade-offs involved, try this exercise. Take the general formula for sampling error:

$$E = z * \text{sqrt } (.25 / n)$$

and recast it to solve for z:

$$z = 2 * E * \text{sqrt } (n)$$

and to solve for sample size:

$$n = .25 * (z^2 / E^2)$$

Now try out various combinations of sample size, error, and confidence level on your pocket calculator to see how they change. Better yet, put these formulas into a spreadsheet program where you can vary the error margin, the z for different confidence levels, and the sample size to see how they interact with one another. What you will find is some good news and some bad news. First, the bad news:

Increasing the sample size a lot decreases the sampling error only a little.

The good news is the converse proposition:

Decreasing the sample size doesn't increase sampling error as much as you might think.

Here is a number to keep in your head as a reference point: 384. That is the sample size you need for a 5 percent error margin at the 95 percent level of confidence.

Double it to 768, and sampling error is still 3.5 percentage points. Cut it in half to 192, and sampling error is still only 7 percentage points.

The question of how much error you can tolerate and what it is worth to trim that error will be considered in the chapter on surveys. We will also look at some cost-effective ways to improve accuracy in surveys. But for now, relax. The next chapter is about using computers to make these things easy.

NOTES

1. *Editor & Publisher International Year Book 1989,* New York. The figures are for the period ending September 30, 1988.

2. John W. Tukey, *Exploratory Data Analysis* (Boston: Addison-Wesley, 1972), 7–26.

3. Personal correspondence from Lydia Saad of the Gallup Organization. The numbers are quarterly averages rounded to the nearest full percentage point.

4. Electronic mail communication from Barbara Pearson, *USA Today,* August 24, 1989.

5. Victor Cohn, *News and Numbers: A Guide to Reporting Statistical Claims and Controversies in Health and Related Fields* (Ames: Iowa State University Press, 1989).

5

✦

Computers

Computers used to be exciting and esoteric. Now they are mundane and ubiquitous. Reporters who applied them to investigative analysis liked to brag in print that they were doing "computer-assisted reporting."[1] In a world where almost everything is computer assisted, that no longer means a lot, although a gap has developed between older and younger journalists. Older journalists have not adopted the new tools as eagerly and thoroughly as younger ones, who learn the current technology in journalism school.

Word processing has made it possible for the once-specialized tasks of editing, typesetting, proofreading, and page composition to be merged. The Internet has greatly reduced the number of physical trips a reporter needs to make to the library or other archives. And e-mail has made news sources more accessible. Each of these applications is a form of computer-assisted reporting.

This chapter, however, is concerned with none of those obvious applications. Its purpose is to convince you that the computer is important as an analytical tool. As background, we shall now indulge in a little bit of nostalgia.

COUNTING AND SORTING

Bob Kotzbauer was the *Akron Beacon Journal*'s legislative reporter, and I was its Washington correspondent. In the fall of 1962, Ben Maidenburg, the executive editor, assigned us the task of driving around Ohio for two weeks, knocking on doors and asking people how they would vote in the coming election for governor. Because I had studied political science at Chapel Hill, I felt sure that I knew how to do this chore. We devised a paper form to record voter choices and certain other facts about each voter: party affiliation, previous voting record, age, and occupation. The forms were color coded: green for male voters, pink for females. We met many interesting people and filed daily stories full of qualitative impressions of the mood of the voters and descriptions of county fairs and autumn leaves. After two weeks, we had accumulated enough of the pink and green forms to do the quantitative part. What happened next is a little hazy in my mind after all these years, but it was something like this:

On a library table in Akron, we spread out the forms and sorted them into three stacks: previous Republican voters, Democratic voters, and nonvoters. That helped us gauge the validity of our sample. Then we divided each of the three stacks into three more: voters for Mike DiSalle, the incumbent Democrat; votes for James Rhodes, the Republican challenger; and undecided. Nine stacks, now. We sorted each into two more piles, separating the pink and green pieces of paper to break down the vote by sex. Eighteen stacks. Sorting into four categories of age required dividing each of those eighteen piles into four more, which would have made seventy-two. I don't remember exactly how far we got before we gave up, exhausted and squinty-eyed. Our final story said the voters were inscrutable, and the race was too close to call.

The moral of this story is that before you embark on any complicated project involving data analysis, you should look around first and see what technology is available. There were no personal computers in 1962. Mainframe computing was expensive and difficult, not at all accessible to newspaper reporters. But there was in the *Beacon Journal* business office a machine that would have saved us time if we had known about it. The basic concept for it had been developed nearly eighty years earlier by Dr. Herman Hollerith, the father of modern computing.

Hollerith was an assistant director of the United States Census at a time when the census was in trouble. It took seven and a half years to tabulate the census of 1880, and the country was growing so fast that it appeared that the 1890 census would not be finished when it was time for the census of 1900 to be well under way. Herman Hollerith saved the day by inventing the punched card.

It was a simple three-by-five-inch index card divided into quarter-inch squares. Each square stood for one bit of binary information: a hole in the square meant "yes" and the absence of a hole meant "no." All of the categories being tabulated could fit on the card. One group of squares, for example, stood for age category in five-year segments. If you were 21 years old on April 1, 1890, there would be a card for you, and the card would have a hole punched in the 20–24 square.

Under Hollerith's direction, a machine was built that could read 40 holes at a time. The operator would slap a card down on its bed and pull a lid over it. Tiny spikes would stop when they encountered a solid portion of the card and pass through where they encountered holes. Below each spike was a cup of mercury. When the spike touched the mercury, an electrical contact was completed, causing a counter on the vertical face of the machine to advance one notch. This machine was called the Tabulator.

There was more. Hollerith invented a companion machine, called the Sorter, which was wired into the same circuit. It had compartments corresponding to the dials on the Tabulator, each with its own little door. The same electrical contact that advanced a dial on the Tabulator caused a door on the Sorter to fly open so that the operator could drop the tallied card into it. A clerk could take the cards for a whole census tract, sort them by age in this manner, and then sort each stack by gender to create a table of age by sex distribution for the tract. Hollerith was so pleased with his inventions that he left the Bureau and founded his own company to bid on the tabulation contract for the 1890 census. His bid was successful, and he did the job in two years, even though the population had increased by 25 percent since 1880.

Improvements on the system began almost immediately. Hollerith won the contract for the 1900 census, but then the Bureau assigned one of its employees, James Powers, to develop its own version of the punched-card machine. Like Hollerith, Powers left to start his own company. The two men squabbled over patents and, eventually, each sold out. Powers's firm was absorbed by a component of what would one day become Sperry Univac, and Hollerith's was folded into what finally became IBM. By 1962, when Kotzbauer and I were sweating over those five hundred scraps of paper, the *Beacon Journal* had, unknown to us, an IBM counter-sorter that was the great-grandchild of those early machines. It used wire brushes touching a copper roller instead of spikes and mercury, it sorted 650 cards per minute, and it was obsolete even before we found out about it.

By that time, the Hollerith card, as it was still called, had smaller holes arranged in 80 columns and 12 rows. That 80-column format is still found in many computer applications, simply because data archivists got in the habit of using 80 columns and never found a reason to change, even after computers permitted much longer records. I can understand that. The punched card had a certain concreteness about it, and, to this day, when trying to understand a complicated record layout in a magnetic storage medium, I find that it helps if I visualize those Hollerith cards with the little holes in them.

Computer historians have been at a loss to figure out where Hollerith got the punched-card idea. One story holds that it came to him when he watched a railway conductor punching tickets. Other historians note that the application of the concept goes back at least to the Jacquard loom, built in France in the early 1800s. Wire hooks passed through holes in punched cards to pick up threads to form the pattern. The player piano, patented in 1876, used the same principle. A hole in a given place in the roll means hit a particular key at a particular time and for a particular duration; no hole means don't hit it. Any piano composition can be reduced to those binary signals.[2]

After counting and sorting, the next step is to perform mathematical calculations with the encoded data. These operations require the basic pieces of modern computer hardware: a device to store data and instructions, machinery for doing the arithmetic, and something to manage the traffic as raw information goes in and processed data come out. J. H. Muller, a German, designed such a machine in 1786, but lacked the technology to build it. British mathematician Charles Babbage tried to build one starting in 1812. He, too, had good ideas that were too far ahead of the available technology. In 1936, when Howard Aiken started planning the Mark I computer at Harvard, he found that Babbage had anticipated many of the challenges. Babbage, for example, foresaw the need to provide "a store" in which raw data and results are kept and "a mill" where the computations take place.[3] Babbage's store and mill are today called "memory" and "central processing unit" or CPU. The machine Babbage envisioned would have been driven by steam. Although the Mark I used electrical relays, it was basically a mechanical device. Electricity turned the switches on and off, and the on-off condition held the binary information. It generated much heat and noise. Pieces of it were still on display at Harvard's Science Center in 2001.

Mark I and Aiken served in the Navy toward the end of World War II, working on ballistics problems. This was the project that got Grace Murray Hopper started in the computer business. Then a young naval officer, she rose to the rank of admiral and contributed some key concepts to the development of computers along the way.

Parallel work was going on under sponsorship of the Army, which also needed complicated ballistics problems worked out. A machine called ENIAC, which used vacuum tubes, resistors, and capacitors instead of mechanical relays, was begun for the Army at the University of Pennsylvania, based in part on ideas used in a simpler device built earlier at Iowa State University by John Vincent Atanasoff and his graduate assistant, Clifford E. Berry. The land-grant college computer builders did not bother to patent their work; it was put aside during World War II, and the machine was cannibalized for parts. The Ivy League inventors were content to take the credit until the Atanasoff-Berry Computer, or ABC machine, as it came to be known, was rediscovered in a 1973 patent suit between two corporate giants. Sperry Rand Corp., then owner of the ENIAC patent, was challenged by Honeywell, Inc., which objected to paying royalties to Sperry Rand. The

Honeywell people tracked down the Atanasoff-Berry story, and a federal district judge ruled that the ENIAC was derived from Atanasoff's work and was therefore not patentable. That's how Atanasoff, a theoretical physicist who only wanted a speedy way to solve simultaneous equations, became recognized as the father of the modern computer. The key ideas were the use of electronic rather than mechanical switches, the use of binary numbers, and the use of logic circuits rather than direct counting to manipulate those binary numbers. These ideas came to the professor while having a drink in an Iowa roadhouse in the winter of 1937, and he built his machine for $6,000.[4]

ENIAC, on the other hand, cost $487,000. It was not completed in time to aid the war effort, but once turned on in February 1946, it lasted for nearly ten years, demonstrating the reliability of electronic computing, and paved the way for the postwar developments. Its imposing appearance, banks and banks of wires, dials, and switches, still influences cartoon views of computers.

Once the basic principles had been established in the 1940s, the problems became those of refining the machinery (the hardware) and developing the programming (the software) to control it. By the 1990s, a look backward saw three distinct phases in computing machinery, based on the primary electronic device that did the work:

First generation: vacuum tubes (ENIAC, UNIVAC)
Second generation: transistors (IBM 7090)
Third generation: integrated circuits (IBM 360 series)

Transistors are better than tubes because they are cheaper, more reliable, smaller, faster, and generate less heat. Integrated circuits are built on tiny solid-state chips that combine many transistors in a very small space. How small? Well, all of the computing power of the IBM 7090, which filled a good-sized room when I was introduced to it at Harvard in 1966, is now packed into a chip the size of my fingernail. How do they make such complicated things so small? By way of a photo-engraving process. The circuits are designed on paper, photographed so that a lens reduces the image—just the way your camera reduces the image of your house to fit on a frame of 35 mm film—and etched on layers of silicon.

As computers got better, they got cheaper, but one more thing had to happen before their use could extend to the everyday life of such nonspecialists as journalists. They had to be made easy to use. That is where Admiral Grace Murray Hopper earned her place in computer history. (One of her contributions was being the first person to debug a computer: When the Mark I broke down one day in 1945, she traced the problem to a dead moth caught in a relay switch.) She became the first person to build an entire career on computer programming. Perhaps her most important contribution, in 1952, was her development of the first assembly language.

To appreciate the importance of that development, think about a computer doing all its work in binary arithmetic. Binary arithmetic represents all numbers with combinations of zeros and ones. To do its work, the computer has to receive its instructions in binary form. This fact of life limited the use of computers to people who had the patience, brainpower, and attention span to think in binary. Hopper quickly realized that computers were not going to be useful to large numbers of people so long as that was the case, and so she wrote an assembly language. An assembly language assembles groups of binary machine language statements into the most frequently used operations and lets the user invoke them by working in a simpler language that uses mnemonic codes to make the instructions easy to remember. The user writes the program in the assembly language and the software converts each assembler statement into the corresponding machine language statements—all of them "transparent" or out of sight of the user—and the computer does what it is told just as if it had been given the orders in its own machine language. That was such a good idea that it soon led to yet another layer of computer languages called compilers. The assembly languages were machine specific; the compilers were written so that once you learned one, you could use it on different machines. The compilers were designed for specialized applications. FORTRAN (formula translator) was designed for scientists and remained a standard for many years. COBOL (common business-oriented language) was produced, under the prodding of Admiral Hopper, and lasted for several decades as the world standard for business applications. BASIC (beginners all-purpose symbolic instruction code) was created at Dartmouth College to provide an easy language for beginners.

To these three layers—machine language, assembler, and compiler—has been added yet a fourth layer. Higher-level special purpose languages are easy to use and highly specialized. They group compiler programs and let the user invoke them in a way that is almost like talking to the computer in plain English. For statistical applications, the two world leaders at the turn of the century were SPSS (Statistical Package for the Social Sciences) and SAS (Statistical Analysis System). If you are going to do extensive analysis of computer databases, sooner or later you will probably want to learn one or both of these two higher-level languages. Here is an example that will show you why:

You have a database that lists every honorarium reported by every member of Congress for a given year. The first thing you want to know is the central tendency, so you write a program to give you the mean and the standard deviation. A FORTRAN program would have required twenty-two steps. In

SAS, once the data have been described to the computer, there are just three lines of code. In SPSS there is only one. With the Windows version of SPSS, you can do it with just five mouse clicks. The software responds to the clicks by writing code transparently in the background. (But you can set the program to print out the code so that you will have a record of all your points and clicks.)

So much has become transparent for end users that computing is starting to look like magic. Every computer needs a system for controlling its activity, directing instructions to the proper resources. Starting with the first of the third-generation IBM mainframe computers, the language enabling the user to control the operating system was called JCL, for Job Control Language. Now "job control language" has become a generic term to mean the language used to run any operating system. (On second-generation mainframes, which could only work on one job at a time, we filled out a pencil-and-paper form telling the computer operator what tapes to mount on what drives and what switches to set on which positions.) These operating systems also included some utility programs that let you do useful things with data like sorting, copying, protecting, and merging files.

One other kind of software is needed for batch computing. If you are going to send the computer a list of instructions, you need a system for entering and editing those instructions. Throughout the 1960s and part of the 1970s, instructions were entered on punched cards. You typed the instructions at a card-punching machine and edited them by throwing away the cards with mistakes and substituting good ones. Today the instructions are entered directly into computer memory and edited there with a word processor. If you do mainframe computing, you will have to learn one of the editor systems available for that particular mainframe. Personal computer programs have their own built-in editors, and you can learn them at the same time you learn the underlying program. You can also use the word processing program with which you are most familiar to write and edit computer programs.

COMPUTERS TODAY

The first decision to make when approaching a task that needs a computer is whether to do the job on a mainframe or on a personal computer. The second is what software to use. Software can generally be classified into two kinds: that which operates interactively, generally by presenting you with choices from a menu and responding to your choices, and that which operates in batch mode, where you present a complete list of instructions and get back a complete job. Some statistical packages offer aspects of both, and point-and-click menu-driven programs have become the most popular. But it is still good to know the underlying code. Pointing and clicking is convenient much of the time, but journalists who take the trouble to become code writers have fuller control and flexibility than those who are limited to clicking on menu choices.

The threshold of size and complexity at which you need a mainframe keeps getting pushed back. As recently as the early 1980s, a mainframe would routinely be used to analyze a simple public opinion survey with, say, 50 questions and 1,500 respondents. By the 1990s, personal computers powerful enough to do that job more conveniently were commonplace in both homes and offices. By the turn of the century, mainframes were still useful for very large and complex databases, but even then their use was mainly to slice out subsets of data for detailed analysis on a desktop or laptop computer.

For most journalists, the entry-level computer applications (after word processing and Internet searching) are spreadsheets and database programs. The best way to get to know a spreadsheet (examples: Lotus, Excel) is to use one as your personal check register. As a journalist or potential journalist, you are probably more comfortable with words than numbers and don't get your checkbook to balance very often. A spreadsheet will make it possible and may even encourage you to seek out more complicated applications. For example, you can create a spreadsheet model for a hypothetical tax return. Then when legislators debate changes in the tax law, you can quickly show how each proposal would affect different hypothetical taxpayers.

To understand what a database program (examples: Access, FoxPro) is good for, imagine a project requiring data stored on index cards. The school insurance investigation described in chapter 1 is a good example. A database program will sort things for you and search for specific things or specific relationships. One thing it is especially good for is maintaining the respondent list for a mail survey, keeping track of who has answered, and directing follow-up messages to those who have not. A database system is better at information retrieval than it is at systematic analysis of the information, but many reporters have used such systems for fairly sophisticated analysis.

Those who design computer software and those who decide what software to use have difficult choices to make. Life is a trade-off. The easier software is to learn and use, the less flexible it is likely to be. The only way to gain flexibility is to work harder at learning it in the first place. It is not the function of this book to teach you computer programming, but to give you a general idea of how things work. To do that, this next section is going to walk you through a simple example using SPSS.

To ensure that the example stays simple, we'll use only ten cases. But the data are real enough, and they include both continuous and categorical variables. What we have here is a list of the ten U.S. presidents who served in the second half of the twentieth century. The continuous variable is his average Gallup approval rating over his entire service (a summary and compilation of data used in the previous chapter). The categorical variable is political party, 1 for Democrat, 2 for Republican. Here is what the complete database looks like:

Name	Rating	Party	Inaugural Year
Truman	45.28	1	1944
Ike	65.03	2	1953
JFK	70.10	1	1961
LBJ	55.10	1	1963
Nixon	49.02	2	1969
Ford	47.19	2	1973
Carter	45.48	1	1977
Reagan	52.79	2	1981
Bush	60.86	2	1989
Clinton	55.10	1	1993

Before we do anything with it, let's visualize a couple of concepts. In dealing with any set of data, the first thing you need to identify is the unit of analysis. In this case, the unit is the individual president. Each line in the data is a *unit of analysis* and each gives summary data for one president. Another word for unit of analysis is *observation,* which is the term used in SAS manuals. Yet another is *case,* a term preferred by the writers of SPSS instructions. Each case or observation in the previous example is one line or *record,* to use a common data-processing term. In a larger data set, you might have more than one record per case. When data were entered on punched cards, the standard record length was 80 characters, which was the width of the standard Hollerith card. Now your data entry medium is more likely to be a magnetic card or disk, and there is less restriction on record length and therefore less need to have more than one record per case. However, 80 characters is still a good length if you are likely to want to look at your data on a computer screen. The typical word processor shows an 80-character screen, and if you have to edit the data, the word processor with which you are most familiar can be the best way to do it. Another practical length is 132 characters, the number that will fit on a wide-carriage printer.

If you have trouble picturing the concepts of "record" and "unit of analysis," imagine that your data are entered on three-by-five index cards. Each card is a record. What does each card stand for? Is it a person, as in a public opinion poll? A political contribution? A piece of real estate? Whatever it is, that is your unit of analysis or "case," if you are using SPSS; "observation," if you are dealing with SAS.

Here are some other things worth noticing about the simple data set in our example. The identity of each case comes first. In this data set, we have four *fields.* The first is a text *string,* and the other three are *numeric.* Computers are better at manipulating numeric data and, where we have a choice, we usually prefer all numbers. An identification field is not used for manipulation, as a rule, and so we don't mind not having numbers there. (If your data set has string variables, SPSS can be set to automatically recode them into numbers.)

Another thing to note about this data set is that it is in *fixed format.* In other words, each field of data lines up (with left justification for text strings, right justification for numbers) vertically. If we think of the character fields as vertical columns, the identification in this particular set always occupies columns 1 through 7, Gallup approval rating is in 12 through 16, political party in 22, and inaugural year in 27 through 30. Many analysis systems, including both SAS and SPSS, are so forgiving that they don't require this much attention to "a place for everything and everything in its place." They can be made to recognize variables just by the order in which they appear, provided the values are *delimited.* Spaces, commas, tabs, or other characters can be used as delimiters. In the old punched-card days, raw data was hard to read with the human eye because we liked to cram the fields together, cheek to cheek. Storage media are now cheap enough that we can give the variables some breathing space.

Now think for a moment about what we might want to do with this data set. One obvious thing is to calculate the mean and standard deviation for presidential popularity. That way, we can see if Republicans or Democrats are the most popular. We would also be interested in knowing the trend over time. Here is the entire SPSS program for doing all of that. The program would be the same whether we were dealing with 10 cases or 10,000.

DATA LIST FILE = 'A:PRES.TXT'/NAME 1–7 (A) RATING 12–16
    PARTY 22 YEAR 27–30.
DESCRIPTIVES RATING.

Only two statements. No more. Here's what they do:

1. DATA LIST. This is a format statement. It tells SPSS to look in A drive's root directory for the file named "PRES.TXT." How did the file get there? I put it there with my word processor. It then tells SPSS that the first variable is named NAME, that it is found in positions 1 through 7, and that it is alphanumeric rather than numeric (the default). Then each of the other variables is named and its location given.
2. DESCRIPTIVES. This simple command tells SPSS to report the minimum and maximum value for the named variable, plus the mean and standard deviation.

Here is what the output looks like:

Descriptive Statistics

	N	Minimum	Maximum	Mean	Std. Deviation
RATING	10	45.28	70.10	54.5945	8.4856
Valid N (listwise)	10				

Next let's get a stem-and-leaf plot, part of the SPSS procedure EX-PLORE, in order to get a better visualization of the distribution:

RATING *Stem-and-Leaf Plot*

Frequency	Stem & Leaf
4.00	4 . 5579
3.00	5 . 255
2.00	6 . 05
1.00	7 . 0

Stem Width: 10.00
Each leaf: 1 case(s)

The plot quickly tells us the distribution is positively skewed—that is, when extreme cases happen, they are on the positive side. The modal category is ratings in the 40s, while the median is halfway between 52 and 55—in other words, 53.5.

Naturally, we want to know which party has had the most popular presidents. That can be done with either a single line of code or five mouse clicks. The code is easier to show than the clicks:

MEANS TABLES = RATING by PARTY.

Either way, the result looks like this:

Report

RATING

PARTY	Mean	N	Std. Deviation
Dem	54.2123	5	10.1241
GOP	54.9767	5	7.6909
Total	54.5945	10	8.4856

Republican presidents have been slightly more popular. SPSS offers several ways of comparing that difference to what chance variation would have produced in a sample with those standard deviations. The difference turns out to be quite insignificant.

Another way to compare the parties would be to turn popularity into a categorical variable by dichotomizing at the median of 53.5. Again, you can do it with one line of code or five mouse clicks. Here's the code:

RECODE RATING (0 thru 53.5 = 1) (else = 2) into RATECAT.

My use of caps for procedures and variable names is merely cosmetic. SPSS code is not case sensitive.

With PARTY and RATECAT both categorical variables, you produce a crosstab for a different evaluation of the two parties:

Rating Dichotomy * Party Cross-Tabulation

			PARTY Dem	GOP	Total
Rating Dichotomy	Low	Count	2	3	5
		% within Party	40.0%	60.0%	50.0%
	High	Count	3	2	5
		% within Party	60.0%	40.0%	50.0%
Total		Count	5	5	10
		% within Party	100.0%	100.0%	100.0%

This time, the Democrats look a little better than the Republicans. They have had three presidents with rating averages in the upper half, while the Republicans have had only two. How could this happen? Two of the popular Democrats, Clinton and Johnson, were just barely above the median. The two Republicans in the upper half were the first George Bush and Eisenhower, and they were both toward the top of the range. This illustrates the cost of reducing continuous data to categories. You lose some important information.

Let's close this demonstration with two more computer tricks. With simple lines of code or a few mouse clicks you can convert the presidential approval ratings to rank orders and to standard deviation units (z-scores). That enables you to generate a report that ranks the presidents by their popularity and gives each one's standardized score so that you can see how far above or below the mean he was.

The SPSS procedure SUMMARIZE yields the following table:

Case Summaries

	PRESIDENT	RATING	RANK of RATING	z-score (RATING)
1	JFK	70.10	1.000	1.82727
2	Ike	65.03	2.000	1.23000
3	Bush	60.86	3.000	.73784
4	LBJ	55.10	4.000	.05957
5	Clinton	55.10	5.000	.05947

6	Reagon	52.79	6.000	−.21283
7	Nixon	49.02	7.000	−.65710
8	Ford	47.19	8.000	−.87272
9	Carter	45.48	9.000	−1.07413
10	Truman	45.28	10.000	−1.09736
Total N	10	10	10	10

Notice how the z-scores are positive for values above the mean and negative for those below. John F. Kennedy was nearly two standard deviations above the mean, while both Carter and Truman were full standard deviations below the mean.

Finally, SPSS makes it easy to visualize the data with pictures. Figure 5.1 shows the trend in presidential popularity across time. The years are those when each president first took office, while the popularity figures are the mean across his entire term.

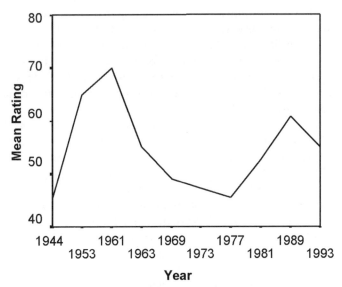

Figure 5.1 Variation in Mean Presidential Popularity across Time

SPSS AND SAS COMPARED

Both SAS and SPSS have been around for a long time. My first encounter with such user-oriented, higher-level languages was at Harvard in 1966, where faculty members in the department of social relations had written a language called DATA-TEXT for Harvard's IBM 7090.[5] They worked on a government grant and gave the product away to anyone for the cost of a blank tape, then about $10. It never really caught on because, to make it fast and efficient, they wrote it mostly in the 7090's assembler language. That meant that when the third generation of computers came along, it could not be quickly adapted. By the time the Harvard folks got around to it, SPSS, written in FORTRAN and therefore readily transportable, had passed it in popularity. Today, SPSS is a booming business, based in Chicago, the academic home base of Norman Nie, its chief founder. SAS, meanwhile, based in Cary, North Carolina, became the chief rival to SPSS.

Both systems are constantly being improved and expanded, and so any comparison between them risks becoming quickly outdated. However, there were, at the start of the twenty-first century, fundamental differences in approach traceable to the respective corporate cultures of SAS and SPSS, which did not seem likely to change over time.

SAS was more of a programmer's system; SPSS was better suited to the nonprogrammer. In the trade-off between flexibility and ease of use, SAS leaned more toward flexibility. If you were going to analyze data often—that is, more than two or three times a year—it could be worth the trouble to master SAS. With SPSS you did not have to think like a programmer. Some steps that SAS kept visible in order to force you to understand what was happening in the computer were made transparent by SPSS. This was particularly true where crosstabs were concerned. Labeling and setting up tables was much easier in SPSS.

SAS justly gained fame for its file management capabilities. If you had large and complicated bodies of data to work with on a mainframe, SAS was great at letting you reshape them and get them into workable form. Both SAS and SPSS were, by the late 1980s, capable of reading complicated formats, some of which will be discussed shortly.

The weakest point for SAS was its manuals. Those produced in the 1980s were written by programmers for programmers, and, until you learned to think like a computer programmer, they were hard to read. The SAS folks cranked these out so fast that they sometimes did not get the manuals organized well. An early introduction to SAS-PC, for example, told you clearly, with four-color illustrations, how to save a program file, but it never mentioned how to retrieve it once it was saved. SPSS manuals were more readable. Best of all, SPSS had Marija Norusis, a gifted writer on computing and statistical method, who produced a series of books for SPSS that integrated the explanation of computer technique and statistical method, which is the logical way to learn this stuff.[6] It lets you mix learning and doing in a way that constantly rewards your efforts.

Both SAS and SPSS had only minor differences in their mainframe and PC languages. After learning one, you could easily switch to the other.

Starting in 1988, I stopped introducing students to the mainframe and let them learn first on the PC because the feedback is faster and the student has a greater sense of control. Both SAS and SPSS had systems for exporting their system files—files with the format and label instructions already carried out—between mainframes and PCs. And at the mainframe level, SPSS and SAS could read each other's system files, a clever move designed to encourage users of one to switch to the other without worrying about losing the value of their existing data libraries.

The SAS versus SPSS story is a fine example of the power of competition in a free market system. Each keeps trying to outdo the other. Many users, afraid of being left behind in some new development, maintain a bilingual capability.

COMPLEX DATABASES

A database that follows the model of the ten presidents used earlier in this chapter is straightforward and easy to work with, no matter how large it gets. If we had 2,000 cases and 2,000 variables (4 million pieces of information), the logic and the programming would be exactly the same as we used with 10 cases and 5 variables. Such a database is called *rectangular.* Every case has the same number of records and the same number of variables.

There are two fairly common types of nonrectangular files: (1) files with different numbers of records per case, and (2) files that are *hierarchical* or nested. In the first of these two cases, a file can be treated as if it were rectangular, with the variables that would have been in the missing records defined as "missing." Both SAS and SPSS provide for automatic treatment of missing values. When calculating percentages, for example, they use the number of nonmissing values as the base. For example, if you had a file describing the 83 residents of a dormitory, and if 40 were classified as males, 40 as females, and the gender of 3 was unknown, either system would report 50 percent males and 50 percent females unless you specified "missing" as a separate category.

But sometimes an unequal number of records does not denote missing values. It may just mean different quantities of whatever is being measured. A hierarchical file is one way of dealing with this situation. Suppose the government created a computer file based on reports filed by manufacturing companies on their disposition of toxic waste. The unit of analysis (or case or observation) would be a single plant. Then there might be one record for each toxic chemical emitted, with each record showing how much of the chemical was discharged in each of several sectors of the environment—for example, land, water, air, or recycling facility. A plant that dumped a lot of different chemicals would have more records per case than a plant that dumped a few. Both SAS and SPSS are equipped to handle this situation.

Let's complicate this example a little bit more. Suppose there is one report for each corporate entity that emits toxic waste. The first record in each case would have information about the corporation, its size, location of headquarters, industrial classification, and so on. Call this Record Type 1.

For each of these corporate records, there is a set of plant records, one for each plant. This would be Record Type 2, and it would contain information about the plant, including geographic location, size, product line, and so forth.

For each plant record, there would be yet another set of records (Type 3), one for each toxic chemical discharged. Each of these records would give the generic name for the chemical, any trade names, the amount, and an indication of its form (gas, liquid, or solid).

Finally, for each chemical record, envision one more set (Type 4), one for each method of disposal used for that particular chemical—that is, ground, water, air, recycling. Each of these records could give details on the time, place, and manner of each emission.

If all of that sounds complicated, it is. However, there is some good news here. The good news is that a flexible analysis package like SAS or SPSS can deal with this kind of file, and, even better, it can let you choose the unit of analysis.

Hierarchical files are created by people who don't have the slightest idea what the analyst will eventually be interested in, and so the files are designed to leave all possibilities open. The advantage is that you can set your unit of analysis at any level in the hierarchy. Suppose, for example, you want the individual plant to be the unit of analysis. The computer can spread the corporate data across all of the plant cases so that you can use the corporate variables in comparing the characteristics of different plants. Or if you want the individual chemical emission to be the unit of analysis, you can tell the computer to spread the corporate and plant data to cover each emission. You do that by creating a rectangular file first. After that, the rest of the analysis is straightforward.

One common form of file manipulation is to aggregate cases to create a higher level of analysis. The ten-president database used in this chapter began as a database of hundreds of public opinion polls that all asked the same question about presidential approval. The "aggregate" procedure in SPSS can create a new database that combines those individual polls into a new dataset where the president is the unit of analysis and the approval rating is the mean from all of those individual polls taken during his term.

COMMUNICATION AMONG COMPUTERS

Twenty years ago, the first law of computers seemed to be "Everything is incompatible." Today, compatibility, while not universal, is usually close at hand.

Although computers use binary formats to hold and process information, there are a number of possible ways to do it. The smallest unit of information is the binary "bit," meaning one piece of on-off, yes-no, open-closed information. By stringing several bits together, one can encode more complicated pieces of information, and the standard convention is to string them together in groups of eight. Each group of eight is called a "byte." When a computer manufacturer tells you that a machine has 512K of random access memory, it means 512 kilobytes or 512,000 bytes. A byte is also the equivalent of a letter, number, or special character on the keyboard. For example in the Extended Binary-Coded Decimal Interchange Code (EBCDIC), standard on IBM mainframes, the eight-bit expression 11010111 stands for the letter "P." Another coding system, the American Standard Code for Information Exchange (ASCII), is used on most personal computers. Right there you can sense some problems if you try to move data from one kind of computer to another, but they have been mostly anticipated by the designers of the communication equipment. If you move data between a mainframe and a personal computer, the communication software takes care of the ASCII–EBCDIC conversion, and you seldom have to be aware of the difference.

How do you get data from one place to another? The size of the data set that can be conveniently moved by e-mail or downloaded from Internet archives keeps increasing, as technology brings improvements to both bandwidth and data compression. Many private and government agencies now supply data on CD-ROMs. A compact disk can hold, for example, all the names, addresses, and detailed participation histories of all the voters in North Carolina.

Data formats are more standardized in a personal computer, and you seldom have to worry about the details of how information is laid out on a disk. Excel is very good at reading delimited text files, and SPSS can read Excel.

DATA ENTRY

How do data get onto the tape or disk medium in the first place? Someone types them in. When you have data that you generated yourself, through a survey, field experiment, or coding from public records, you can type it in yourself, using your favorite word processor, especially if you have a word processor that keeps track of the columns for you so that you can be sure that each entry in a fixed format is going to the right place. Save it in ASCII code, unformatted, and read it directly on a personal computer or upload it through a modem to a mainframe. For any but small-scale projects, however, it is better to send the data to a professional data entry house. The pros can do it faster and with fewer errors than you can. Normally, data entry suppliers verify each entry by having it done twice, with a computer checking to make certain that each operator read the material the same way. A variety of optical character readers is also available to machine-read printed or typed materials or special pencil-and-paper forms. Using an OCR to get from printed material to computer-readable data is fairly easy but always takes some editing.

THE NERD FACTOR

Computers are so fascinating, in and of themselves, that it is easy to get so absorbed in the minutia of their operation that you forget what you started to use the computer for in the first place. The seductive thing about the computer is that it presents many interesting puzzles for which there is always an answer. And if you work with it long enough and hard enough, it will always reward you.

Most of life is not that way. Rewards are uncertain; you never have complete control. And so it becomes tempting to concentrate on the area where you do have control, the computer and its contents, to the exclusion of everything else. Neither academics nor journalists can afford to become that narrow. The computer needs to be kept in its place: as a tool to help you toward a goal, not as the goal itself.

You can't learn everything there is to know about computers, but you can learn what you need to know to get the story. You will find that concepts and procedures that you do not use more than once are quickly forgotten, and that you will build two kinds of knowledge: things you need to know and do yourself, and things for which you can find ready help when you need it. Be a journalist first, and don't use the computer to shut out the world.

NOTES

1. The term was still in use as recently as 2001. For example, "underground tanks leak even more than they did before the laws went into effect, according to a computer-assisted investigation by the *Kansas City Star*." "Leaking Gasoline Tanks Release Danger Below," *Kansas City Star*, April 22, 2001, 1.

2. Many of these historical details come from Robert S. Tannenbaum, *Computing in the Humanities and Social Sciences* (Rockville, Md.: Computer Science Press, 1988).

3. G. Harry Stine, *The Untold Story of the Computer Revolution* (New York: Arbor House, 1985), 22.

4. Allan R. Mackintosh, "Dr. Atanasoff's Computer," *Scientific American* (August 1988): 90–96. See also the biography by a veteran journalist, Clark R. Mollenhoff, *Atanasoff: Forgotten Father of the Computer* (Ames: Iowa State University Press, 1988).

5. *The Data-Text System: A Computer Language for Social Science Research, Preliminary Manual* (Cambridge, Mass.: Department of Social Relations, Harvard University, 1967). Leader of the Data-Text team was Arthur S. Couch. Some members later worked on the creation of SPSS.

6. For example, look for the most recent version of Marija J. Norusis, *The SPSS Guide to Data Analysis* (Chicago: SPSS, Inc.). Version 10 was published in 2000.

6

+

Surveys

Sometimes your data analysis skills will be applied to data that have been collected by others. At other times you will have to collect it yourself. The most widely used method is survey research, more popularly known as public opinion polling (although many applications involve special populations rather than the general public). A survey has the following elements:

1. An information goal or set of goals
2. A definition of a population to be studied
3. A sample
4. A questionnaire
5. A collection method (personal interview, telephone interview, self-administered questionnaire)
6. Coding and analysis

Getting to an information goal was discussed in chapter 1. This chapter is about the mechanics of getting to that goal by the survey method.

SAMPLING

General Principles

The kind of sample you draw depends, of course, on the method of data collection. If you are going to do it by mail, you need a sample that includes addresses. If by phone, you need phone numbers. If in person and at home, you can get by without either of these, at least in the opening stages. You will probably use instead the census count of housing units.

Regardless of the method, the basic statistical rule of sampling still applies:

> *Each member of the population to which you wish to generalize must have a known chance of being included in the sample.*

The simplest way to achieve this goal is to give each member of the population an equal chance of inclusion. It needs to get more complicated than that only if you wish to oversample some minority segment. The purpose of oversampling is to make certain that you will have enough to allow you to generalize to that minority. For a study on race relations, for example, you might want equal numbers of minorities and nonminorities, even though the minorities are only 15 percent of the population. You can do that and still generalize to the population as a whole if you weight your oversample down to its proportionate size in the analysis. That is simpler than it sounds. Three lines of SAS or SPSS code are all it takes to do that trick. Here's an SPSS example:

```
COMPUTE wtvar = 1.
IF (race ~ = 1) wtvar = .3.
WEIGHT by wtvar.
```

The first line creates a weighting variable for every case and initializes it at 1. The second causes the computer to check each case to see if it is a minority. If it is, its WTVAR is changed to .3. The third line weights the data.

For now, however, we'll consider only equal probability samples. It is easy to think of ways to do it in theory. If you want a representative sample of adults in your hometown, just write all their names on little pieces of paper, put the slips of paper in a steel drum, stir them up, and draw out the needed number. If you live in a small enough town, that might actually work. But most populations are too big and complex. So samples are usually drawn in stages on the basis of existing records.

Telephone Samples

One of the big advantages of telephone surveys is that the existing records make it quite convenient. Let's start with the simplest kind of telephone sample, one drawn directly from the phone book.

1. Cut the back off a telephone book so that it becomes a stack of loose pages.
2. Prepare a piece of cardboard (the kind the laundry wraps shirts around will do nicely) by cutting it to the size of the page and making

four or five holes sized and shaped so that each exposes one name and number.

3. Decide how many calls you need to attempt to get the desired number. Divide the total by the number of holes in the cardboard. Call that number n, the number of pages you will need.
4. Divide the number of pages in the phone book by n. The result is i, the interval or number of pages you have to skip between sample pages.
5. Start at a random page between 1 and i. Slap the cardboard over it and hit the exposed numbers with a highlighter pen. Repeat the procedure with every ith page.

What if you land on a business number? Many cities have business and residential numbers segregated in their phone books. If yours doesn't, you will have to increase your draw so that you can throw away the business numbers and still have enough. The total number you draw will depend a good deal on the characteristics of your town, and so some experience will help. But a draw of twice the number you hope to complete is a reasonable start. Some of the people in the book will have died or moved away, some will not be at home when you call, and some will refuse to be interviewed.

As easy as this sounds, it still includes only one stage of the sample. Drawing a phone number gets you to a household, but more than one member of your target population may share that number. You need a way to randomly choose a person within the household. The equal-probability rule is still your best guide. Several methods have been devised that require you to ask the person who answers the phone to list all the eligible respondents—for example, persons 18 and older—at that number. Then, using some random device, you choose one and ask to speak to that person. A simpler way is to ask how many persons who meet the respondent criteria specification are present and then ask in what month their birthdays fall. With that list, you can choose the person with the next birthday. Because birthdays occur pretty much at random (and because astrological sign does not correlate with anything), each person in the household has an equal probability of selection.

Right away you can think of two things that might go wrong:

1. Nobody is at home when you call.
2. The husband answers the phone, but the next-birthday person is the wife, and she works nights or is otherwise unavailable.

The simple solution is to call another number in the first instance and interview the husband in the second instance. But stop and think! What happens to your equal-probability criterion if you do that? It is violated, because you will have introduced a bias in favor of people who are easy to reach. To maintain the equal-probability standard, you have to follow this rule:

Once a person is in the sample, you must pursue that person with relentless dedication to get his or her response. Any substitution violates the randomness of the sample.

For no-answers, that means calling back at different times of the day and week. For not-at-homes, that means making an appointment to catch the respondent when he or she is at home.

Of course, there has to be some limit on your hot pursuit. And you need to treat all of your hard-to-get potential respondents equally. To chase some to the ends of the earth, while making only desultory attempts at others, would violate the randomness principle. So you need a formal procedure for calling back and a fixed number of attempts. Set a level of effort that you can apply to all of your problem cases.

Your success will be measured by your response rate. The response rate is the number of people who responded divided by the number on whom attempts were made. If you dial a working telephone and nobody ever answers, that represents one person on whom an attempt was made—even though you may know nothing about the person.

What is a good response rate? Years ago, when the world was a gentler and more trusting place, response rates of more than 80 percent were commonplace in personal interview surveys, and that became more or less the standard. By the late 1980s, researchers felt lucky to get two out of three. By 2000, one out of three started to seem respectable. But the problem is that as the response rate falls below 50 percent, the danger increases rapidly: The people you miss might differ in some systematic and important way from the ones who were easier to reach.

An example will illustrate why this is so. Suppose your information goal is to learn how many members of the National Press Club are smokers. Your mail survey has a response rate of 80 percent. Now assume a major bias: Smoking has become a mark of low sophistication and ignorance. Smokers, loath to place themselves in such a category by admitting their habit, are less likely to respond to your questionnaire. Their response rate is 10 percent, compared to 50 percent for nonsmokers. The following table is based on a fictional sample of 100.

	Smokers	Nonsmokers	Total
Respond	2	40	42
Nonrespond	18	40	58
Total	20	80	100

As you can see, the true value in the population is a smoking rate of 20 percent. But among those who responded, it is only about 5 percent (2/42).

That's an important underestimate. If you go back to the nonrespondents for a second wave of data collection, you are more likely to pull in smokers, simply because there are proportionately more of them to be found. The fewer nonrespondents, the less room is left in which the bias can hide.

Because every research project is subject to the first law of economics— that is, nobody has enough of anything to do everything—you have to consider a trade-off in your design between sample size and sample completeness. Follow this general rule:

> *A small sample with a good completion rate is better than a large sample with a bad completion rate.*

One reason for this rule is a healthy fear of the unknown. You know the effect of shrinking the sample on your error margin. But the error introduced by systematic nonresponse is unknowable.

A Better Telephone Sample

The method just described has a couple of flaws. If you choose each listed household with equal probability of selection in the first stage and select a member from the chosen household with equal probability in the second stage, that doesn't add up to equal probability. Why not? Because households come in different sizes. Assume that the first household in your sample has one adult of voting age and the second has three. Once the second sampling stage is reached, the selection of the person in the first household is automatic, while the people in the other household must still submit to the next-birthday test. Therefore, the single-person household respondent has three times the probability of being selected as any of the three persons in the second household. The best solution is to use weights. The person you choose in the three-person household is representing three people, so count him or her three times. (That's relatively speaking. More specific advice on weighting will come in the analysis chapter.)

Here's another complication in telephone sampling: In this age of telecommunications, some households have more than one telephone line. The extra one may be for the children, a computer, a fax machine, or a home office. Or it could be a cell phone. If two phones are listed, the two-phone household has twice the probability of inclusion. You can correct for that by further weighting, but first you have to know about it, and you can do that by asking. Just make one of your interview questions, "Is your household reachable by more than one telephone number, or is this the only number?" If there is more than one, find out how many and weight accordingly.

If you do all of the previous, you will have a pretty good sample of people whose households are listed in the phone book. Is that a good sample? Yes, if all you want to generalize to is people listed in the phone book. Most of the time you will have a more ambitious goal in mind, and a phone book sample can mean trouble. On average, across the United States, 15 percent of the working residential numbers will be missing from the phone book. That proportion varies widely from place to place, so check it out in your locality. Most of the nonpublished numbers belong to people who moved in since the phone book was published. Others are unlisted because the householder wants it that way. Maybe he or she is dodging bill collectors and former spouses or is just unsociable. Either way, such people are out of your sampling frame.

There is a way to get them back in. It is called *random digit dialing,* or RDD. You can draw your own RDD sample from the phone book, using the listed numbers as the seed. Follow the procedure with the holes in cardboard as before. But this time, instead of dialing the published number, add some constant value to the last digit—say, 1. If you draw 933-0605 in the phone book, the sample number becomes 933-0606. And it could be unlisted! That method, called "spinning the last digit," will produce a sample that comes very close to fulfilling the rule that each household have an equal chance of being dialed.

Of course, some of those numbers will be business numbers. And some will be nonworking. If a human voice or a recording tells you that the number belongs to a business or is nonworking, you can pitch it out of the sample. Unfortunately, not all nonworking numbers are connected to a recording machine. Some just ring into empty space, like the philosopher's tree falling in the forest where no human ear can hear. That means you really can't figure an absolute response rate (successes divided by attempts on real people), because you don't know if there is a real person associated with the number the interviewer hears ringing. Best bet in that case: Specify some reasonable number of attempts on different days and at different times. Then if there is no answer, chuck it out of the base. But remember, you will have to redefine your sample base, not as all possible numbers, but as all numbers verified to be working. That is a big difference, but it is still a rate worth calculating, because you can use it to compare your completeness from one survey to another.

Using the telephone directory as an RDD seed is convenient, but it may not be a completely random seed. In a larger city, the three-digit prefixes are often distributed in some geographic pattern that might correlate with the socioeconomic characteristics of the subscribers. As a result, certain prefixes (or NNXs, as the phone company calls them) will have more unlisted numbers than others. An area with an unusually high proportion of unlisted numbers is underrepresented in the book and will still be underrepresented in any RDD sample drawn from that seed.

The best solution to this problem is to avoid the phone book altogether. Obtain from your local telephone company a list of the three-digit prefixes and an estimate of the number of residential telephones associated with each, plus a listing of the working ranges. Phone companies tend not to assign numbers at random but to keep them together in limited ranges. You can save time and effort if you know those ranges and don't have to waste time dialing in the vast empty spaces. From those data, you can estimate how many calls you need to complete from each NNX, and you can write a short program in BASIC or SAS to generate the last four digits of each number randomly but within the working ranges. Sound like a lot of trouble? Not really. Here is a BASIC program for printing 99 four-digit random numbers:

10 FOR I = 1 TO 99 20 PRINT INT (RND * 8000) 30 NEXT

This method works for large areas, including states, provided the number of telephone companies is limited. Maryland is relatively easy because most of the state is covered by one company. North Carolina is tough, having more than thirty companies to contend with.

Telephone sampling has become such a specialized task that many survey organizations prefer not to do it themselves and instead contract the job out to a sampling specialist who charges by the number. A statewide sample for one-time use for a few hundred dollars was a typical price in 2001.

Household Sampling

The discussion of telephone sampling assumed that the universe of telephone households and the universe of all households are one and the same. If you have the good luck to be doing survey research in Sweden, that's just about true. Telephone penetration there is 99 percent. Canada is good, too, with 97 percent. In the United States, however, only 94 percent of households have telephones. In some states in the South, coverage is much lower. The range in 1999 was from 88 percent in Mississippi to 97 percent in Maine.[1]

For some news stories, a telephone sample won't do. You may need the nontelephone households because you want the downscale segment represented. Or you may have to visit the respondent in person if you want the interviewer to show an exhibit, such as a copy of a newspaper, or size up the person's appearance, or walk in the house and inspect the contents of the refrigerator. The objective of equal probability for all can be met for personal interviews, but with some difficulty.

If you are going to do 1,500 personal interviews in your state or town, you will want to *cluster* them to reduce field costs. Like telephone samples, personal interview samples are based on housing units. You can even use the phone book. Draw a sample of telephone listings in the manner already described, but with this difference: divide the number selected by five. That gives you a sample that, after allowing for not-at-homes and refusals, would yield 300. But those are 300 clusters, not 300 interviews.

Send an interviewer to each address, with the following instructions:

1. Do not attempt an interview from the listed address.
2. Stand with your back to the listed address, turn right and take the household next door. (If in an apartment building and there is no unit to the right, go downstairs one flight and start with the last one on the left, then work to the right.)
3. Continue in this manner. If you come to a corner, turn right, working your way around the block, until you have attempted five housing units.

An even better way is to send a crew out into the field to prelist the units in all of the clusters. In that way, the interviewer doesn't have to waste time figuring out the instructions, and you have time to resolve any ambiguities.

Because the household that forms the seed for this sample is skipped, those not listed in the directory have an opportunity to be included. There is still a bias, however, against neighborhoods with high proportions of unlisted numbers or no telephones at all.

Using the Census

When your population is too scattered to be covered by one or any other convenient number of phone books, or when you are concerned by the no-telephone/unpublished-number bias, consider skipping phone books and working directly from census counts.

Assume that you want a statewide survey. Draw the sample in stages. Start with a listing of counties and their populations. If your survey is about voting, use the number of registered voters or the turnout in the last comparable election instead of total population.

Your goal is to choose sample counties with representation proportional to population. Divide the population by the number of clusters needed. If you plan to attempt 1,500 interviews (and hope for 1,000 at a 67 percent response rate), you will need 300 clusters of 5. Take North Carolina, for example. Its voting-age population in the 2000 census was 6,085,281 and it has 100 counties. Dividing the total voting-age population by 300 yields 20,284 That will be the *skip interval*. Now take a walk with your pencil down the list of counties and find out in which counties each 20,284st person falls. Start with a random number between 1 and 20,284. Where to get such a random number? Books like this one used to publish long lists of computer-generated random numbers just to help out in such cases. With personal computers and calculators so handy, that is no longer necessary.

Once you have learned BASIC, you can use its random-number generating capability. Meanwhile, just grab your calculator and multiply two big, hairy numbers together. Skip the first digit, and read the next five. If they form a number equal to 20,284 or smaller, use it. If not, move one digit to the right and try again. If necessary, enter another big hairy number, multiply and try again. Let's assume you get 13,137 (which is what I just drew by following my own instructions). Call this number the *random start*.

To show you how this works, I am going to walk you through a lot of numbers very quickly. But don't even think of looking at the next few paragraphs until you have the concept. Here is another way to get it. Imagine all of North Carolina's people lined up in a long queue, by county, in alphabetical order. The object is to find the 13,137th person in the line, and then every 20,284st person after that. If we count them off that way, we will collect 300 people, and we will know what counties they came from. Each of those persons represents one sampling point in his or her county. The object of this exercise is simple: to find out how many sampling points, if any, each county gets. By basing the selection on people, we will automatically give each county representation according to the size of its adult population. Some small counties, with adult populations less than the 20,284 skip interval, will be left out. But some will fall into the sample by chance, and they will represent all of the small counties.

If you understand the concept, it's okay to go ahead and look at the example. Or you can wait until such time as you need to actually draw a sample. The example is just to show the mechanics of it.

Here is the top of the list of North Carolina's 100 counties and close estimates of their 2000 adult populations, derived from early census figures.

County	Adults
Alamance	99,679
Alexander	25,370
Alleghany	8,606
Anson	18,906
Ashe	19,556
Avery	13,837

Your first task is to find the county with the random start person—in this case, the 13,137th person. That's easy. It is Alamance. Subtract 13,137 from the Alamance population, and you still have 86,542 adults left in the county. Your next person is the one in the position obtained by adding 13,137 and 20,284. But don't bother to do that addition. Just subtract 20,284 from the 86,542 still showing on your pocket calculator. The result shows how many Alamance County people are left after the second sample hit. There are still 66,258 to go. Keep doing that and you will find that Alamance gets four sampling points and has 5,406 people left over.

Subtract 20,284 from that remnant, and you get negative 14,878, which means that your next selected person is the 14,878th one in the next county, Alexander. Keeping track of this process is simple. To get rid of your negative number, just add in the population of Alexander county. Now subtract 20,284 and you have 10,492 left. Because this remainder is less than 20,284, Alexander gets no more sampling points.

To get rid of the negative, add in the population of the next county. Little Alleghany County doesn't quite reach the Skip Interval even with Alexander's leftovers added in, and there is still a negative remnant. No sampling point at all for Alleghany County. Add in Anson County. It has enough population for one hit, but with 17,720 left over, it doesn't quite qualify for a second. Subtracting the skip interval yields the negative that shows how far into the next county our target person waits. And so on and on. If you follow this procedure all the way through North Carolina, you would end up with exactly 300 sampling points.

If you are clever with Excel, there is no need to do this by hand. You can set up the spreadsheet to do the subtracting and selecting for you. Head your columns "County," "Adults," "Hits," "Integer," and "Remainder." In the first column, type the name of the county. The second gets the adult population. In the third, put in a formula that subtracts RS (random start) from the population and divides the remainder by I (skip interval). Use actual numbers for RS and I, not references to cells, so that they will stay constant when you copy the formula.

The formula for the fourth column is INT(C2), which converts the value in the previous column to an integer by truncation.

For the final column, we have to figure out how many adults are left over. The formula = B2 − (4 * 20,284) − 13,137 calculates it. Notice that instead of the 4, we could have put the cell reference, but there is no need to, because we won't be copying cells in the first row. We have to get past the random start first.

Now it starts to get easy. For the second row of data (third row in the spreadsheet, counting the labels) put this formula in C3: = (B3 + E2) / 20,284. (The = sign is needed to tell Excel that it's a formula and not a label.) For D3, just copy the formula in D2 to convert the result in C3 to an integer.

Now to wrap it up. In E3, write this formula: = (E2 + B3) − (D3 * 20,284). As you can see, it adds the remainder from the previous step to the new county's population, then subtracts a sum equal to the number of hits for that county times I or 20,284. This yields the remainder to add to the population of the next county.

Now all you have to do is copy the formulas in C3, D3, and E3 to the rows below, and the entire sample stage will be done for you. The column of integers will tell you how many sampling points you have in each county.

For each of those chosen counties, you next need to get the detailed census maps that show tracts. In this stage of the selection you give each tract an equal probability of selection, regardless of its size. That makes it easy. If a county needs five sampling points, add up the number of tracts and divide by five to get the skip interval (I). Choose a random start. Take every *i*th tract or district.

In the final stage, choose blocks with probability proportional to population. It is the same procedure used to choose the counties, only on a smaller scale. The blocks become your sampling points.

Now you need to devise a rote procedure for choosing a starting point in each block. You can't let the interviewer choose it, because he or she will pick the nicest looking or the most interesting looking place. Tell her or him to find the northeast corner of the block and then choose the second dwelling to the right. Starting with the corner house is considered a bad idea because corner houses might be systematically different—more valuable in some older neighborhoods, less valuable in others because of the greater exposure to traffic. In neighborhoods without clearly defined blocks, you will have to use some other unit, such as block group. Maybe you will have to throw a dart at a map to get a starting point. Just remember the first law of sampling: Every unit gets an equal chance to be included.

When the starting point is chosen, give the interviewer a direction, and then take five dwellings. If you can prelist them in the field first, so much the better.

In multistage sampling it is important to alternate between selection proportional to population and equal probability of selection. That adds up to equal probability for the individuals finally chosen. Leslie Kish gives the arithmetic of it in his authoritative work on the subject.[2] I can explain it with an example.

Consider two blocks of high-rise apartments. Block A has 1,000 households. Block B has 100.

If you live in Block A, you have 10 times the probability of having your block chosen.

But here is the equalizer: The same number of interviews is taken from each block. So once the blocks are chosen, a person living in Block B has 10 times the probability of being interviewed as a person in a selected Block A. The bottom line: equal probability for all.

When you cluster a sample to save time and trouble in the field, the arithmetic of sampling changes. Kish gives the mathematics for figuring it exactly. For a rough rule of thumb, figure that clustering cuts efficiency by about a third. In other words, a cluster sample of 1,000 would yield about the same margin of error as a pure probability sample of 666.

Some of the efficiency that is lost in clustering is regained by *stratifying*. The procedure I have described for North Carolina ensures that sampling points will be geographically scattered, that no major county will be left out, and that the biggest counties will have respondents in proportion to their size. Because none of those things is left to chance, you get some improvement over simple randomness.

Samples of Limited Areas

For the 1967 Detroit riot survey, John Robinson designed a sample that used census and city directory data without clustering. Because the geographic area was so small, there was no great advantage to clustering households. But we did cluster within households. Teenagers, as well as adults, were included in the sample, so Robinson specified that half the eligible respondents would be interviewed in each home. They were chosen by making a numbered list, based on sex and age, and then taking all of the odd (or even) numbers. Making participation a family activity helped boost cooperation, although it created some difficulty in protecting privacy. A city directory was used to obtain the addresses, and Robinson devised a procedure for getting unpublished addresses. Each interviewer checked the house next door to the house in the sample. If that house was not listed in the directory, interviews were taken there as well. To the extent that unlisted houses next door to randomly chosen houses are a random sample of all unlisted houses, that brought them into the sample with correct representation.

Bias in Telephone and Home Samples

The people most difficult to reach tend to be those at the bottom of the socioeconomic scale. Interviewers don't like to go into bad neighborhoods, and telephone penetration is also less in those kinds of neighborhoods. Telephone surveys introduce an additional bias against less-educated people, who are less likely to cooperate with a telephone interviewer once they are reached on the telephone. In some kinds of surveys, this does not make a lot of difference. If it is a marketing survey, the nonrespondents tend to be nonbuyers as well. If it is a voting survey, they are likely to be nonvoters. But the upper-class bias can be a serious defect for many surveys for journalistic purposes. If the topic involves a social problem, the people most affected by the problem may be the ones least likely to be reached by a survey.

In Miami, when Juanita Greene, George Kennedy, and I studied the black community before any rioting had taken place there, we were surprised to find our data telling us that two-thirds of all the blacks in Miami were female. This was the first time we had encountered the problem of the invisible black male. How can one handle such a profound bias in the sample?

We considered several choices:

1. Weighting. We could weight up the males we did get to make them represent the males we didn't get. Problem: Chances are pretty good that the ones we didn't get are different, maybe a lot different, from the ones who could be found.
2. Throw the data away. Problem: We didn't know how to collect data that would be any better.
3. Redefine our sampling frame and generalize only to the stable, visible black population. Problem: Redefining the missing males out of the survey doesn't really make them go away.

We chose the third option, and Greene used conventional reporting methods to write a separate story on Miami's invisible black males and the social and political forces that kept them out of sight. She showed with anecdotes what we could not show with data: that the family structure and the welfare regulations forced poor males into a state of homelessness and/or disaffiliation with families. That strategy covered that base and left us free to write about the data from the survey with frank acknowledgment of its limitations. And it suggests a pretty good general rule:

When writing about a social problem that involves people who are going to be underrepresented in your survey, find some other reporting method to include them in the story.

Knowing when a survey can't carry all of the freight will keep you from deceiving yourself and your readers.

Sampling in Mail Surveys

Mail and Internet surveys are usually done for special populations. Getting the mailing list can take some reportorial ingenuity. When Mike Maidenberg and I did a five-year follow-up survey of people who had been arrested in the first major student protest of the 1960s—at Sproul Hall on the campus of the University of California in 1964—we worked from alumni records. But first we had to know who had been arrested, and the courts had expunged the records of every person who was under the age of 21 at the time of the arrest. Fortunately, obtaining the order to expunge had taken some time, and local newspapers had printed their names while they were still available. A search of those contemporary newspaper accounts produced the needed list of names, which we then compared with the alumni list for current addresses.

USA Today needed a list of inventors for a story on the current state of American ingenuity. It obtained a list for a mail survey by checking the U.S.

Patent Office for recent registrations. Mail surveys are commonly used to profile delegates to the major party nominating conventions, and the names and addresses are available from party headquarters. Surveys of occupational groups, such as police officers and airline pilots, have been done by using lists obtained from their professional associations.

Sometimes the target group will be small enough that no sampling is needed. You can attempt to collect data from each member of the group. But the basic rule of sampling still applies: Completion is more important than sample size. If your target population has 8,000 names and addresses, you can send a questionnaire and get perhaps 2,000 back. That 2,000 is a sample, and not a very representative one. But if you sampled every fourth name to begin with, sent 2,000 questionnaires, and did vigorous follow-up to complete 1,500 of them, you would have a far superior sample.

When you sample from a small population, the margin for sampling error is reduced somewhat, though not as much as you might think. George Gallup liked to explain it with an image of two barrels of marbles. One barrel holds 200,000 marbles, the other 2,000. In both barrels half the marbles are black and half are white, and they are thoroughly mixed. Scoop out a handful from either barrel and your chances of getting close to a 50-50 mix are about the same. Each individual marble has an even chance of being black, regardless of the size of the barrel from which it came.

But when the population is very small, the chances of sampling error are appreciably reduced. The rule of thumb: If your sample is more than one-fifth of the population being sampled, try the correction factor.[3] The formula is

$$\text{sqrt } (1 - (n / m))$$

where n is the sample size and m is the population from which it is drawn. Work it out, and you'll see that if your sample of 2,000 is drawn from a population of 8,000, the error margin is 87 percent of what it would be if the population were of infinite size.

Possibility Samples

There are situations where scientific sampling is not possible, but there is still some point in using some kind of random selection. Intercept or shopping mall interviews are an example. There is a crowd of people and no way to get them to hold still for sample selection. But you can pick a random point in the mall and a random number—say, 4. Stand at the random point and count the people who cross an imaginary line and then intercept the fourth one. That at least prevents the choice from being made by the interviewer, who is likely to prefer people who look interesting, attractive, sexy, or otherwise appealing. Since the probability of any given shopper crossing your random point is unknown, it is not a true probability sample, but it at least eliminates interviewer selection as a source of bias. This technique was used by Al Gollin to sample participants in mass political demonstrations when he was with the Bureau of Social Science Research.[4] Stanley Milgram used it for assessing the helpfulness of people encountered on city streets.

ASKING QUESTIONS

The answers you get depend on the questions you ask. In recent years, because of an increasing awareness of the sensitivity of certain kinds of issues to the design of the survey instrument, it is necessary to question not only the wording of survey questions but also the order and manner in which the questions are asked. Survey questions are carefully framed in everyday language to be understood by everyday people, and yet the survey situation is quite different from everyday conversation. Listen to somebody else's spontaneous conversation on an elevator or in a taxi and notice its structure. It is full of redundancies. Its questions and answers cover the same material over and over, as the participants reduce ambiguity and converge on a narrow area where both desire some level of precision in understanding. Consider the redundancy checks in your own telephone conversations. Notice how a phone conversation usually ends with each party repeating what he or she is going to do next as a result of the conversation, even though that ground has already been well covered. Instinctively, we know how difficult oral communication is, and we build in the redundancies as a form of error checking.

Questions in survey research are put in a much different framework. The purpose is to measure a response to a stimulus, and so the stimulus must be formulated in a way that can be repeated from one respondent to another so that each respondent is reacting to exactly the same thing. The questioner cannot improvise or recast the question to fit the existing knowledge or interest of the respondent. Each item has to be delivered just the way it left the question factory.

That procedure pays off in precision, but it comes at the cost of creating an unnatural situation in which the full power of oral communication is not realized. The survey question-asking situation is so unnatural that Howard Schuman, in his 1986 presidential address to the American Association for Public Opinion Research, argued for de-emphasizing, or even ignoring altogether, the raw frequencies or *marginals* in survey results. No survey number means very much, he said, without another number to compare it to. Knowing that 60 percent of the conference attendees liked the conference program would be good news, he said, if the average for previous conferences had been 40 percent. But "if the average over the past years had been 80 percent, this year's organizers might well hang their heads in shame."[5]

The Referendum Model

Schuman's view is contrary to most journalistic practice, which is to treat polls as an ongoing referendum in which the people instruct their representatives on how to act. That model can lead editors, politicians, and readers alike to overestimate both the power of the survey question and the knowledge and attentiveness of the typical citizen.

And yet the referendum model is not always invalid. If it were, polls would not predict elections as accurately as they do. And questions on many public policy issues would not show the robustness that they do. By robustness I mean that some questions keep giving the same answers, no matter how you twist or tamper with them.

That leads to the first law of question writing:

Never pass up a chance to borrow or steal a question that has worked for somebody else.

The advantages are several. If it worked for somebody else, it is more likely to work for you. And you already have another population and/or another time with which to compare your population at your time.

Here is another general rule:

Do not frame a question to fit a headline that you hope to write.

Some of my best friends are newspaper editors, but I hate writing questions with them when they are looking ahead to the kind of headline that they hope to get. An editor's question about the public's response to the president's latest tax proposal might read something like this:

Which of the following best describes your response to the president's tax proposal:

1. I like it.
2. I sort of like it.
3. Drop dead!

The hope is that the headline writer can later say something like "People to Prez: Drop Dead!"

Even if you tried such questions, you would find that most of the time respondents will shy away from the catchy headline-grabbing response in favor of a more conventional one. And you have hopelessly biased the question by changing its tone in mid-thought, leaving it badly out of balance. It just does not pay to try to put catchy phrases in your respondents' mouths.

Open-Ended Questions

The other extreme, putting no phrases in the respondent's mouth by asking a question that is open-ended, is equally impractical for most journalistic purposes. When an open-ended question is asked, the answers have to be recorded, coded, and categorized in some way if they are to be summarized. Just developing the coding scheme can be a long and tedious process. You have to look at the answers produced and figure out ways to classify them. Once a classification scheme is worked out, you then must go over each response and decide where it fits in the scheme. In a business with daily deadlines, there are just two situations where open-ended questions are useful:

1. When you use them to generate quotes to liven up a story. You don't need to code or classify them in that case.
2. When the response is a number—for example, "How many years have you lived at this address?" Quantitative information can be entered directly into the computer, as long as the unit is consistent.

In most other situations, open-ended questions are a poor option for journalistic surveys. When under deadline pressure, you have to constrain the responses to categories that can be counted and compared in the computer with a minimum of human processing. And so the closed response categories become an important part of the question, both leading respondents to the categories that you picked in advance and shunting them away from all the possibilities you are not giving them. It is a big responsibility.

Non-Attitudes

The chief disadvantage of the closed-end response is that the respondent with no knowledge of the subject can pick one of the proffered choices as readily as one who is well versed. Indeed, the social pressures of the interview situation encourage it. The interviewer defines the roles: I give questions, you give answers. And the system forces everyone into a category. Many journalists are disappointed when large numbers of respondents' answers fall into the "don't know" category and argue for question protocols that force a respondent to decide. But all that such a practice does is contribute to self-delusion. Lots of people really don't know, and as a journalist/researcher you should feel that it is as important to know and count them as it is to identify the people with firm intentions. Thus the rule: "Don't know" is data.

Cherish it as much as the data from people who do know. More than twenty-five years ago, Philip Converse started worrying about the measurement of what he later called "non-attitudes" when he was a survey respondent and no-ticed himself hastening to give answers to questions on topics about which he knew or cared little, just so he could fulfill his role in the social encounter and get it over with. That led to a career-long interest in the subject and some sem-inal work that has led to a greater appreciation for "don't know" as valuable data.[6] Later, two other University of Michigan researchers, Howard Schuman and Stanley Presser, experimented with questions that contained explicit invi-tations to admit to not knowing. They found that the relative proportion of pro and con positions often remained unchanged, but the number of don't knows increased substantially.[7] How do you invite the respondent to admit not know-ing? Here is an example:

"Do you think the United Nations has been doing a good job or a poor job in dealing with the problems it has had to face—or haven't you followed this closely enough to have an opinion?"

To demonstrate the importance of including this escape hatch, Schuman and Presser, along with George Bishop of the University of Cincinnati, asked people to give their opinions on some things that don't exist, such as "The Public Affairs Act." Almost a third expressed an opinion. When the es-cape hatch was added to the question, fewer than 10 percent pretended knowledge of the nonexistent act.[8]

Another way to avoid the non-attitude problem is to put a "don't know" filter ahead of the question. Ask a simple knowledge question first—for ex-ample, "Have you read or heard anything about . . ." If the answer is no, don't bother the respondent with a question on that topic.

Interest groups that use polls to generate political support for their causes often have extremely esoteric concerns that they try to fit to the referendum model. They do it by drafting a very long question that ex-plains the issue and then asks the respondent to take a side. Not a good idea! You just can't create instant education that way and then general-ize to what the rest of the public would think if it were well informed. The question becomes so complicated that it is almost impossible to word objectively. And the instantly educated respondent thus created is not representative of anybody. The instant education makes the respon-dent different from other ignorant respondents, without bringing him or her up to speed with those who have studied and thought about the is-sue. It is far better to identify those who are already well informed, and then ask them what they think.

Journalists are particularly likely to fall into the trap of thinking that their concerns, interests, and knowledge are reasonably representative of the population as a whole. They're not! If you are reading this book, that alone marks you as a peculiar, even deviant, subset of the population of journal-ists and journalism students, not to mention the population as a whole. Never generalize from yourself. For that matter, never generalize from

Chapel Hill, Cambridge, Topeka, or any interesting place where you happen to live. Representativeness is elusive, and it is somewhere else.

The Middle-Category Problem

When the Harris Survey asked for a rating of the president's performance, the choices given were "excellent, good, fair, or poor." When the Gallup Poll asks the question, the choices are "approve or disapprove." Neither has a clear middle category.

Both sets of possible responses were designed for journalistic application. Being a journalist usually means having a low tolerance for ambiguity. Politicians and other news sources are always trying to fuzz things up. Journalists are supposed to make things clear. Therefore, it seems natural to frame response categories into discrete, either-or binary choices. But the argument against this forced choice is the same as the argument for inviting "don't knows." Some respondents really belong neither in the pro nor in the con but right in the middle. The Gallup and Harris questions for rating the president's performance were written in a time when most pollsters saw it as their duty to try to force the respondents out of the middle. The current trend is to treat the middle as a legitimate category and include it in the response choices.

Schuman and Presser found that inclusion of the middle does not affect the balance of pro and con, and it does not affect the size of the don't-know category. If some people are most comfortable in the middle, our dedication to truth should compel us to respect that instead of trying to manipulate them into a firmer position. Forcing them out of the middle actually causes us to lose data, because it can mask a real mushiness in attitudes that might be important to know about.[9] Although inclusion of the middle alternative need not be an absolute rule, consider it in those cases where you have reason to suspect that the middle represents an important part of reality. On the simplest questions, an invited "don't know" can provide a refuge for the middle. Example: "Should the President send troops to stop the rioting in Xandu, or haven't you thought enough about the situation to say?"

The Balanced Question

A balanced question presents two alternatives with similar structures. An unbalanced question gives one side and then asks the respondent to agree or disagree (or approve or disapprove). For a complicated issue, the balanced question might take the "some people say" form. Example:

"Some people say the President should be doing more to balance the federal budget. Others say he's done enough already. Which comes closest to your opinion—that he should be doing more, or that he's done enough already?"

The unbalanced form: "Do you agree or disagree with the following state-ment: The President should be doing more to balance the federal budget."

Then there is a balanced version with a middle category: "Has the Presi-dent's action in reducing the national debt been too much, about right, or too little?"

The balanced form is generally better when you are looking for a refer-endum and your main purpose is to identify a majority or plurality view. However, there are at least two situations where the unbalanced form is jus-tified:

1. *Index construction.* Some dimensions are too important to be left to one question. You can reduce error by asking a number of questions on the same topic and then combining them into an index. That index can give you a nice continuous measure of whatever you are measur-ing and provide a check on respondent consistency. An agree-disagree list can generate a lot of index items in a hurry.
2. *Creating a simple independent variable.* Often the referendum is less important than knowing how one attitude affects another or how an opinion affects a behavior such as voting. In that case, the goal is not to ask an unbiased question but to ask a question in a way that mea-sures the target attribute and splits the population more or less evenly so that you can use it in a cross-tabulation.

In exit polls, which use self-administered questionnaires (SAQs), an agree-disagree list of issues creates a number of variables that can be cross-tabulated against actual vote. In that situation, you don't care about the ref-erendum; you just want to know what issues helped which candidates, what the relative effects of the issues were. To do that, you have to frame the questions to produce binary responses that will divide the population into roughly equal categories.

Here's a rather extreme example. Once in a Florida primary, busing to achieve school desegregation was an issue. We needed an agree-disagree question that would serve as an independent variable in the analysis. Op-position to busing was so strong, however, that it was hardly a variable at all, and so the question had to be loaded in a way that would make it a vari-able. Agree or disagree: "If the courts require busing to integrate schools, we might as well close the public schools." For that extreme statement, there was enough variance for cross-tabulation.

Response Set

Unbalanced questions make poor referenda because of a tendency for some respondents to be "yea-sayers." In a telephone interview an impatient respondent may agree to anything just to get the interview over with. When lists of items are written for possible index construction, the respondent may be more influenced by the form of the question than by the content. In psychological testing it is customary to reverse the polarity for alternate questions. For example, an agree-disagree list might include both "The *New York Times* is fair," and "The *New York Times* is biased." Some people will agree to both, but at least the yea-saying is compensated for.

Even in the absence of an obvious pattern, response set can cause problems. In 1960 and 1973, different sociologists tried these two agree-disagree statements in the same survey: "It's hardly fair to bring children into the world the way things look for the future." And "Children born today have a wonderful future to look forward to." A disquieting proportion of the people who agreed with the first also agreed with the second.[10] Schuman and Presser tried a split-sample experiment, where half were asked to agree or disagree with "Individuals are more to blame than social conditions for crime and lawlessness in this country." The other half were asked for agreement or disagreement to the reverse: "Social conditions are more to blame than individuals for crime and lawlessness in this country." Each version drew a solid majority of agreement.[11] The maddening thing is that the acquiescence bias, as Schuman and Presser called it, is inconsistent. It doesn't turn up for all issues and questions in a predictable manner.

One situation where you can expect it to cause trouble is when the questions are obviously being used to evaluate something or somebody—an institution or a political candidate, for example. If the favorable answer is an agreeing one (or the one on the left in a self-administered questionnaire), the respondent will expect that pattern in the following items and interpret them with that expectation in mind. Reversing the polarity just encourages the respondent to misinterpret the questions; keeping the polarity constant is the safer course.[12]

Order of Response Categories

Even when a question is balanced, the order in which the balanced response categories are offered can make a difference. Investigators have found evidence of both primacy effect (favoring the first choice) and recency effect (favoring the last choice). Schuman and Presser report that recency effects are by far the more common. Stanley Payne first noticed recency effects in some split-sample experiments he did for the American Petroleum Institute in the 1940s.[13] Schuman and Presser replicated some of those questions more than 30 years later, and the order effects were still there. A sample: "Some people say that we will still have plenty of oil 25 years from now. Others say that at the rate we are using our oil, it will all be used up in about 15 years. Which of these ideas would you guess is most nearly right?" In the 1979 replication, the number believing there was plenty of oil jumped by 13 percentage points when that choice was given last. Schuman and Presser found such order effects in about a third of the items they tested, but they could not discern a pattern that would give a clue to what causes such effects or when to expect them.[14]

A different kind of order effect can occur when a respondent is asked to judge a series of items in comparison with each other. If you are ever a contestant in a beauty contest, try to avoid being the one judges see first. When *USA Today* screened television pilots for test audiences in Dallas in advance of the 1989–1990 season, the viewers gave the lowest ratings to the shows they saw first. Anticipating an order effect, *USA Today* rotated the shows so that they were seen in different order by different groups. Thus *Major Dad* was rated 7.7 on a 10-point scale by a group that saw it before viewing any other shows. But a group that saw two other shows first, and therefore had something to compare it to, gave *Major Dad* an 8.8.

Rotation is also a good strategy in a survey interview. If the respondent is asked to rate a list of candidates or a list of issues, reverse the order for half the interviews. Experiments at the University of Chicago, the University of Michigan, and elsewhere have shown that unrelated questions can also be affected by what came before. Something in the content of a previous question can sometimes start a train of thought or set a mood that affects the response to the next. Unfortunately, nobody has found a way to predict these effects. The careful approach, when replicating a question from another survey, as you were advised to do at the start of this chapter, is to look for context that needs replicating as well.

Continuous Variables

More information is collected and more sophisticated analysis is feasible if you frame questions with response choices that fit on a continuum. But it is not easy to do, especially on the telephone. In personal interviews or with mail or Internet questionnaires, you can show a picture of a ladder with the steps numbered from 1 to 10 and ask the respondent to position an attitude on the ladder. Or you can show rows of numbers, 1 through 7, with the 1s and 7s headed by words of opposite meaning: biased-unbiased, brave-timid, exciting-boring, honest-deceitful, and so forth. The odd-numbered scale includes a middle point, and the respondent can mark it with a pencil or point and click with relative ease.

Telephone interviewing can do the same if the topic is one that is easily visualized. Using the familiar academic grading scale of A through F is helpful. *USA Today* experimented with it briefly. The question: "Using a grading scale of A, B, C, D, and F, where A is 'excellent' and F is 'very poor,' and using any of the grades in between, how would you grade the job George Bush has done as President so far? Would you give him an A, B, C, D, or F?"

Scales of 1 to 10 can also work on the telephone if the subject matter is familiar and the scale is given an explicit anchor. "On a scale of 1 to 10, with 10 being the best possible performance and 1 being the worst possible, how would you rate the President's speech on drugs last night?" Such a question would, of course, be asked only of people who saw or heard the speech.

Yet another way to get some scaling is to loop back after a response to an agree-disagree item and try to split it into strong or not-so-strong agreement or disagreement. But that procedure is time consuming and induces respondent fatigue. You can get away with it on one or two questions, but not with a long list in a telephone interview.

For a key variable, however, it is worth going to some trouble. The National Opinion Research Center question on political party affiliation is a classic. Following a scheme developed at the University of Michigan, it converts the simple Republican-Democrat dichotomy into an ordinal variable:

Generally speaking, do you usually think of yourself as a Republican, Democrat, Independent, or what?

(If Republican or Democrat) Would you call yourself a strong (R or D) or not a very strong (R or D)?

(If Independent) Do you think of yourself as closer to the Republican or Democratic party?

The result is a seven-point continuum from strong Republican to strong Democrat. It is a lot of trouble to ask, but worth it if you are studying changes in party loyalty and affiliation over time.

Threatening Questions

You can ask about the darndest things in surveys: riot participation, sexual behavior, drug use, all kinds of antisocial behavior. The telephone provides an advantage over the personal interview because you don't have to look at the respondent. And you can create a social situation where it seems natural and easy for the respondent to tell you about his or her bad behavior.

One way is to deliberately load the question to elicit the admission. In the Detroit riot study, the question assumed that everybody was a rioter, and that the interviewer was just asking for details—for example, "How active were you in the riot . . . ?" Then there is the everybody-does-it gambit, reminding the respondent that the behavior asked about is fairly common. "A lot of people yell at their spouses some of the time. Did your spouse do anything in the last seven days to make you yell at (him/her)?" That wording also suggests that your yelling was your spouse's fault, not yours.

Students in my advanced reporting class measured cocaine use in Orange County, North Carolina, by asking a graded series of questions on substance

use, starting with tobacco, beer, and wine and working up through hard
liquor, amphetamines or tranquilizers (uppers or downers), marijuana, and
finally cocaine and heroin. The early questions about legal drugs set up a
pattern of disclosure that could be maintained when the illegal drugs were
asked about.

For a survey to determine the incidence of date rape, another class used
the telephone to recruit respondents who would agree to fill out and return
a mailed SAQ. They were warned in advance that it contained some sexually
explicit questions. In addition to asking directly about rape, the questions
asked about more detailed behavior, including one that amounted to the legal definition of rape: "Have you ever had sexual intercourse with a woman
without her consent?" Like the cocaine question, this came at the end of a
series asking about more benign behaviors. Far more males admitted to non-
consensual intercourse than would admit to rape when the word itself was
used, which raised some interesting issues about the social definition of rape.

Questions about prosocial behavior can be threatening if the respondent
failed to perform the approved action. To coax out admissions of nonperformance, it helps to build some excuse into the question. "Did you happen
to vote in the last election, or did something come up to keep you from voting?" Even with that wording, past voting is generally overreported. "Do you
use a seat belt when you drive, or are you one of those people who hate being strapped down?" can encourage an admission of nonperformance. Even
better would be asking about a specific time—in other words, "the last time
you drove." That way the person could admit to not performing a desirable
behavior just once without seeming to be a total nonperformer. The standard newspaper industry question on readership asks if the respondent read
the newspaper "yesterday" for the same reason.

DEMOGRAPHICS

Every ongoing polling operation should have a standard list of demographic
categories and should stick to it. Making comparisons across time is an important way of enriching your data, and you need consistent categories to
do it. Here are the demographics you should collect as a minimum:

1. *Gender.* Two categories will do.
2. *Race.* Find out whether the respondent is black, white, or something
   else. The something else could include Asian or Native American, but
   not Hispanic. The designation of Hispanic refers to national origin,
   not race, and there are in fact Hispanics who are white, black, Asian,
   and Indian. So ask about Hispanic origin as a separate question, before you ask about race.

3. *Age.* Ask for exact age. You can set the categories in the analysis. It is important to maintain flexibility here, because the relevant age categories can depend strongly on the news topic. There is a myth among pollsters that asking for exact age irritates the respondent and ruins cooperation. When *USA Today* switched from asking age category to asking exact age, the refusal rate went from 0.33 percent to 1.5 percent—an increase of 9 refusals in an 800-person survey. That's not too much to pay for the ability to set whatever cutting points the analysis requires.[15]

4. *Education.* Asking for exact number of years in school preserves your flexibility. But the categories you will usually end up with are these: grade school (0–8), some high school (9–11), high school graduate (12), some college (13–15), college graduate (16), and postgraduate (17+). In North Carolina, some older people got high school diplomas with only 11 years of school, so a more detailed question has to be asked.

5. *Income.* This one is usually saved for last, because the refusal rate is relatively high. Because of inflation, it is impossible to set categories that will make a lot of sense over time. A common format is to have the interviewer read a list of categories after having asked the respondent to "stop me when I get to your category." Usually, total household income before taxes, not the respondent's own income, is requested. Experiments with this question have shown that the more different kinds of income are asked about, the more income surfaces. For many newspaper surveys, however, education is enough of an indicator of socioeconomic status so that income is not needed, unless it is particularly relevant to the story—for example, one on tax policy.

6. *Religion.* The common categories are Protestant, Catholic, Jewish, Other, and None. In the parts of the South where half the population is Baptist, the Protestants can be subdivided into Baptist and Other.

7. *Work.* To see how complicated occupation codes can get, check the codebook for the General Social Survey.[16] It would be nice if you could sort people into blue collar, white collar, and professional categories, but too many jobs are hard to classify. You can, however, ask whether a person is working, unemployed, retired, keeping house, or going to school.

8. *Marital status.* Married, never-married, widowed, divorced, separated.

9. *Region of socialization.* Sometimes the kind of place in which a person grew up is relevant to your story. For consistency, consider using the regions of the United States as defined by the Bureau of the Census. You'll find them on the inside cover of the *Statistical Abstract of the United States.*[17]

SIZE OF PLACE

Don't ask this one. Just code it from what you already know about the respondent's city, county, or zip code. A useful distinction is between urban and nonurban, defined as counties that are part of Metropolitan Statistical Area and those that are not. Even a state with no large cities, such as North Carolina, can end up with a neat half-and-half division on that dimension.

COLLECTING THE DATA

Data are collected in person, by mail, and by telephone. Technology keeps bringing new methods. Both personal and telephone interviews can be assisted by a computer that stores both the questions and the answers. As Internet penetration climbs past 50 percent, surveys by e-mail will gain in popularity.

Two basic strategies have been tried for using the Internet, despite its low penetration compared to telephones. One is to use statistical weighting to compensate for the absence of non-Internet households. The first step is to find out what demographic groups are underrepresented in the Internet sample. Then members of those groups who are in the sample are counted more than once to represent their peers who do not have access to the Internet. This method will become less risky, and even less necessary, as Internet penetration increases.

A more ambitious method is to draw a sample by conventional means, find out (by asking them) which members do not have Internet access, and then give it to them by providing computers and training in their use. To make it pay, the sample has to be used over and over again. To keep it from wearing out respondents, it has to be very large so that subsamples can be used for most projects. This method is capital intensive, but at the start of the twenty-first century, there were entrepreneurs bold enough to try it.

The most accessible methodologist on mail and Internet surveys is Don A. Dillman, author of *Mail and Internet Surveys: The Tailored Design Method* (New York: John Wiley & Sons, 1999). If you are seriously considering doing your own mail or Internet survey, put this book down and go get the current edition of Dillman.

TRAINING INTERVIEWERS

Whether interviewing is done in person or by telephone, the interviewer must know both the elements of social science data collection and the specific aims and characteristics of the study at hand. A survey interview is a conversation, but it is an unnatural conversation. As any reporter knows, you could take the respondent to the corner bar, spend some time over a couple of beers, and get a better idea of the person's attitudes.[18] Such a conversation would generate insight, but not data. To produce quantifiable data, you have to train individual differences out of the interviewer so that the questions will produce the same responses, no matter who is asking them. The technical term for this consistency is *reliability*. Achieving it may come at some cost to *validity* or the essential truth of the answers you get. But without reliability, you can't add one interviewer's apples to another's oranges. So you train the interviewers to behave in uniform ways that squeeze the subjectivity out of the process.

The interviewers have to be taught to read the questions exactly as read. If the question as read does not yield an answer, the interviewer is allowed to use neutral probes—for example, "un-hunh," "Could you be a little more specific?" or just an expectant pause. Suggesting a response is not allowed. "You mean you approve of the way President Bush is doing his job?" is not a neutral probe.

Interviewers are allowed some freedom, however, in the introductory part of the interview. You will write a script for them that opens the conversation and requests the respondent's cooperation, and it is okay for the interviewer to use it with improvisation. But when the data collection part begins, he or she must stick to the script.

Some of the questions from potential respondents can be anticipated: who is paying for this survey, will my name be published, and so forth. It is a good idea to make a list of the expected questions and recommended answers for each interviewer to have at hand during the data collection. For some excellent examples of the written instructions with which interviews can be fortified, see Don A. Dillman's book *Mail and Telephone Surveys: The Total Design Method*.[19] Dillman has turned his attention to self-administered forms of data collection, but this older book still has good advice for researchers who use live interviewing by telephone.

Help your interviewer trainees to become familiar with the questionnaire by role playing. Pick one to interview another in front of the group. Then do it again, with you acting as a particularly difficult respondent.

Reassure your trainees that most people enjoy being interviewed. It is not necessary to act like a detective on a secret mission. If yours is a prestigious media company, mentioning its name in the opening pitch will help convey the feeling that a good cause is being served by participation.

CATI SYSTEMS VERSUS PAPER AND PENCIL

If you have the resources, a CATI system saves time and improves accuracy. Computer Assisted Telephone Interviewing requires a personal computer or a mainframe terminal at each station. In its simplest form, you program the questions on a floppy disk and make a copy for each interviewer. The questions appear on the screen, and the interviewer punches the answers into the computer and they are written onto the same floppy disk. At the end of the evening, the disks are collected and the data compiled on a master disk. If your personal computers are part of a network, the answers can be directed to the file server as they are collected, and you can make running frequency counts. Some mainframe and networked systems even allow for questionnaires to be revised online to respond to news events that break while a survey is in progress.

If you use pencil and paper, design the form so that the answers are recorded on a separate sheet of paper. A vertical format makes data entry easier. I prefer a three-column answer sheet with the response spaces matched horizontally to the question sheets. That reduces printing costs because you need one questionnaire per interviewer, not one per respondent. And the answers will usually fit on one piece of paper, front and back, which eliminates a lot of tiresome page turning during data entry.

Before finalizing a questionnaire and answer sheet, show the answer sheet to the person who will be responsible for data entry to make certain that it is workable. When data were entered on punched cards, it was standard practice to precode the answer sheets so that the eventual column location of each item was indicated from the start. Now that data entry folks work with direct computer input, that is not as necessary. But check it out anyway to make sure you have not left any ambiguities.

CALLING BACK

You will need to develop a paper trail to keep track of each interview attempted. The more advanced CATI systems can do most of this work for you and even manage the sample. Otherwise, you will have to keep interview attempts sorted into these categories:

1. Completions.
2. Appointments to call back the next-birthday person.
3. Busy signals and nonanswers that need to be tried again.
4. Refusals, nonworking numbers, business numbers, and other outcomes for which substituting a number is allowed.

Naturally, you will want to keep track of all of these outcomes so that you can spot inefficiencies in your operation and work to improve it.

How many times should you attempt to contact a nonanswer before you give up? Three times on different days and at different times of day would be good. Journalists working under deadline pressure can't always manage that. When I supervised the Carolina Poll, conducted by the students at the University of North Carolina at Chapel Hill, we used three call-backs spaced a minimum of an hour apart. That usually forced one of the attempts to another day. Even then, cleaning up the last few cases could be messy, and the Carolina Poll sometimes switched to a quota sampling method for the last 10 or 20 percent of a project.

Comparing completion rates from different surveys is quite difficult because there are so many different ways of calculating them. The American Association for Public Opinion Research (AAPOR) has established a set of standardized definitions that is most helpful and gets updated from time to time. Your best source for the current version is the AAPOR Web site, www.aapor.org.[20]

QUOTA SAMPLING

Quota sampling got a bad name when it was blamed for the wrong election forecasts made by all of the major polls in 1948. In fact, other mistakes contributed to that spectacular error as well. Quota sampling still lives on in a less dangerous form when it is used in combination with probability sampling for the last stage of respondent selection. And it was still the standard method for most polls in Europe at the start of the twenty-first century.

Probability sampling is used to choose a cluster: a cluster of homes or blocks in a personal interview sample, or a cluster of telephone numbers from a single NNX in a telephone sample. In its loosest form, the quota sampling method allows the interviewer to select whoever is most readily available from then on, subject to loose age and sex quotas. A simple way of setting the quota is to instruct the interviewer to speak to the youngest male at each household. That compensates for the relative difficulty of finding young people and males at home. If there is no young male present, the interviewer asks for the youngest female.

In a slightly more rigorous form, call-backs are still made at the household level to reduce the bias from nonanswers and busy numbers, but the sample frame is limited to whoever is at home once the phone is answered. Again, the youngest male is asked for (females are more likely to answer the phone).

Sometimes the pressures of the news will limit the time available for fieldwork to a single night, in which case quota sampling at the household level and instant replacement of unavailable households will be necessary. The bias in favor of people who are easy to find may or may not be important. For political topics, it often is. If you notice instability in a series of competing pre-election polls, try dropping the one-nighters from the comparison and see if what is left looks more consistent.

COLLECTING DATA BY MAIL

Mail surveys are slow. And they can be surprisingly expensive. You have to do more than get a list, write a questionnaire, send it out, and then wait for the postman to bring you the results.

A mail survey should not be too short. It will seem trivial and not worth bothering about. If too long, it will seem like too much work. One sheet of 11- by 17-inch paper, folded to make four letter-size pages, is about right. Enclose a come-on letter and a stamped, addressed return envelope. Mark the letter or the questionnaire with a visible code so you will know who has responded, and explain the purpose of the code—along with any assurances of confidentiality you want to give—in the come-on letter. At the same time you prepare this material, prepare a reminder postcard, to be sent five days after the original mailing without waiting to see who responds unprompted. (Naturally, the card will include some apologetic language: in other words, "If you have already responded, please accept our thanks.") After two weeks, send a reminder letter with a fresh copy of the questionnaire to the nonrespondents.

A personal computer database program like Access is useful for managing the mailing list and keeping track of the returns. The trick is to get a healthy response rate of two-thirds or better. So always choose a sample small enough to leave the time and resources for vigorous follow-up—including pleading phone calls, if necessary—to motivate nonrespondents.

MIXED-MODE SURVEYS

Mixing mail and telephone methods works well when you need to show an exhibit for the respondent to judge: a sample product, a newspaper layout, or a photograph of a blooming celebrity, for example. You can use random digit dialing sampling for the initial contact, get the respondent to agree to accept the mailing, and then call him or her back to ask questions about the mailed material. Again, a personal computer is helpful in keeping track of who has agreed to do what.

The *USA Today* 1989 fall television evaluation project was a mixed-mode survey, in that the telephone was used for the initial contact and for asking questions to identify frequent TV viewers. Then respondents who met the criteria were offered $40 to come to a central location to watch the shows and evaluate them on a self-administered questionnaire. The respondents had already passed one level of telephone screening. The research supplier who recruited them maintained a list of thousands of people who had expressed interest in evaluating products. With such a group it is sometimes difficult to know to whom you can generalize:

heavy TV viewers in Dallas who are interested in product evaluation and could use $40 and aren't doing anything else that night. There is no problem with doing that so long as readers are advised and no pretense is made that the group represents the nation's TV watchers as a whole. They are still likely to be more representative than your average jaded newspaper TV critic.

MAKE-OR-BUY DECISIONS

Any news organization that does a lot of polling sooner or later has to make what business schools call the make-or-buy decision. Is it better to farm the polling out to a firm that specializes in the work or to do it yourself?

The important thing to recognize about this decision is that it is not all or nothing. Different pieces of a project can be separated and done in-house or sent out. The general rule to remember is this:

Doing work in-house hides costs and reveals inefficiencies. Work sent out has visible costs and hidden inefficiency.

Sampling is a piece of a survey project that is easily severable. So is the fieldwork. You give the supplier a sample and a questionnaire and he or she gives you back a stack of completed questionnaires. Putting the questionnaires into computer-readable form is readily farmed out to a data entry specialist. Analysis is not so readily delegated. That is really a journalistic function and something that should be done by the news organization's own people.

Doing it all yourself may look cheap, but that's because you aren't counting the whole cost: overhead for your plant and equipment, for example, and the salaries of all the people in your organization who will help you. The main reason for doing it yourself is to maintain control, to restrict the journalistic functions to journalists. Survey research is a powerful tool, and a news organization can keep it under control by keeping it in-house.

NOTES

1. Federal Communications Commission, Industry Analysis Division, Common Carrier Bureau, "Trends in Telephone Services," December 2000.

2. Leslie Kish, *Survey Sampling* (New York: John Wiley, 1965).

3. This rule and the correction factor come from Hubert M. Blalock, *Social Statistics* (New York: McGraw-Hill, 1960), 396.

4. Described in Philip Meyer, *Precision Journalism*, Second Edition (Bloomington: Indiana University Press, 1979), 306.

5. Howard Schuman, "Ordinary Questions, Survey Questions, and Policy Questions," *Public Opinion Quarterly* 50, no. 3 (Fall 1986): 437.

6. Philip E. Converse, "Attitudes and Non-Attitudes: Continuation of a Dialogue," 17th International Congress of Psychology, 1973.

7. Howard Schuman and Stanley Presser, *Questions and Answers in Attitude Surveys: Experiments on Question Form, Wording and Content* (New York: Academic Press, 1981).

8. Cited in John P. Robinson and Robert Meadow, *Polls Apart: A Call for Consistency in Surveys of Public Opinions on World Issues* (Cabin John, Md.: Seven Locks Press, 1982).

9. Some distinguished social scientists agree with me. See Seymour Sudman and Norman M. Bradburn, *Asking Questions: A Practical Guide to Questionnaire Design* (San Francisco: Jossey-Bass, 1982), 141.

10. Cited in Robinson and Meadow, *Polls Apart,* 124.

11. Schuman and Presser, *Questions and Answers in Attitude Surveys,* 208.

12. Philip Meyer, "Defining and Measuring Credibility of Newspapers: Developing an Index," *Journalism Quarterly* 65, no. 3 (Fall 1988).

13. Stanley Payne, *The Art of Asking Questions* (Princeton, N.J.: Princeton University Press, 1951), 133.

14. Schuman and Presser, *Questions and Answers in Attitude Surveys,* 72.

15. Calculated by Jim Norman on the basis of seventeen surveys by Gordon Black for *USA Today.*

16. *General Social Survey, Cumulative Codebook* (Roper Center, University of Connecticut), updated annually. Available on the World Wide Web.

17. *Statistical Abstract of the United States* (Washington, D.C.: U.S. Government Printing Office). Published annually in both print and Web versions.

18. The beer-hall analogy was used by Elizabeth Noelle-Neumann, "The Public Opinion Research Correspondent," *Public Opinion Quarterly* 44, no. 4 (Winter 1980): 591.

19. (New York: John Wiley & Sons, 1978), 260–67.

20. In 2001, the information was under the home-page heading "Ethics and Standards."

7

✛

Lurking Variables, Part I

The standard statistics textbooks put a lot of emphasis on significance testing, but the real action in statistics lies elsewhere. The important part is in the search for cause-and-effect relationships.

It's done in two steps. First you look for covariance—that is, evidence that one variable tends to track with another. Then you try to figure out what besides straightforward causation might account for it. Nothing happens in the real world without multiple causes, and the simplified models that we use to understand it can mislead us if we are not careful.

An obvious example can be found in stories about racial profiling. These have become a staple of investigative reporting, and they are usually based on simple one-way cross-tabulations. Reporters demonstrate that blacks are stopped in greater numbers than the black proportion in the population would suggest, and they rest their case. But that gives them no defense against a counter-hypothesis—that blacks deserve to be stopped in greater numbers because they engage in more illegal behaviors than white drivers.

There is a simple way to test this alternative hypothesis. If the police are really prejudiced, if they really arrest blacks on flimsier evidence than they require for whites, then, in a fair court system, fewer black arrests would result in conviction. Dan Browning of the *Star Tribune* newspaper in Minneapolis looked for just that possibility.

And he found it. After analyzing five years of arrest data, Browning reported that for crimes requiring police discretion, blacks were less likely than whites to be sentenced—a strong indicator that their arrests were indeed less justified.[1]

The other much-investigated form of racial profiling, discrimination against minorities by mortgage lenders, could be tested in similar fashion. It's easy to show that blacks are denied loans more often than whites. Holding income constant is standard procedure, but data representing other possible lurking variables are harder to come by, such as credit history. Minorities, because of past discrimination, may be less likely to have inherited wealth and therefore have less net worth to give lenders confidence in their ability to repay.

If banks really discriminate, it would mean that they are passing up creditworthy minorities in favor of riskier nonminorities. If they do not discriminate, the charges could easily be refuted by showing that the default rates for minorities and nonminorities are either equal or greater for minorities. I have never seen a lending institution make this defense, but it would at least be good for a reporter to inquire about it. Even a "no comment" would be enlightening.

Before looking at more complicated strategies for finding lurking variables, let's get some basic points about data analysis out of the way. Most public opinion data are not analyzed beyond simple reporting of the marginal frequencies. And some news media find that it is hard to get even that right.

The marginals give basic factoids: the number and percentage of people who have given each of the possible responses to each of the questions in the survey. Determining this basic information is not as clear-cut as it sounds, however, and a few policy decisions must be made in advance.

First among them is the problem of dealing with answers of the don't-know, no-opinion, and no-answer variety. Do you leave them in the base for calculating percentages, or do you take them out? It can make a difference. Suppose you ask five hundred people, "On the whole, do you approve or disapprove of the way the mayor is handling his job?" and you get the following distribution:

Approve	238
Disapprove	118
Don't know	104
No answer	40

If you base the percentages on the total sample of 500, you find:

Approve	48%
Disapprove	24
Don't know	21
No answer	8

The total in this case is 101 percent because of rounding errors. No need to be compulsive about that. If survey research were a totally precise and reliable instrument, you might be justified in reporting fractional values. But it isn't, and using decimal points gives a false sense of precision that we ought to avoid.

Now looking at the previous percentages, the sensation-seeking beast that lurks in all of us spots an opportunity for an exciting lead: "Mayor Frump has failed to gain the approval of a majority of the adult residents of the city, an exclusive *Daily Bugle* poll revealed today."

However, it is possible to give the mayor his majority support by the simple expedient of dropping the "no answers" from the percentage base. Using the same numbers based on the 460 who responded to the question, we find:

Approve	52%	
Disapprove	26	
Don't know	23	(n = 460)

Mayor Frump suddenly looks better. Much of his looking better, of course, is based on the artificial distinction between a minority and a majority. The four-point difference would not seem nearly as important if the range were, say, from 42 to 46. And since no election is involved here, the question of majority support is not particularly germane. Moreover, the apparent majority or lack of it could be due to sampling error. Artificial as the distinction may be, however, it is one that can quickly catch the reader's eye and one that will be overemphasized, despite your best efforts to keep it in perspective. The choice of a base for computing percentage is therefore crucial.

There is yet a third possibility, basing the percentages on the total number of people who have opinions about the mayor:

Approve	67%	
Disapprove	33	(n = 356)

Now the mayor looks very good indeed, especially when we consider the likelihood that the "don't know" segment is also the least informed. The public relations staff at City Hall can leap on this and claim, with some justification, that informed citizens approve of the mayor by a ratio of two to one.

DECIDING WHAT TO COUNT

So here you sit with a survey containing perhaps two hundred questions, and each of them is subject to three different interpretations. You are a writer of news stories, not lengthy scholarly treatises. What do you do? A rule set forth in the previous chapter is so important that it is worth repeating here: "Don't know" is data.

The soundest procedure is to base your percentages on the nonblank answers, as in the second of the three examples cited previously. It is theoretically justifiable because not answering a particular question is in somewhat the same category as not responding to the entire questionnaire. The reasons for no answer are varied: The interviewer may have been careless and failed to mark that question or failed to ask it, or the respondent may have refused to answer. In any case, failure to answer may be treated as not being in the completed sample for that particular question. You should, of course, be on the lookout for items for which the no-answer rate is particularly high. They may be a tip-off to a particularly sensitive or controversial issue worth alerting your readers about; and you will, of course, want to warn the reader whenever you find meaningful responses that are based on considerably less than the total sample.

Usually, however, the no-answer rate will be small enough to be considered trivial, and you can base your percentages on the nonblank answers with a clear conscience and without elaborate explanation.

The don't-know category is quite different. The inability of a respondent to choose between alternatives is important information, and this category should be considered important data—as important as that furnished by people who can make up their minds. In an election campaign, for example, a high undecided rate is a tip-off that the situation is still unstable. In the example just examined it suggests a substantial lack of interest in, or information about, the mayor—although these are qualities best measured more directly.

Therefore, you should, as a matter of routine, include the don't-knows in the basic frequency count and report them. When you judge it newsworthy to report percentages based on only the decided response, you can do that, too. But present it as supplementary information: "Among those with opinions, Mayor Frump scored a substantial . . ."

When you do your counting with a computer, it is an easy matter to set it to base the percentages on the nonblank answers and also report the number of blanks. If you are working with SAS or SPSS, the frequency procedures will automatically give you percentages both ways, with the missing data in and out.

BEYOND THE MARGINALS

Either way, you can quickly size up your results if you enter the percentages on an unused copy of the interview schedule. Before going further, you will want to make some external validity checks. Are males and females fairly equal in number? Does the age distribution fit what you know about the population from other sources, such as census data? Does voting behavior fit the known results (allowing for the expected over-recall in favor of the winning candidates)? With any luck, each of these distributions will fall within the sampling error tolerances. If not, you will have to figure out why and what to do about it. Once you know the percentage who gave each of the alternative responses to each of the questions, you already have quite a bit to write about. *USA Today* can produce a newspaper column from three or four questions alone. However, the frequencies—or marginals, as social scientists like to call them—are not the entire story. Often they are not even very interesting or meaningful, standing by themselves. If I tell you that 61 percent of the General Social Survey's national sample said in 1998 that the government spends "too little" on improving the environment, it may strike you as mildly interesting at most, but not especially meaningful. To put meaning into that 61 percent figure, I must compare it with something else. If I tell you that in a similar national sample nine years earlier, 73 percent gave that response, you can see that something interesting is going on in the nation. And that is just what the General Social Survey did show in the years 1989 and 1998. A one-shot survey cannot provide such a comparison, of course. However, if the question has been asked in other surveys of other populations, you can make a comparison that may prove newsworthy. That is one benefit of using questions that have been used before in national samples. For example, a 1969 survey of young people who had been arrested in December 1964 at the University of California sit-in used a question on faith in government taken from a national study by the Michigan Survey Research Center. The resulting comparison showed the former radicals to have much less faith in government than did the nation as a whole.

INTERNAL COMPARISONS

Important opportunities for comparison may also be found within the survey itself. That 75 percent of Miami blacks are in favor of improving their lot through more political power is a fact that takes on new meaning when it is compared to the proportion who favor other measures for improvement. In a list of possible action programs for Miami blacks, encompassing a spectrum from improving education to rioting in the streets, education ranked at the very top, with 96 percent rating it "very important." Violent behavior ranked quite low on the list.

And this brings us anew to the problem of interpretation raised in the opening chapter of this book. You can report the numbers; pad some words around them, the way wire-service writers in one-person bureaus construct brief stories about high school football games from the box scores; and let it go at that, leaving the reader to figure out what it all means. Or you can do the statistical analog of reporter's leg-work and dig inside your data to find the meaning there.

One example will suffice to show the need for digging. A lot has been written about generational differences, particularly the contrast between the baby boomers and the rest of the population. And almost any national survey will show that age is a powerful explanatory variable. One of the most dramatic presentations of this kind of data was made by *CBS News* in a three-part series in May and June of 1969. Survey data gathered by Daniel Yankelovich, Inc., was illustrated by back-to-back interviews with children and their parents expressing opposite points of view. The sample was drawn from two populations: college youth and their parents constituted one population; noncollege youth and their parents the other. Here is just one illustrative comparison: Asked whether "fighting for our honor" was worth having a war, 25 percent of the college youth said yes, compared to 40 percent of their parents, a difference of 15 percentage points.

However, tucked away on page 186 on Yankelovich's 213-page report to CBS, which formed the basis for the broadcasts, was another interesting comparison. Among college-educated parents of college children, only 35 percent thought fighting for our honor was enough to justify a war. By restricting comparison to college-educated people of both generations, the level of education was held constant, and the effect of age—that is, the generation gap—was reduced to a difference of 10 percentage points.

Yankelovich had an even more interesting comparison back there on page 186. He separated out the noncollege parents of the noncollege kids to see what they thought about having a war over national honor. And 67 percent of them were for it. Therefore, on this one indicator we find a gap of 32 percentage points between college-educated adults with kids in college and their adult peers in noncollege families:

Percentage Saying "Honor Worth Fighting a War"

College youth	25
	10% difference
College parents of college child	35
	32% difference
Noncollege parent of noncollege child	67

Obviously, a lot more was going on there than just a generation gap. The education and social-class gap is considerably stronger. Yankelovich pursued the matter further by making comparisons within the younger generation. "The intra-generation gap, i.e., the divisions within youth itself," he told CBS a month before the first broadcast, "is greater in most instances than the division between the generations."

The same thing has turned up in other surveys. Hold education constant, and the generation gap fades. Hold age constant, and a big social-class gap—a wide divergence of attitudes between the educated and the uneducated—opens up. Therefore, to attribute the divisions in American society to age differences is worse than an oversimplification. It is largely wrong and it obscures recognition of the more important sources of difference.

CBS, pressed for time, as most of us usually are in the news business, chose to broadcast and illustrate the superficial data that supported the preconceived, conventional-wisdom thesis of the generation gap.

HIDDEN EFFECTS

Three-way cross-tabulation to create statistical controls can be a powerful tool for bringing out effects that were invisible before. When Jimmy Carter ran for president in 1976, the reporters, using old-fashioned shoe-leather methods, wrote that his religious conviction was helping him among churchgoers. Then the pollsters looked at their numbers and saw that frequent churchgoers were neither more nor less likely to vote for Carter than the sinners who stayed home on Sunday.

These data from a September 1976 Knight Ridder poll illustrate what was turning up:

	Highly Religious	Not So Religious
Carter	42%	38%
Ford	47	52
Not voting or DK	11	10
Total	100	100

Carter support was four points greater among the "highly religious" than among the "not so religious" (42 to 38). But the difference was not statistically significant. As it turned out, however, the shoe-leather guys were right. There was a religion effect if you knew where to look for it. Carter had a strong appeal to young people, and young people tend to be less religious. Carter's religiosity did not have much effect on older people, whose political beliefs were well established. The religion appeal worked mainly on the young. Variables that conceal effects this way have been called "suppressor and distorter variables" by Morris Rosenberg.[2] The way to find the effect is to look at Carter support by churchgoing behavior within each age group. When that was done, a strong church effect favoring Carter appeared among those aged 18 to 41.

	Highly Religious	Not So Religious
Carter	49%	38%
Ford	43	52
Not voting or DK	8	9
Total	100	100

The two previous examples are rather complicated, and you can't be blamed for scratching your head right now. Let's slow down a bit and poke around a single survey. I like the *Miami Herald*'s pre-riot survey as a case study because of its path-breaking nature and because the analysis was fairly basic. We shall start with a simple two-way table. A two-way (or bivariate) table simply sorts a sample population into each of the possible combinations of categories. This one uses age and conventional militancy among Miami blacks. In the first pass through the data, age was divided four ways, militancy into three.

				Age		
		15–24	25–35	36–50	Over 50	Total
	Low	23	28	34	45	130
Militancy	Medium	65	60	65	56	246
	High	23	44	38	19	124

Because the marginal totals are unequal, it is hard to grasp any meaning from the table without converting the raw numbers to percentages. Because militancy is the dependent variable, we shall base the percentages on column totals.

				Age		
		15–24	25–35	36–50	Over 50	Total
	Low	21%	21%	25%	37%	26%
Militancy	Medium	59	45	47	47	49
	High	21	33	28	16	25
	Percentage					
	of N	22	26	27	24	100

The marginal percentages are based on the total 500 cases. Thus we see at a glance that 26 percent are in the low-militancy category, 49 percent in the medium group, and 25 percent in the high group. Age is distributed in nearly equal categories. Looking across the top row of cells, we can also see that the proportion of low militancy tends to increase with age. And the greatest percentage of high militancy is found in the 25–35 group.

There are too many numbers here to throw at your readers. But they mean something (the chi-square value—computed from the raw numbers—is 20, which, with 6 degrees of freedom, makes it significant at the .003 level). And the meaning, oversimplified—but honestly oversimplified, so we need make no apology—is that older people aren't as militant as younger people. We can say this by writing with words and we can also collapse the cells to make an easier table.

		Age	
		15–35	Over 35
	Low	21%	31%
Militancy	Medium and high	79	69
	Total	100	100

This table also eliminates the marginal percentages. The sums at the bottom are just to make it clear that the percentages are based on column totals.

The problem of figuring which way the percentages run may seem confusing at first, but eventually you will get the hang of it. To make it easier, most of the tables in this book base the percentages on column sums. Thus the dependent variable—the quality being dissected—is listed across the rows. No law of social science requires this arrangement. We could just as logically put the dependent variable in columns and figure percentage across rows. In some cases, to clarify a distribution, you may want to base percentage on the table total—that is, the sum in the corner of the margins. But for now we shall standardize with the dependent variable reported across rows and the percentages based on totals down the columns.

STANDARDIZING YOUR TABLES

With this standard presentation, you can quickly gain the habit of letting your eye rove from left to right to find the percentage difference. The table comparing the proportion of younger and older people among the militants shows that older people have half again as many conservatives or low militants among them as younger people have: 31 percent versus 21 percent. And that is a fairly good way to explain it to the reader.

But if it takes you some time to develop your table-reading skill so that the figures leap off the page at you, bright and meaningful, consider the plight of the reader. Your practice and skill at interpretation do not help him or her, and so you have to reduce things to words or to bare numerical essentials, or both in combination. One way to ease the burden on the reader is to give him or her one-way tables, created by lopping off the less dramatic half of the two-way table. Even then, you should add some words to tell what the numbers are saying. Here is how the relationship between militancy and age could be presented:

Militancy and Age: Older people tend to be more conservative than younger people.

	15–35 Years	*Over 35 Years*
Conservative (%)	21	31

The other half of the table, the percentage nonmilitant in each category, is implied. And the table makes clear that the numbers are percentages within age categories.

What about the don't-knows? Shouldn't there be cells in the table for them? Not in this case. The militant was operationally defined as someone who gave militant answers to six of the eight questions in the index. "No answer," therefore, counted as a nonmilitant answer. Had the number of blanks for any one of the items been unusually high, some theoretical problems could have been raised. They weren't. In a few cases, interviewers failed to record age, and those cases were automatically eliminated from the table.

Now we must reflect a bit on what we have added to the reader's knowledge here. We have made a comparison between young and old and demonstrated that militancy is found more frequently among the young. That in itself is something of an achievement because it provides a fuller description of the phenomenon of militancy than was available before we produced the table. Age and militancy are related.

Can we go beyond that and assume that the relationship involves causation? Nothing in the numbers themselves demonstrates that the relationship is a causal one. To make the leap to a causal assumption, we have to use some logic, a bit of intuition, and common sense. And that, you may remember from an earlier chapter, is why we keep referring to one variable as the dependent variable and the other as the independent variable. This description is the most parsimonious and conservative one available. We can say that we are looking for evidence that militancy *depends* on age, without committing ourselves to talking about causation. The statement that the amount of militancy depends on age is purely a descriptive one. (Or, if the row comparisons had turned out to be about equal, we could have said that militancy does not depend on age.)

Now let us look at this particular table and bring some logic to bear on it. If there is a relationship between the two variables, then it could be because one of them is a cause of the other. But which way does the causal arrow run? In this case, it is easy to eliminate the hypothesis that militancy causes age. Chronological age, more's the pity, is fixed and unchangeable, so the arrow must run the other way. Other readily measured attributes possess the same advantage in deducing causality: sex, race, and birth order within the family are examples. Because they are unchangeable, we can assume that they are causes and not effects, if there is causation.

For illustration, we return to the case of the Miami blacks. Militancy can't cause people to be young, but the reverse proposition, that being young causes them to be militant, also lacks a good deal. What we really want to know is what it is about being young that makes people militant.

The way to find out is to look first for other dimensions where young people differ from old: education, for example. People in all social classes tend to be better educated than their parents. Among Miami blacks more than 24 years old, 25 percent had high school diplomas. Only 12 percent of their fathers were high school graduates. Furthermore, we can expect militancy to increase with education.

Knowing this, we then suspect that it may not be youth per se that causes militancy, but merely the fact that young blacks are better educated, and that better education is the real cause of militancy. To test this idea, we first verify our suspicion that education is related to militancy. And indeed it is. Reducing the table to a newspaper-compatible form produces the following evidence that militancy increases with education.

	Education			
	Grade School	Some High School	High School Graduate	Beyond High School
Militant (%)	16	23	32	38

(The full table, with seven categories of education and three of militancy, has a chi-square value of 33, significant at the .001 level with 12 degrees of freedom.)

At first glance, education seems to have even more to do with militancy than does age. Perhaps age is not a "real" factor at all. Maybe it is simply a cause of education, which is then the more direct cause of militancy.

To test this idea, we introduce what Morris Rosenberg calls a test factor.[3] Another word for it is *control*. As in the CBS report, we want to control for age—this time to examine the relationship between militancy and education. Controlling for age means to hold its effect constant by looking at the effect of education on militancy within each age category. This process is analogous to the laboratory scientist who, by repeating his experiment in a variety of temperatures, makes certain that variation in room temperature is not affecting his chemical reaction.

TABLES WITH THREE DIMENSIONS

The result of such an examination is a three-way table: militancy by education by four layers of age. In physical printout, it is a two-way table repeated for each educational category—the only way that a three-dimensional table can be reproduced on two-dimensional paper.

Several things might happen:

1. The education–militancy relationship could disappear within each of the age groups. If so, age, not education, is the cause of militancy. Age, in fact, is a common cause of both education and militancy and the apparent education–militancy relationship is spurious.
2. The education–militancy relationship could remain in each of the age categories. In this case, age and militancy are both links in the causal

chain. Logic tells us that age, being fixed, comes first. Therefore, youth causes education and education causes militancy.

3. The education–militancy relationship could disappear in some of the age categories and remain the same or become stronger in others. If so, some kind of interaction effect is operating. There are special circumstances in which age and education work together to increase militancy—more, perhaps, than simple addition of their separate effects would account for.

Which of the previous really happened in the Miami case?

To make it easy, we'll again collapse the tables to one dimension, looking at the percentage militant in each age group, starting with the youngest. Remember, we are looking not at one table, but four.

| | | Education | | | |
		Grade School	Some High School	High School Graduate	Beyond High School
	Age 15–24	*	15	25	36
	Age 25–35	*	25	39	48
Militant	Age 36–50	17	32	33	*
(%)	Age over 50	14	15	23	*

*Number in cell too small to compute percentage

As you can see, education and militancy are related in all age categories. The second of the three hypotheses is sustained. It is not the ebullience of youth so much that produces militant attitudes. Rather, it is the greater educational opportunity open to young people, which in turn increases their militancy. This finding fits neatly into a larger theoretical framework of rising aspirations: Education moves people closer to goals and increases their expectations. Higher expectations, left unfulfilled, produce frustration and militancy.

This example deals with a relationship between what Rosenberg calls a "property" (age) and "disposition" (militancy). Properties are unambiguous, things an individual is or isn't: white, German-born, grammar school graduate, blue-collar worker, 2000 Gore voter, digital-television owner, teetotaler, licensed airplane pilot, pack-a-day cigarette smoker. Dispositions are more difficult to get a grip on because they are qualities that need the presence of special situations in order to be activated. The black militant—that is, a black person scoring high on the militancy scale—may or may not express his or her disposition by behaving in a militant manner, depending, normally, on the external situation he or she faces at any given moment. But the disposition is there and it is measurable. One of the things that some social scientists try very hard to do is to establish relationships between dispositions and behavior. Another school, however, holds that dispositions—

the attitudes, values, and personality traits within the person—have much less to do with behavior than does the external situation.

It is generally much easier to establish the relationship between a property and a disposition than to predict actual behavior, as in the case of the age-education-militancy chain. However, you can find news applications of both types, although you may find that you are unable to interest your editors or your readers in attitudinal relationships until dispositions are manifested in newsworthy behavior. We become interested in what blacks, students, or public school teachers are thinking after they riot, eject the dean from his office, or go on strike. Nevertheless, a news organization that takes the new methods seriously will try to monitor the attitudinal developments before matters reach the overt, obviously newsworthy, man-bites-dog level. If a man biting a dog is news, a man thinking about biting a dog is a potential scoop.

If a disposition is the dependent variable—that is, the thing being studied—you then can quickly find yourself in the business of searching for relationships between one disposition and another. In the *Miami Herald's* pre-riot survey of early 1968, one of the important dependent variables was disposition toward violence. It was measured with two questionnaire items, one dealing with general approval of violence to advance black goals and the other asking about the respondent's own intent to participate in such violence should the opportunity arise. The two items were combined to form a four-part index, ranging from "violent"—those who both favored violence as an idea and were ready to participate themselves—to those who were opposed to both the concept and the personal act. It was then tested against a number of specific grievances to find out, first, whether grievances really do dispose people toward thoughts of violence, and, if so, which grievances had the most effect.

One of the more clear-cut tables showed quite plainly that disposition toward violence was associated with dissatisfaction over one's personal housing situation.

		Attitude toward Housing		
		Happy	Unhappy	
	Violent	7%	12%	
Attitude	Near violent	8	18	
toward	Ambivalent	25	24	
Violence	Opposed	69	45	
	Total	100	100	(*n* =478)

However, young people tend to be more educated and more discontent and also more violent. The question arises, then, whether discontent with housing really has an effect on feeling toward violence, or whether the two variables are merely common effects of a more complicated bundle of attitudes that involved being young and black. So the table was run again, this time controlling for age. To conserve cases, the four violence categories were collapsed to two and the tables were reduced to one dimension apiece for simplicity.

		Attitude toward Housing	
		Happy	Unhappy
	Age 15–24	21%	33%
Violent	Age 25–35	19	29
or Near	Age 36–50	12	40
Violent	Age over 50	12	20

The relationship persists in each age group, though it comes on significantly stronger in the middle-aged, 36–50, group. Therefore, at least two things are probably going on here: first, youth, or something about youth, causes people to feel and express grievances over housing and the grievances in turn stimulate favorable attitudes toward violence. But look at the third age category. Housing is strongest as an explanatory variable for violence in that age group for which it is most relevant: These are people in the middle-to-late child-rearing years for whom being deprived of satisfactory housing can be the most frustrating. Thus bad housing makes these people disposed toward violence despite their age; age, negatively associated with violence (the greater the age, the less the violence) has thus had a suppressor effect in the previous two-way table, which tested for the effect of housing dissatisfaction on violence.

Or, recasting this statement in shorter sentences:

Disposition toward violence decreases with age.
Disposition toward violence increases with housing dissatisfaction.

Among middle-aged people, housing dissatisfaction relates so strongly to disposition toward violence as to outweigh the violence-suppressing effect of age. When you can pinpoint a group in which special circumstances make a relationship stand out with extra power and clarity, you have a strong potential for an important news story. In Miami, urban affairs writer Juanita Greene found that housing frustrations for people in the child-rearing years were grounded in objective reality. The gap between housing need and housing availability was large, and it was not being closed. This kind of spotting of special situations, by the way, is something that social scientists, in their quest for general theoretical principles, do not often do very well. "Social science has been justly criticized," says Rosenberg, "for its neglect of situational factors. One may know that general principles obtain, but one does not know whether these principles have predictive value in specific circumstances."[4] Digging for specific circumstances may fit the instincts of the journalist better than those of the social scientist. Academic reluctance to ferret out the mundane details needn't inhibit us at all as we look for the traditional who, what, when, where, why, and how.

Before leaving the violence-by-housing and satisfaction-by-age tables as compressed previously, scan this combination table once more to see how quickly you are becoming accustomed to letting the numbers leap off the page, bearing their message to you. Your eye automatically scans from left to right to show that housing attitudes relate to violence attitudes in all age groups. But you can also scan it vertically to see how attitudes favoring violence tend to fade with advancing age. The percentage disposed to violence fades from 21 to 12 among those happy with housing conditions and from 33 to 20 among those unhappy with housing conditions. Furthermore, the exception, that 40 percent violent among the unhappy 36–50 group, cries out for attention and explanation.

If, on the other hand, you still have to stop and puzzle out the meaning, don't worry. You are, after all, in the business of writing with words, not numbers. But facility with the numbers will come with practice, particularly as you apply them to work of your own and not just to examples printed in a book. You may also take comfort from this thought: You are avoiding, so far, the danger of becoming so fluent with numbers that you begin to lose your ability to put their meaning into words that newspaper readers can understand and appreciate. This hazard is well known to social scientists, especially among students getting a grip on quantitative methods for the first time. They sometimes reach a stage in which they resent the fact that they can't simply send the computer printout to the publishers and have its significance instantly appreciated and spread upon the record for all the world to see. It doesn't work that way for them, and it especially doesn't work that way for us in journalism. We write with words, but we must learn to read in numbers.

MORE THAN ONE INDEPENDENT VARIABLE

We have now seen some of the things that can happen to a simple two-variable relationship when a third variable, related to both, is introduced. One more example deserves some examination. This is the case where the third variable is not really a test or control variable but acts as a second independent variable. In other words, we find two things that relate to the phenomenon under study, and their impact appears to be cumulative. There are ways to sort out the relative contribution of the two independent variables. However, in a newspaper story, about all you need to get across is that they exist, that they affect the dependent variable, and that their effect is cumulative.

In the five-year follow-up study of Berkeley arrestees, for example, an effort was made to determine what made some of the former student radicals—a minority, as it turned out—become relatively conservative in their political behavior. A political conservative in this context was someone who voted for Hubert Humphrey in 1968 (no one in this group voted for Nixon). A vote for Humphrey represented an act within the political system and not a protest, as a write-in vote for Eugene McCarthy, Dick Gregory, Eldridge Cleaver, Pat Paulsen, or a deliberate nonvote would be.

Several factors were associated with a Humphrey vote, of which two are worth mentioning here as examples: a general low level of self-perceived radicalism and the acquisition of a spouse since the 1964 arrests.

Among all those arrestees who responded to the mail survey, 33 percent voted for Humphrey. Among those who got married after the sit-in, 43 percent voted for him. Among those who placed themselves in the lower two-thirds on a self-anchoring scale of radicalism, 49 percent voted for Humphrey.

Immediately, the hypothesis suggests itself that the less radical are the more likely to do conventional things like getting married, and these two independent variables—marriage and low self-assessed radicalism—are telling us the same thing. It seems likely that radical students, being dedicated to their causes, would have little time or inclination for such a conventional institution as marriage. In fact, however, there was no significant difference in the marriage rate of the high-radical group and the low-radical group. What difference there was indicated that those who were still single five years later tended to rank somewhat lower in radicalism.

This lack of correlation between the two independent variables means, then, that their effect must be cumulative. The existence of both conditions, low radicalism and marriage, should produce a higher rate of Humphrey voting than either condition separately. It did, and the effect was easily demonstrated with numbers that could be interpreted to readers:

Forty-three percent of the married subjects voted for Humphrey.
Forty-nine percent of the low-radicalism subjects voted for Humphrey.
Sixty-one percent of the married, low-radicalism subjects voted for Humphrey.

From these examples, you can see how the introduction of a third variable to elaborate on what you already know about a two-variable relationship can do three basic things:

1. It can spot a spurious relationship. Example: People who eat candy have a lower death rate than those who do not eat candy. Therefore, eating candy causes longevity? No. Children eat candy, and children have yet

to face the death-causing infirmities of old age. Control for age, and the relationship between candy eating and death rate disappears.

2. It can isolate the conditions in which the relationship is strongest and most important. Example: Newspaper readership in a southern city declines among younger age groups, a finding that raises the suspicion that the paper is losing touch with the educated younger generation. But when the relationship is controlled for education, nearly all of the young-readership decline is found to be among the least educated. This discovery opens a whole new line of inquiry, directed at the possible substitution of television for newspapers among the uneducated young, and a projection of future trends as the number of uneducated young people continues to dwindle.

3. Chains of causation can be sorted out and interactive or cumulative effects discovered. Example: Among Miami blacks in 1968, those scoring highest on a measure of political effectiveness tended to score high on conventional (as opposed to radical) militancy. Both measures also were positively correlated with income. Treating income as a separate independent variable demonstrated that it and political efficacy tended to operate cumulatively: Each made a separate contribution to increased militancy.

Until this chapter, when you thought of a variable, you probably thought of a single question item in the interview schedule. And most of the time that is exactly what a variable will be. However, you must learn early in the game not to let your imagination be limited by single-item variables. It often makes sense to combine two or more to create an entirely new measure.

NEW VARIABLES FROM OLD

One of the classic combined variables in social science literature is status inconsistency. Take two measures of socioeconomic status, education and income, for example. People who rank high in both or low in both are status consistent. Those who are high in one but low in the other are status inconsistent. And, research has shown, status-inconsistent people are different. It is a useful variable.

Another way to create new variables from old is in scale or index construction.[5] The new variables are not really "new," in that they involve a different property or disposition. Rather, they provide a more accurate and flexible indicator of what you are trying to measure. To return to the black militancy example, its eight items are a better collective measure of the disposition than any single item is. One obvious advantage is that you can rank order the individuals in the sample according to the number of militant answers given.

The choice of which of the available intercorrelated items to use in the index may be somewhat arbitrary, but you needn't worry about it. As Paul Lazarsfeld has pointed out, indices measuring the same phenomenon tend to be interchangeable.[6] Shifting combinations of indicators will mean that some people will fall into or out of the defined group with each change. However, the different combinations are not likely to make any substantive change in the results when you look for relationships with another variable. We could take any four of the eight conventional militancy items and use them for a dichotomized index and still find that conventional militancy correlates with education. Then we could take the other four, try again, and again get the same general finding.

For this reason, there is usually little need to use as many as eight items in an index. Two or three will often do quite as well. And, in the case of socioeconomic status, you may often find cases where you will be content to use education as the only indicator. Sometimes the response rate is low on the income question, and occupation involves a difficult (though not insurmountable) coding problem. But both correlate well enough with education that for many research purposes, you can get by with education alone.

You don't see many poll stories based on indices. That's a pity because index construction can add to the power and interpretability of polling data. And you should start to think about ways of analyzing survey data that go well beyond the basic frequency count—how many people gave each answer to each question—and even beyond simple bivariate comparisons, such as how high-income people compare to low-income people, city dwellers versus suburbanites, and so forth. How can such painstaking analysis be made to fit into the time constraints of journalism?

It is easier than you might think. Even though the bulk of what you write from survey data will probably be based on the marginal frequencies and simple two-way relationships, it pays to stay alert to situations where deeper analysis can be useful.

One very basic tactic is to recode your variables so that the numerical values form rank order indices. For example, an item on prospective riot behavior might be originally coded:

Probably would join	1
Probably would not join	2
Not sure	3

To make the numbers stand for a rough approximation of propensity to riot, this item can be recoded:

Probably would join	3
Not sure	2
Probably would not join	1

When all the continuous or roughly continuous variables are thus coded, the computer can produce a correlation matrix—every item correlated with every other item. Statistically, of course, that is unsound in most cases. The assumptions underlying correlation (Pearsonian r) include interval scaling. Aside from such necessarily continuous variables as education, income, and age, most social science variables can only be ordinally scaled at best. But the computer doesn't know what kind of scales or indices your numbers represent. It will produce a correlation matrix that will have enough approximate validity to be useful as a searching device. Your eye can scan the rows and columns of correlation coefficients and when unexpectedly high values turn up, you can ask yourself why, and then run contingency tables to find out what is going on. You would not, of course, consider reporting correlation coefficients in the newspaper. It is simply a tool to alert you to relationships that you might otherwise not have noticed or not thought to have looked for.

INDEX CONSTRUCTION

The correlation matrix can also guide you in the construction of scales out of several variables. If you think that several questionnaire items all tap a common characteristic, such as disposition toward violence, dissatisfaction with local government services, or racial prejudice, then you can get a quick estimate of their validity as an index by seeing whether they intercorrelate.

How do you tell what items are suitable for a scale? You want them to have low intercorrelations, in the neighborhood of .2 to .5. If the intercorrelations are too high, the items are redundant, measuring too much the same thing. If they are too low, they are measuring different things. There are several statistical tests to guide you in building indices. Cronbach's alpha is available in SPSS. It provides an estimate of the extent to which all of the items are measuring the same underlying characteristic. How does it do this? For a direct explanation, you need a statistics test. For most purposes, it is enough to think of it as a measure of internal consistency. A low alpha score means that you probably have an apples-and-oranges problem—that is, the items in your scale are not really measuring the same thing. The accepted interpretation of Cronbach's alpha[7] is that an alpha of .7 means that a scale is good enough for exploratory research, and if it is .8 or more, you can use it in a confirmatory application.[8] The same SPSS routine that produces it will also tell you how badly you need each item in the scale. It looks at each one in turn and tells you how much alpha will be reduced if the item is dropped. You would not want to bother newspaper readers with this information, but it can be good for your own peace of mind.

This quick search for things that hang together can be carried a step further with a factor analysis program that combs through a correlation matrix and picks out the clusters of variables that stick together with the most mathematical precision. The logic of factor analysis assumes that your variables are surface manifestations of some underlying condition and the optimum alignment of the intercorrelated variables will show what these underlying situations are. The trouble with this particular tool is that it is so powerful that it will cause factors to surface for you, whether or not they are real. So you have to look at it with a skeptical eye and ask yourself whether they make any intuitive or theoretical sense. When they do, you can use them as scales to construct variables that will usually work better than single-item indicators.

An example of a case in which this procedure was successful is the 1968 Detroit study of black attitudes in the 1967 riot area. A number of items that dealt with possible courses of actions toward black achievement were intercorrelated and factor analyzed. The program called for orthogonal factors to be extracted—a shorthand way of saying that the items within each factor should correlate with others in that factor, but that the separate factors should not be intercorrelated. Thus each factor represents a separate dimension unrelated to the others.

In the Detroit study, the first two factors extracted made good sense. The first was labeled "black power," and its strongest components were positive responses to statements such as "blacks should get more political power by voting together to get officials who will look out for the Negro people" and "blacks should get more economic power by developing strong businesses and industries that are controlled by blacks."

The second factor was labeled "black nationalism." (The computer, it should be noted, does not invent these labels. You have to do it yourself.) Its strongest components included agreement with statements such as "It is very important for blacks to avoid having anything to do with white people as much as possible" and "It is very important for blacks to be ready to fight alongside other blacks and participate in riots if necessary."

Finally, it was shown that a sizable majority of Detroit blacks subscribed to the black power idea, as defined in the conservative, self-help sense, and that very few were disposed to black nationalism. That these two dimensions were different and unrelated things was news to many whites, who were accustomed to thinking of the extreme forms of militancy as differing only in degree from the black power concept. It is a difference in kind, not in degree.

Although the discovery was accomplished through factor analysis, the proof did not rest on this rather intricate and difficult-to-explain tool. Indices of black power and black nationalism were constructed, collapsed into categories for contingency tables, and run against one another to verify the absence of a relationship. This step was necessary not only for simplification, but as a check against the misuse of factor analysis. For our purposes especially, it should only be used to discover clues to things that can be described in a more straightforward manner.

There are other tricks that can be done with a correlation matrix. When there are several independent variables associated with the dependent variable, it is a shortcut for sorting out the effect of each by computing what is called the partial correlation coefficient. For example, in a survey of voters in Muncie, Indiana, in 1964, the correlation between political interest and income was .212, suggesting that people with money have more at stake in political decisions and therefore pay more attention to politics. On the other hand, income and education were very definitely correlated ($r = .408$), and there was a small but significant link between education and political interest ($r = .181$). Using contingency tables, it is possible to test the relationship between political interest and income by looking at it within categories of education. But that means another trip to the computing center. Partial correlation offers a quicker way to estimate the effect of holding education constant. You can find the formula in a statistics textbook for doing it on the back of an old envelope, or you can get SPSS to do it for you with a few points and clicks.

The correlation matrix has one other special application if you have panel data. It can, sometimes, give you an easy way to spot the direction of causation. Suppose you have interviewed the same people in two projects a year apart. Each survey shows a relationship between interest in local politics and time spent reading the morning paper. The question bothering you is which comes first in the causal chain (if one does come first; it could be a case of mutual causation). Out of the correlation matrix, you find that there is a significantly stronger relationship between interest in politics at Time 1 and newspaper reading at Time 2 than there is between newspaper reading at Time 1 and interest in politics at Time 2. The predominant direction of causation, then, is from interest in politics to newspaper reading. See figure 7.1.

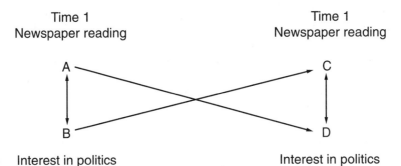

Time 1
Newspaper reading

Time 1
Newspaper reading

A

C

B

D

Interest in politics

Interest in politics

Figure 7.1   Newspaper Reading and Interest in Politics
Note: If correlation AD is greater than correlation BC, newspaper reading is more a cause of interest in politics than an effect.

You may have noticed by now that you are beginning to see social science methodology in a somewhat new light. With any luck, it should begin to look like something you can do, rather than just passively observe and write about.

There is another corner that we have turned in this chapter. We have not, you may have noticed, made a big deal of significance testing in the discussion of survey analysis. And we have put a lot of emphasis on digging and searching procedures that don't quite square with the pure model of hypothesis testing that was presented earlier in this book.

Is this, then, the point of transition from scholarship to journalism? Not exactly. The better, more creative scholars know that the search for probable cause is where the action is in survey research, and statistical testing is trivial by comparison. The tests help you guard against the temptations of overinterpretation. But analysis of tables, with the introduction of third variables to go behind the superficial, two-variable relationships, is your protection against wrong interpretation. It is also your opportunity to discover causal sequences and explanations of the way things work in your community that you didn't suspect existed before.

In classical scientific method, you form a hypothesis, test it, and, if it fails the test, reject it and go on to something else. You don't keep cranking in epicycles, as Ptolemy did, until you have a clumsy, nonparsimonious explanation to fit the observable data. Nevertheless, the rule against making interpretations after the fact, after the data are in and the printed-out tables are on your desk, is by no means ironclad. There is room in social science for serendipity. If the data give you an idea that you didn't have before, you need feel no guilt at all about pursuing it through the tables to see where it leads. Rosenberg notes that cases of serendipitous discoveries are plentiful in both the natural and the social sciences. He cites one of the best and most original concepts to emerge from modern survey research as an example: relative deprivation, uncovered by Samuel Stouffer in his research for *The American Soldier.*[9]

Stouffer did not enter this survey with the idea that there might be such a thing as relative deprivation. The idea had not occurred to him, and the survey was not designed to test it. But numbers came out that were so unexpected and so surprising that it was necessary to invent the idea of relative deprivation in order to live with them. One of the unexpected findings was that northern blacks stationed in the South, despite their resentment of local racial discrimination, were as well or even better adjusted when compared to those stationed in the North. Another discrepancy turned up in the comparative morale of soldiers in units with high promotion rates and those in units with low chances of promotion: The low-promotion group was the happiest.

One parsimonious concept, relative deprivation, fit both of these situations. The black soldiers stationed in the South compared themselves to the black civilians they saw around them and found themselves better off. The high-promotion units had more soldiers who saw others being promoted and therefore felt more dissatisfaction at not getting ahead than soldiers in units where no one got ahead.

When the apparent discrepancies turned up, did the analysts shout, "Eureka!" and appreciate their importance in the history of social science? No. Instead, they delayed the report and went over the numbers again and again, hoping that some clerical error or something would show that the black soldiers and the low-promotion soldiers were not so happy after all. There is a moral here for journalists. We are not charged with the awesome responsibility of making an original scientific discovery. We do have the responsibility of challenging and testing the conventional wisdom. And if the conventional wisdom says one thing and our data say another, we should, if the data are well and truly collected and analyzed, believe our data.

Rosenberg also has an answer for the methodological purists who say that after-the-fact interpretation is too much like Ptolemaic epicycle building. Accidental discoveries, he points out, are nullifiable. If you find something surprising, you can use your contingency tables to creep up on it from another direction to see if it is still there. Stouffer found something surprising in the attitude of black soldiers, invented the concept, and then tested it elsewhere in his data on the high- and low-promotion units.

A journalistic example is also available. When the Knight Newspapers surveyed Berkeley arrestees five years after the arrests, one of the interesting findings was that females who had been radicalized by the Sproul Hall affair tended to hold on to that radicalization more than did males in the ensuing years. This finding, based on one table, led to the hypothesis that for a female to become a radical involves a more traumatic separation from the values and attitudes of her family than it does for a male, and that she therefore holds on to the radical movement as a family substitute. The theory was testable from other data in the survey. If it were true, females should have a greater proportion of parents who disapproved of the activity that led to their getting arrested. Furthermore, those females with disapproving parents should be more likely to retain their radicalism.

Checking these two propositions required a new two-way table (sex by parent approval) and a three-way table (radical retention by parental approval by sex) and one trip to the computing center. It turned out that there was a small sex difference (though not statistically significant) in favor of males having parental approval. However, the effect of disapproving parents on radical retention was the same for boys and girls. So the theory was, for the purposes of this project at least, nullified.

"The post-factum interpretation," says Rosenberg, "is thus not the completion of the analysis but only the first step in it. The interpretation is made conditional upon the presence of other evidence to support it."[10]

Thus it is not necessary to fall back on a journalistic excuse for using the computer as a searching device instead of a hypothesis-testing tool. The journalistic excuse would be that we are in too much of a hurry to be as precise as sociologists, and, besides, our findings are not going to be engraved on tablets of stone. Let us think twice before copping out like that. If we were really backed up against the wall in a methodological argument with scientific purists, we might have to take that last-resort position. Meanwhile, we can make the better argument that we are practical people, just as most sociologists are practical people, and therefore, when we spot the germ of an idea glimmering in our data, we need not shrink from its hot pursuit.

NOTES

1. Dan Browning, *Star Tribune*, "Testing Police Strategy and Claims of Racial Profiling," July 23, 2000.
2. Morris Rosenberg, *The Logic of Survey Analysis* (New York: Basic Books, 1968).
3. Rosenberg, *The Logic of Survey Analysis*.
4. Rosenberg, *The Logic of Survey Analysis*, 139.
5. Some social scientists make a distinction between scales and indexes. An index is based on a set of variables that have some theoretical relation without necessarily being intercorrelated. For example, a consumer price index could be affected by the price of both bread and gasoline, even though market conditions don't necessarily make the prices of those two items rise and fall together. Items in a scale are intercorrelated, a sign that the items measure the same underlying phenomenon and that accumulating the items provides a measure of the intensity of the phenomenon.
6. Paul Lazarsfeld, *Daedalus* 87, no. 4 (1958).
7. L. J. Cronbach, "Coefficient Alpha and the Internal Structure of Tests," *Psychometrika*, 16 (1951): 297.
8. Jum C. Nunnally, *Psychometric Theory* (New York: McGraw-Hill, 1967), 276.
9. Samuel A. Stouffer et al., *The American Soldier: Adjustment during Army Life* (Princeton: Princeton University Press, 1949).
10. Rosenberg, *The Logic of Survey Analysis*, 234.

8

✛

Lurking Variables, Part II

The main problem with using crosstabs to tease out lurking variables is that unless your sample is very large, you run out of cases very quickly. That's because your method of control is to literally hold constant the suspected lurkers. If you think that a difference between the attitudes of old people and young people is explained by the fact that younger people tend to have had more years of schooling, you can check it out by comparing the age group within similar layers of education. Then you see if the effect is still there when education is not allowed to vary.

In theory, that's fine. But the more you squeeze those layers, the more you risk losing statistical significance just because of the small number of cases within each layer. And if you need to add a second or third control, such as region or race, the numbers get thinner still.

Variables that are measured on interval scales help you to avoid that problem. The information embedded in that level of measurement lets you adjust for different lurking variables instead of literally holding them constant. And that makes regression methods very useful indeed.

To make the transition in your head from cross-tabulation to regression, consider the relationship between a crosstab and a scatterplot. Figure 8.1 shows a plot divided into quadrants, representing the four cells of a two-by-two table. Each data point represents one of the twenty-six communities whose well-being is followed by the Knight Foundation. The vertical axis represents public perception of illiteracy, while the horizontal axis shows actual incidence of low levels of literacy.

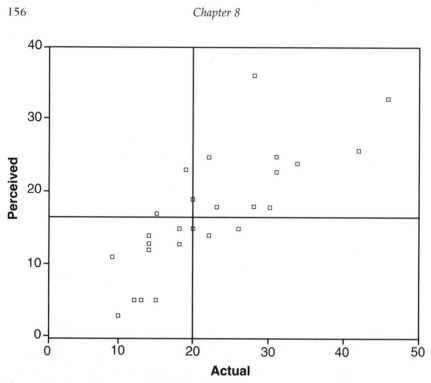

Figure 8.1   Low Literacy and Its Perception

The points cluster around a straight line slanting upward to the right, and
the interpretation is obvious. As real illiteracy increases, so does public perception. The categorical version of these two variables can be obtained by dichotomizing each one at the median. (SPSS will do this for you automatically.)

If we set the cutting points so that 1–16 is low for perception and 1–19
is low for actual illiteracy, we can show the relationship in a crosstab:

		Levels of Illiteracy *Actual*	
		Low	High
	High	17%	79%
Perceived	Low	83	21
	Total	100	100

The table shows less detail, but it is easier to summarize in a simple declarative sentence: 79 percent of the high-illiteracy communities had a relatively high perception of illiteracy, compared to only 17 percent of the low-
illiteracy communities.

As journalists, we like crosstabs for their ease of explanation, but as analysts, we have to appreciate the power of the scatterplot. One thing the scat-

terplot can do for us is yield an equation that describes the trend. The equation in this case is:

$$\text{Perception} = 1.98 + (.686 * \text{Reality})$$

In words, it would be this: The percentage who call illiteracy a "big problem" increases by .686 of a percentage point for every 1 percent increase in the actual proportion of people at the lowest levels of literacy.

That's the kind of statement you can get into a newspaper. Any such observation about a given change in one variable—in this case, perception of the illiteracy problem—associated with a given change in another (actual number of persons with low literacy) is a statement of a linear regression model. If you think of it as a line on a graph, the line will be straight. If you think of it as an equation, it will always take this general form:

$$Y = C + Xb$$

The C in the equation is a constant that anchors the line to a starting point somewhere. The rest of the equation tells you the steepness of the slope.

We can make this easier to visualize by starting with a simple scatterplot. Consider this hypothesis (the newspaper and the data are fictitious): Street sales of the *Miami Journal* pick up whenever a hurricane is spotted near the Cape Verde islands; and these sales tend to increase by some uniform amount as the distance between Miami and the hurricane decreases.[1] From circulation records, we collect eight data points:

Distance	Sales
1,035	2,000
805	3,000
667	4,000
529	4,000
460	6,000
391	8,000
276	7,000
115	8,000

Sure enough, just by scanning the columns we can see that street sales increase as the hurricane gets closer to Miami, but for an even clearer picture we need a plot. We'll show street sales on the vertical or Y-axis and miles on the horizontal or X-axis (figure 8.2).

How to describe what is going on here? We could say that it looks like the profile of an alligator peering out of a swamp. Or that it resembles the Florida Keys in mirror image. Or that it is a pretty good approximation to a straight line. When we take the latter approach, we are invoking something

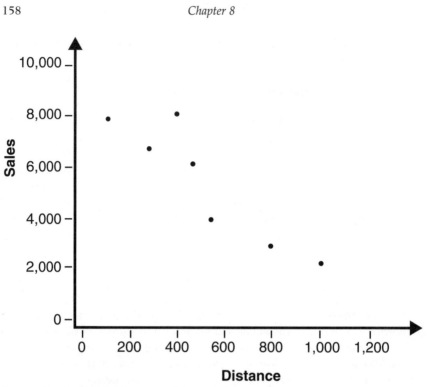

Figure 8.2   Hurricane Distance and Street Sales

called the general linear model, of which simple linear regression is the
principal component.

The model enables us to be quite specific in our description. Any good
statistics text will give you the formula for least squares regression, which
can be used to find and describe the straight line that best fits these data
points. Or you can skip the formula and have a computer do the work for
you—or even a low-cost pocket calculator, such as the TI-55. In this case,
the best-fitting straight line is described by the following equation:

$$Y = 9,150 - (7.3 * X)$$

For most of us, words are easier. Try this: When the hurricane hits, the
Miami Journal will sell 9,150 additional papers on the street. Before it hits,
7.3 fewer papers will be sold for each mile of distance between Miami and
the hurricane.

Now that would be true, of course, only if all the data points were always
right on the line. In fact, they are not. But because they tend to fit a straight
line, the linear model becomes a practical tool for planning purposes, especially if the variation around the straight line is random. If it is, then the
straight line becomes the best guess available, and we can almost hear the

circulation manager saying, "Let's see, the hurricane is 500 miles away, and 500 times 7.3 is 3,650 and 9,150 minus 3,650 is 5,500. Okay, Harry, let's up the street edition press run by 5,500."

Before using this tool, the circulation manager might want some quantifiable indication of how well the linear model fits the data at hand. The statistic telling us that is the correlation coefficient, also yielded by the formula for least squares regression. In this case, the correlation coefficient, also known as Pearsonian r, is $-.930$. How to interpret it? If the correlation were 1 or -1, it would mean that all of the data points were sitting right on the straight line. A positive value means that the line slopes upward to the right; that is, an increase in X yields an increase in Y.

A negative value, which we have here, indicates a downward slope to the right: As X increases, Y decreases. A correlation coefficient of 0 would mean that the data do not fit a straight line at all. They still might be in some easily described pattern. They could form an O or a U or maybe an S, and the pattern might have some predictive value. But it would not fit a linear model.

The correlation coefficient has another useful interpretation. Its square is the amount of variance explained. This concept is so important that we are going to elaborate on it a little bit. First we'll look at our plot again with the best-fitting straight line drawn in figure 8.3.

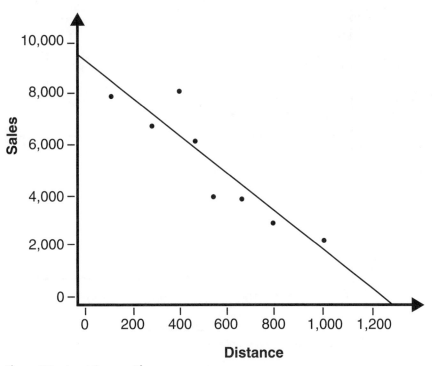

Figure 8.3   Least Squares Line

This line is called the "least squares line" because it, out of all possible straight lines, is the one with the least total of squared vertical distances from each data point to the line. We can illustrate these least squares distances by drawing them in (figure 8.4).

Those vertical lines are the physical representation of unexplained variance. The better the fit that the dots make to the line, the less the unexplained variance. If all the dots were on the line, we could say in plain English, "All of the variation in added street sales can be explained by the hurricane's distance from Miami." As it is, we can say that 86 percent of the variation is explained.

But wait, you say. Every percentage has to have a base somewhere. Where is the base here? Good point. I haven't shown you what we mean by variance. Let's look at the plot again with some different vertical lines (figure 8.5). These show the total variance.

This time the vertical line runs from each data point to a horizontal line representing the mean of Y. Why? Well, suppose you are the circulation manager of the *Miami Journal* and you know a hurricane is coming, but you haven't figured out that its distance from Miami has an effect on sales. All you know is that you sell more papers when there is a hurricane than when there isn't.

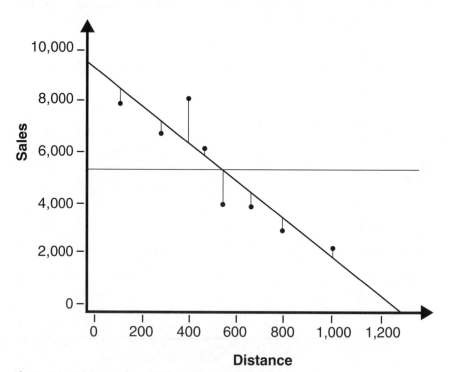

Figure 8.4   Distances from the Least Squares Line

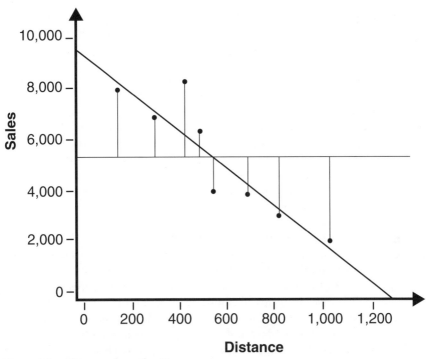

Figure 8.5   Distances from the Mean

How many more? Well, it varies. But your average over the data points, rang-ing from 8,000 copies to 2,000 copies, is 5,250. So if you wanted to minimize your risk of being wrong, and if you had nothing else to go on, you would use that average—the mean, to be more precise about it—as your guess.

And—here's the good part—the measure of your error is the extent to which there is *variance* around that mean.

Now a market researcher comes along, he or she explains the general lin-ear model to you, and a least squares line is found to fit the available data. Now you are smarter: Instead of using the average across the eight data points to make your prediction, you use the regression line. If you had been given the equation for the line before the eight events forming these data points had occurred, your guesses would be much better than if you had just used the mean. How much better? If you measure the distance between each data point and the mean and add those distances up, you'll see how well you did using that way of guessing. Now measure the difference between each data point and regression line. You've done a lot better. And if you calculate the ratio of those two sums, you will find that your guesses were 86 percent better—that is, the total squared distance between the estimates and the reality was reduced by 86 percent when you used the regression line. And that's why a statistician will tell you that distance of the hurricane from Miami explains 86 percent of the variance in added street sales.

THE UNEXPLAINED VARIANCE

That's pretty good, but the persistent researcher is troubled by the thought of that 14 percent of the variance that remains unexplained. Is there any way to reduce it? Yes, because there may be yet another variable for which a measure can be obtained that will further increase the explanatory or predictive power of the model. Wind speed, perhaps. A hurricane with top wind speeds of 150 m.p.h. ought to sell more papers than one that blows at a mere 80 m.p.h., don't you think?

Here's how that information is cranked into the equation. For each data point, we measure the difference between its observed value and the value predicted by the model (represented by the physical distance on the plot from the point to the regression line). This difference is expressed in units of *Y*, or, in this case, in terms of numbers of papers. If we sold more than the model predicted, the difference is positive. If less, it is negative. This difference is called the *residual* and it is the real-world manifestation of unexplained variance. It is what we have left to explain. This residual is what we want our new equation to predict.

So we could make another pair of columns of numbers. *Y* would be the residual from the previous model. And *X* would be the new independent (or predictor) variable, the speed of the wind in miles per hour. And if it worked, we could make another profound statement, which would go something like this: The additional street sales will equal 9,150 papers, plus or minus some other constant introduced by the second step of this regression, minus 7.3 papers for each mile the hurricane is from Miami, plus *X* papers for each m.p.h. of wind speed. And what you will have done is shown the effect of the new variable, after the effect of the first variable is already accounted for or, as we say, controlled.

Multiple regression does something like this, only better. It gives you an equation with this form:

$$Y = C + (b_1 * X_1) + (b_2 * X_2) + (b_3 * X_3) \ldots$$

The coefficients, or *b*s, are estimates of the effect of each of the different independent variables (*X*s) on *Y* when all of the other independent variables are controlled. For the equation to work best, you need independent variables that are not correlated with one another. This assumption is often violated, however. In our hurricane example, it is violated because hurricanes originating around Cape Verde tend to increase their wind speed as they move west. When such intercorrelation exists, there really is no way to sort out the independent effects of each variable. As a practical matter, however, you may improve the predictive power of the equation by adding variables that have some correlation with one another. If predicting the value of *Y* is more important to you than estimating the effect of individual variables in the casual chain, then it makes sense to go ahead.

EVALUATING CIRCULATION PERFORMANCE

Here is a real-life example. The *Philadelphia Inquirer,* fighting a vigorous competitive battle in the 1970s, wanted to evaluate its circulation performance in small geographic areas.

The traditional way to do that is to color a map. One color code is used for average circulation penetration (circulation divided by households), another for areas below average, and a third for those above average. Or there might be five colors to allow for areas that are *way* above or below average. The editor and the circulation director look at the map, their eyes are drawn to the below-average areas, and they notice that these are mostly low-income areas where they shouldn't expect to have average penetration. And they look at the above-average places on the map and observe that older, affluent citizens live there, and that explains that. In short, the map does not help very much.

What they really need is a way to evaluate those small areas that measures circulation performance against the potential—with the potential based on the known demographic characteristics. Multiple regression is tailor-made for that kind of a problem, but you need two things: census data and circulation data based on the census areas.

In the Philadelphia case, circulation data were available for geographic units based on the Census Bureau's minor civil divisions. Demographic data for each of these units, plus circulation and household count, were fed into the model. Out came an equation with a multiple regression coefficient of .795 that explained 63 percent of the variance in *Philadelphia Inquirer* household penetration. These are the variables that did the trick, along with their coefficients:

Variable	Coefficient
Percentage working in Philadelphia	.15
Percentage with income of $15,000 and up	.40
Percentage older families	1.56
Suburban paper penetration	−.06
Population density index	.12

New housing index	.21
Percentage single females	1.54
Percentage automobile commuters	.19
Percentage white	.12
Percentage childless families	−.55
Percentage younger families	.76

And the regression constant was −.35. So the model tells us that for any given small geographic area, you could have predicted the circulation penetration of the *Philadelphia Inquirer* with 63 percent better accuracy than you could have achieved by using the mean if you had the variables listed previously. And to arrive at the prediction, you start with −.35 and add .15 of a percentage point for each 1 percent who work in Philadelphia, plus .4 percent for each 1 percent with incomes of $15,000 and up, and so on.

Some of it, you may notice, does not make sense. Why should *Inquirer* penetration go up if there are a lot of older families and then go up some more if there are a lot of younger families? Blame the multicolinearity problem. The exact contribution of each variable just can't be teased out when variables are intercorrelated. It doesn't matter so much in this application, because what we want to know is how much circulation penetration to expect in each place once the demographics have been accounted for. So we get the computer to print us out a table of residuals.

The residual, you will remember, is the difference, for each data point, between the observed value and the value predicted by the equation. And to discover that difference is the whole point of the exercise. Here is a portion of the table of residuals that the computer supplied:

Unit	Predicted	Observed	Residual
01A	.37	.41	.04
01B	.41	.41	.00
01C	.35	.41	.06
02A	.38	.39	.01
02B	.36	.39	.03
02C	.36	.39	.03
02D	.35	.39	.04
03A	.40	.30	−.10
04A	.39	.34	−.05
04B	.27	.34	.07
05A	.36	.25	−.11
06A	.58	.43	−.15

You can see the value of it. In District 06A, for example, the 43 percent penetration looks good compared to the rest of the area until you see what the regression model predicts. And that makes you want to dig further into what is happening there to see if anything can be done to bring the area up to its circulation potential. The study uncovered a number of places with high unrealized potential in the suburbs around Philadelphia.

NONLINEAR MODELS

Perhaps you have noticed by now that the world was not made in straight lines, at least not in all respects. Many effects are nonlinear. For example, the Harvard Club of New York City features oversize coffee cups that were inspired by Theodore Roosevelt's complaint that the second cup of coffee never tastes as good as the first. I doubt that creating a cup with a capacity equal to two cups solved that problem for most drinkers, but the former president was right about the phenomenon of diminishing returns. Other effects have a delayed reaction until some threshold is reached. For example, a new business might be unprofitable until a critical mass of customers or market share is reached. The first dollars invested return less than later dollars.

When using regression to understand covariance, it is important to always look at the scatterplot first. That will tell you if something nonlinear is going on. If it is a simple curve, you can re-express the independent variable in order to make the model fit. Is this cheating? No, it is simply accepting the way the world works and trying to describe it as parsimoniously as you can.

John Tukey set forth some simple rules for re-expression. If you have an effect that starts off quickly and then slows down, you can show it as a straight line by stretching out the low end of the independent variable's scale and compressing the high end. A logarithmic re-expression is one way of doing that. In his book on exploratory data analysis, Tukey proposed a ladder of re-expression. Try one, and, if it helps, move further on the ladder. If the line bends in the opposite direction, move back. Here is Tukey's ladder.[2]

$$Tukey's\ Ladder$$
$$X^3$$
$$X^2$$
$$X$$
$$sqrt\ X$$
$$Log\ X$$
$$-1/(sqrt\ X)$$
$$-1/X$$
$$-1/X^2$$

When Tukey refers to Log X, he is suggesting the Base 10 logarithm, which treats the distances from 0 to 10, from 10 to 100, and from 100 to 1,000 as all showing the same linear distance on the chart. For an example of how it works, here are scatterplots of the effect of participation rate on state Scholastic Achievement Test (SAT) averages.

As a general rule, states with low participation rates tend to have higher SAT averages. That's because the highest ranking states don't require the test for their own public universities. If the test-taking population is disproportionately composed of high school students hoping to go to Harvard, the scores will be high. But this effect fades very rapidly as the participation rate approaches 30 percent (figure 8.6).

As you can see, the cases are not randomly distributed around the best-fitting straight line. Those with the highest and lowest SAT scores tend to be above the line, while those in the middle sag below. Even so, the line has a decent *r*-squared, .785. And it is defined by an easy-to-understand equation:

$$Y = 1,114 - (2.07 * X)$$

where Y is the predicted SAT average for a state and X is its participation rate. The translation: State SAT averages tend to decline by two points for each 1-percent increase in the participation rate.

That statement is accurate, but it doesn't tell the full story because the effect is not uniform, and the linear model implies a uniform effect. But we can fix that.

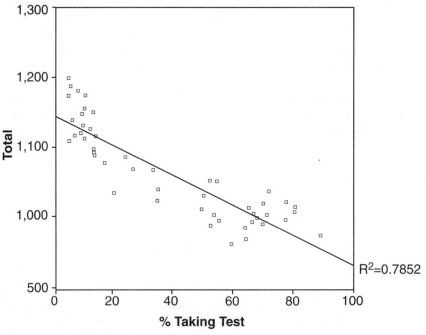

Figure 8.6   Participation Rates and State SAT Averages

Imagine this scatterplot on a rubber sheet. Stretch the left side and compress on the right, and the line straightens out. Re-expressing participation as its logarithm produces the same effect (figure 8.7).

Now we have better random distribution around the best-fitting straight line. The variance explained has improved to 86 percent. And the equation for describing this line is still fairly straightforward:

$$Y = 1,257 - (137 * \text{Log } X)$$

Again, Y is the predicted SAT average and X is the participation rate. This one, however, is not as easy to put into words. State SAT averages drop by 137 points for each 1-point increase in the log of the participation rate. Those numbers on the vertical axis of the chart are not intuitively easy to interpret.

My solution—and some statisticians will disagree with me here—would be to give the simple declarative sentence from the first formula, and then qualify it by describing how the effect is mostly at the low end of the participation rate. The simple version does summarize the general trend, and it is fair to use it as long as you point out that the effect is not uniform across all the levels of participation rate.

Another way to deal with the uneven effect would be to divide the states into two populations, with the cut point at about 40 percent. Below that

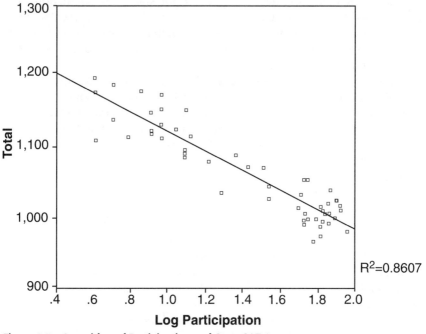

Figure 8.7 Logarithm of Participation and State SAT Averages

level, the effect is almost linear, and above, it is just about nil. It would take a few more sentences to explain, but some audiences would appreciate it.

LOGISTIC REGRESSION

Sometimes we have the luxury of continuous data for our independent variables, but the dependent variable is dichotomous. Medicine, political science, and marketing are areas where this condition is common. The patient is cured or dies, the candidate is elected or defeated, the customer buys or does not. Each of these situations can be coded as a 1 or a 0, but there is no continuous scale.

We can produce something, however, that has the same intuitive appeal as a continuous scale if we think in terms of the probability of 1 or 0 happening. Everybody can relate to, say, an 80 percent probability of being cured, getting elected, or making a sale.

But dealing with probabilities is mathematically messy because, by definition, probability is bounded by 1 for certainty and 0 for impossibility. So logistic regression uses odds instead. Therein lies an interesting story about computers and their power to create new and useful—and also confusing—ways to look at data.

When computers first became available for statistical calculation, they were applied to classical statistics, tools invented from the seventeenth to the nineteenth centuries to evaluate data by hand. Some of these tools were so difficult to use by hand they were hardly ever employed, but they were at least possible before computers.

Multiple regression is one such tool. It offers a way to adjust for each of several independent variables simultaneously so that you can estimate the effect of any one of them on an all-other-things-being-equal basis.

It was a useful tool when statisticians still used pencil and paper. Computers just made it easier. Then one day somebody got an idea. Wouldn't it be wonderful, he or she asked, if we could apply this other-things-being-equal test to a binary variable?

Medicine and political science both have a lot of interesting things to investigate that have this characteristic, from patient survival to election outcomes.

Logistic regression was invented to do for these variables what ordinary regression does for continuous variables. Instead of using a straight-line model, it uses something that looks more like a flattened S. Administer a small dose and nothing happens, increase it, and when the effect does appear, it comes all at once and then further dosage adds no more in the way of results.

It is a lovely model, but it can't be done with pencil and paper. In fact, it can't be done with anything that looks to you and me like arithmetic calculation. Instead, it has to be done with a massive amount of trial runs—iterations, in computer talk—until a combination is found that best fits the logistic model.

It would be nice if the output of a logistic model could be expressed as a probability, a number between 0 and 1 that expresses the likelihood that the effect—patient survival, Republican victory, whatever—will occur. But the model isn't that neat, and if it tries to solve for probability, it sometimes gives answers greater than 1—a logical impossibility.

So its designers set it to solve for something related to probability but with no upper limit: odds.

If you have spent much time at the race track, you probably grasp the difference at once. Here's an explanation for the rest of us:

Draw a card from a jokerless deck, and you have a 1-in-4 chance of getting a heart. The odds of getting a heart are 1 to 3 (one chance you do, for three chances you don't).

Or, to put it another way:

Probability is the target possibility (drawing a heart) divided by all of the possibilities (all four suits): $1/4 = .25$.

Odds is the target possibility divided by all of the *other* possibilities (clubs, diamonds, spades): $1/3 = .33$.

Conversion from one to the other is straightforward:

$$\text{Odds} = P / (1 - P) \quad \text{Probability} = \text{Odds} / (1 + \text{Odds})$$

If the odds are even, we say we have a 50-50 chance, which is an expression of probability. That's the same as 1-to-1 or even odds.

In math notation, that gets shortened to $P = .5$ or odds $= 1$.

Similarly, 75 percent probability is the same as 3-to-1 odds. Again, statisticians don't bother with the "to-1" part and just say the odds are 3.

At the race track, they do use the "to-1" part with this adjustment: they like to avoid fractions. So odds of 1.5-to-1 would be expressed as 3-2. But in statistics, we would just say that odds are 1.5.

And, if you think about it, you will notice that probabilities of greater than 50 percent work out to odds greater than one. Probabilities less than 50 percent are equal to odds less than one.

Computer packages that do logistical regression give you a result that is interpreted as an odds ratio. Here is a simple example from medicine.

A reader wants to know how much a particular course of action is going to change his risk of getting sick. An aging male with untreated hypertension is advised to take medicine for it. Untreated, he is told, he has a 4 percent risk of a stroke or heart attack in the next two years. With treatment, he can lower that risk to 2 percent. That's a *risk ratio* of 2/4 or one-half. Taking the medicine lowers his risk by 50 percent.

Now consider the same story in terms of odds. Untreated, his odds of a stroke or heart attack are 4/96 = .04167. With treatment, the odds are 2/98 = .0204. The *odds ratio* rounds off at .49—close enough to the risk ratio to make no practical difference.

And because it makes no practical difference much of the time, health investigators and social scientists have developed the bad habit of treating the odds ratio and the risk ratio as if they were the same thing. But some of the time, they're not even close.

The difference starts to become important as soon as you leave the set of problems with low probabilities. When the baseline probabilities get much above .10, the odds ratio gives misleading results. (See table 8.6.)

An extreme example is offered by Arnold Barnett in *Technology Review,* published by the alumni of Massachusetts Institute of Technology.[3] Suppose that a black defendant has a 99 percent chance of drawing the death penalty for a particular crime, compared to a 96 probability for a white defendant. The risk ratio is 1.03. In other words, the black defendant has 1.03 times as much chance of getting the death penalty as a white defendant (or .03 times more).

But try converting that to an odds ratio. The probability of .99 is equal to odds of 99 (99/1) and the probability of .96 is equal to odds of 24 (96/4). The odds ratio is therefore 99/24. or 4.1. If you were to write that a black is 4.1 times as likely to be executed as a white, you would be wrong. Very wrong.

Journalists need to understand this because such mistakes creep into the scientific literature. Here is a real-life example. In February 1999, the *New England Journal of Medicine* reported on evidence of race and gender bias in doctors' treatment of heart patients. One piece of evidence was that the odds of blacks being referred for cardiac catheterization were 40 percent less than that of whites.[4]

Table 8.6 Probability Changes versus Odds Changes

Probability	Odds	Probability Change (%)*	Odds Change (%)*
.10	0.11		
.20	0.25	100.00	125.00
.30	0.43	50.00	71.43
.40	0.67	33.33	55.56
.50	1.00	25.00	50.00
.60	1.50	20.00	50.00
.70	2.33	16.67	55.56
.80	4.00	14.29	71.43
.90	9.00	12.50	125.00
.95	19.00	5.56	111.11
.99	99.00	4.21	421.05

*From the preceding value of *o* or *p*

This was true, but the risk ratio was much less dramatic. In fact, 84.7 percent of blacks and 90.6 percent of whites in the set of cases under study were referred for catheterization. That's a risk ratio of 93 percent. In other words, blacks were only 7 percent less likely than whites to be referred.

When the media picked up the story, both print and broadcast, they picked up on the odds ratio and interpreted as a risk ratio, reporting that blacks were 40 percent less likely than whites to get the referrals. In a follow-up editorial, the *Journal* blamed its own authors for presenting the data in a way that was likely to be misinterpreted. But journalists bear some responsibility, too.[5]

Examples of mistaking odds ratios for risk ratios are even found in textbooks.

Odds Ratios in the Analysis of Contingency Tables, by Tamás Rudas, uses a table from a famous work of sociology, Samuel Stouffer's *The American Soldier* from World War II. The table shows that 74 percent of the soldiers based in the North, but only 40 percent of those based in the South, would prefer, if given a choice, to be based in the North. It is obvious that 74 is 1.85 times as great as 40. The simple declarative sentence describing this would be, "Soldiers based in the North are 1.85 times as likely as those based in the South to prefer a camp in the North.

But Michael S. Lewis-Beck, editor of the Sage Publications series in which this work appears, uses the odds ratio for the comparison instead. He correctly calculates the odds ratio as 4.27, but then uses the following sentence: "This odds ratio says that soldiers already in the North are more than four times as likely to prefer a camp in the North as soldiers in the South are." Rudas says approximately the same thing, though not as clearly, in his text.[6]

A similar error is found in an equally surprising place. The *SPSS Base 8.0 Applications Guide* used an example of an election survey where home owners had a 79 percent turnout rate, compared to only 54.4 percent for renters. Without question, that's an advantage for home owners, who are 1.45 times as likely to vote as renters. But the anonymous authors convert those percentages (or probabilities) to odds, correctly finding an odds ratio of 3.161 and incorrectly interpreting it as follows: "Thus, a home owner is roughly three times more likely to vote than a renter."

Wrong. The difference is, of course, only about one and a half times *as likely* or 45 percent *more likely.*[7]

So how can reporters work with odds ratios correctly when even scientists have trouble? The simplest advice I can give is never use or refer to odds ratios in a news story. Express the relationship in terms of risk ratios.

Where the underlying probabilities are below 10 percent, the odds ratio is a close enough approximation of the risk ratio that it's not a problem. When it is higher, you can still convert an odds ratio to a risk ratio, but it takes some work.

It's worth doing. Remember that odds ratios are popular in the first place because logistic regression produces ratios that are adjusted for other intervening factors so that effects can be presented on an all-things-being-equal basis. While risk ratios underlie the odds ratios in theory, they can't be directly teased out.

But a way to produce good approximations has been published by two scientists at the National Institutes of Health.[8] It is a simple formula that a journalist can use:

$$\text{Relative Risk} = \frac{OR}{(1 - P_0) + (P_0 * OR)}$$

P_0 represents the probability of the outcome in the untreated or control group.

I applied it to a famous Harvard study on binge drinking by U.S. college students. In one of the early reports of that study, Henry Wechsler and his colleagues said that frequent binge drinkers were "7 to 10 times more likely than the nonbinge drinkers to not use protection when having sex, to engage in unplanned sexual activity, to get into trouble with campus police, to damage property, or to get hurt or injured."

The statement was keyed to a table of adjusted odds ratios for each of those unpleasant consequences, and they did indeed range from 6.92 to 10.43. But when I used the Zhang-Yu formula to approximate the equivalent risk ratios, the range was lower: from 5.71 to 8.49. That's still an impressive relative risk, but not as impressive as "7 to 10 times."[9]

Journalists might ask, "If it's good enough for scientists, why isn't it good enough for us?" The answer, of course, is that journalists should be skeptical of all sources, even of those with Ph.D.s. The scientists who misuse odds ratios are waking up to the problem, and we should be stirring along with them.

NOTES

1. This example and the accompanying illustrations are adapted from my *Newspaper Survival Book* (Bloomington: Indiana University Press, 1985).

2. John W. Tukey, *Exploratory Data Analysis* (Reading, Mass.: Addison Wesley, 1977), 172. Tukey's Xs are my Ys (to preserve the more common notation for the dependent variable).

3. Arnold Barnett, "How Numbers Are Tricking You," *Technology Review On-Line*, Massachusetts Institute of Technology, 1994.

4. Kevin A. Schulman et al., "The Effect of Race and Sex on Physicians' Recommendations for Cardiac Catheterization," *New England Journal of Medicine* (February 25, 1999): 618–26.

5. "Misunderstandings about the Effects of Race and Sex on Physicians' Referrals for Cardiac Catheterization," *New England Journal of Medicine* (July 22, 1999): 279–83.

6. Advised of the error, Lewis-Beck said, "I have reviewed the quotation and I have to conclude that, while my interpretation of the odds ratio may not be the only correct interpretation, it is one of the correct interpretations." (Personal communication, August 15, 2001.)

7. Alex Reutter of SPSS saw the problem and clarified the difference between a risk ratio and an odds ratio in the *SPSS Base 10.0 Applications Guide.* He included a warning not to use the odds ratio as an approximation of the risk ratio for probabilities below .10.

8. Jun Zhang and Kai F. Yu, *JAMA: The Journal of the American Medical Association* 280 (November 18, 1998): 1690–91.

9. Henry Wechsler et al., "Health and Behavioral Consequences of Binge Drinking in College," *JAMA: The Journal of the American Medical Association* 272 (December 7, 1994): 1672–77. Weschler avoided this problem in later stages of his study by reporting the odds ratios without representing them as risk ratios (personal communication, August 7, 2001).

9

✢

Experiments: In the Lab, in the Field, and in Nature

Editors love field experiments. When I was a young reporter in Miami, a wise but slightly daffy feature editor named Bill Phillips sent me into the streets to test the tolerance of Miamians for boorish behavior. I bumped into hurrying businessmen, I blew smoke into the faces of sweet old ladies, I tied up traffic at a bus stop by spilling a handful of change in a bus doorway and insisting on picking up every last nickel before the bus could move. The reaction of the citizenry was kind and gentle, and I dare any *Miami Herald* reporter to replicate that experiment today.[1] On April Fool's Day, Phillips stationed me at the corner of Miami Avenue and Flagler Street with a string attached to a purse lying on the sidewalk, so that I could snatch it out of the way of any passerby foolish enough to try to pick it up. A photographer hid in a nearby doorway to record the number of times I got punched in the nose. That's another experiment nobody has dared to replicate.

Stunts like these may not be worth turning into generalizable experiments, but there are socially useful and interesting things to be done that have both some degree of generalizability and the mad ring of 1950s *Miami Herald* copy. Some examples:

IGNORANCE ABOUT AIDS

In 1988, Dr. Inge Corless, a faculty member in the health sciences division of the University of North Carolina at Chapel Hill, was preparing a course on Acquired Immune Deficiency Syndrome (AIDS). As part of her research, she discussed with local pharmacists the disease-prevention properties of different types of condoms and discovered a disturbing lack of knowledge among these professionals. To see if her findings were true of a larger group of pharmacists, my advanced reporting class designed an experiment. A team of students sent one of its members to every pharmacy in Chapel Hill and the neighboring town of Carrboro to buy condoms and ask the pharmacist's advice about the best kind for preventing AIDS. A cumulative scale was designed to rank each pharmacist on how much he or she knew. The scale is cumulative because anyone who knows any given fact on the list usually knows the preceding facts as well:

1. Latex is better than animal skin (pores in the latter can admit the virus).
2. Lubricated latex is better than dry latex (less danger of breaking).
3. Lubrication with a spermicide is better than plain lubrication (the spermicide can kill the AIDS virus).
4. The name of the spermicide that kills the AIDS virus in laboratory tests is Nonoxynol-9.

Only 40 percent of the pharmacists knew all of these simple facts. Worse yet, some of them advised the student buyers to buy the lambskin condoms, which are both the most expensive and the least effective in preventing AIDS.

This was a simple and easily generalizable field experiment, for several reasons. First, no inferences about causation or correlation were necessary. The simple rate of ignorance was newsworthy by itself. The students did test some hypotheses about the causes of ignorance by comparing chain stores with independent pharmacies and older pharmacists with younger ones. No meaningful differences were found, nor were they necessary for newsworthiness.

The second boost to generalizability comes from the fact that all of the pharmacies in the defined area were tested. Sampling was involved within the pharmacies because the person on duty when the student condom buyer appeared represented all of the pharmacists who worked there. Overall, those pharmacists could be taken as representative of those on duty during hours convenient for student shoppers.

The resulting story, published in the *Durham Morning Herald*, had two useful social effects.[2] It spurred local pharmacists to become better educated, and it contributed directly to the AIDS education of the newspaper's readers.

THE UNDERAGE DRINKING CRACKDOWN

A more complicated research design was executed by an earlier class in 1982. The purpose of this one was to test the effectiveness of a Chapel Hill police crackdown on illegal beer purchases by persons under eighteen. This time, a causal inference was sought. The hypothesis: When the police crack down, beer sales dry up. To test it, beer sellers in neighboring jurisdictions were used as a control. A secondary hypothesis was also tested: Police are more likely to watch on weekend nights, and so violations will be more frequent on week nights.

In Chapel Hill, there was no sampling. Every convenience store and tavern was visited. Controls were drawn from the yellow pages section of the phone book and accumulated in order of their proximity to Chapel Hill until a matching number was reached. The buyers were all eighteen years old, so that no laws would be broken. The variable being measured was whether the sellers of beer would verify the age of these young people by asking for identification. Verification is sufficiently salient to teenagers that they have a slang term for it: *carding*.

A total of 246 attempts to buy beer was made. The overall rate of carding in Chapel Hill on a Saturday night was 22 percent, a number that, standing alone, suggests that the police crackdown was not very effective. However, the carding rate outside Chapel Hill was only 6 percent, revealing a significant effect after all.

The rate of carding in Chapel Hill dropped on Monday night to 7 percent and was no longer significantly different from the rate outside Chapel Hill. Bottom line: The police crackdown did have a selective effect on weekends, none at all on other times, and there were still plenty of opportunities for illegal drinking by minors.

Executing such a field experiment is not as simple as it sounds. The field workers have to be trained so that they follow uniform behaviors that will generate quantifiable data. We had each eighteen-year-old accompanied by an upperclassman or graduate student who observed and recorded the outcome of each test. We also had a rule against drinking on the job by our field force. That led to some awkward social situations. "We were the only customers in the bar," one of the supervisors reported. "The waitress was very nice and served Wendy a beer and then sat across the bar to talk to us. Wendy would casually pick up her glass and then set it down again without taking a sip. I avoided looking the waitress in the eye by staring out the glass door to the parking lot." The students left abruptly, pretending to pursue a friend spotted in a passing car.[3]

Some journalists are uncomfortable with the ethical considerations in such deception. Participant observation is, however, a time-honored tradition in both journalism and social science. And, at least where monitoring of public service is concerned, even so stringent an ethicist as Sissela Bok gives qualified approval where the monitoring leads to higher standards of public protection.[4]

Field experiments are satisfying in their directness. Instead of asking about social behavior in a survey, you get a chance to observe it straightforwardly.

When the hypothesis is clearly formulated in advance, you can design the experiment to test the hypothesis in the most efficient way and use randomization or test a total population so that error variance is minimized.

RULES FOR EXPERIMENTATION

The rules for experimental research have been well codified over the years, starting with John Stuart Mill's nineteenth-century proposals for scientific method.[5] However, some of the essential principles are intuitively apparent. Thomas D. Cook and Donald T. Campbell cite the story of a seventeenth-century experiment by a group of Frenchmen to test Pascal's theory of atmospheric pressure. They were looking for the cause of the Torricellian vacuum. A tube is filled with mercury and turned upside down, with its lower end in a dish of mercury. The column of mercury falls until it is about 30 inches high, and a vacuum remains in the space above it. What supports the column? Pascal thought it was the weight of the air pressing on the mercury in the dish. On a fall day in 1648, seven Frenchmen took two tubes, two dishes, and lots of mercury to a mountain. At the bottom of the mountain they set up the two tubes and found that the column of mercury was about 28 inches tall. Then, leaving one tube with an observer, they carried the other one 3,000 feet up the mountain and took another measurement. This time the mercury was less than 24 inches tall. They then varied the conditions on the mountaintop, taking measurements at different places and inside a shelter. All yielded the same number. On the way down, they stopped at an intermediate height and got an intermediate reading. At the bottom their observer there verified that the mercury in his tube had not changed. Then they set up the tube from the mountaintop one more time and saw that it now gave the same reading as the one that had been there at the bottom all the time.

Pascal's theory was supported. The second column of mercury had served as a control, showing that the different readings on the mountain were due to the elevation, not to something that had happened generally in the atmosphere during their climb. By taking measurements in all the different conditions they could think of, the experimenters were checking for rival hypotheses. And by taking a measurement halfway down, they were showing a continuous effect. Their example, say Cook and Campbell, "is redolent with features of modern science."[6]

MODERN EXPERIMENTAL DESIGN

For the drinking-age experiment to have been as careful as the one performed by those seventeenth-century researchers, we would have had to do it twice:

once before the police crackdown and once after. That would rule out the possibility that there is some ongoing condition in Chapel Hill that explains its higher Saturday-night carding rate. Experimental designs can take a great variety of forms, and it helps to keep track of them if you make diagrams. Here is one, adapted from Samuel Stouffer,[7] whose pathbreaking study of American military men in World War II was cited in the previous chapter:

	Time 1	Time 2
Experimental Group	X_1	X_2
Control Group	Y_1	Y_2

The experimental condition—police crackdown in the Chapel Hill example—is introduced between *Time 1* and *Time 2* for the experimental group only. In theory, the Xs and Ys are equivalent to start with, but in practice those conditions may be difficult or impossible to achieve. If you have enough control over the situation, you can randomize assignment to group X or group Y, but the police crackdown was not random, and it covered only Chapel Hill. So the next best thing was to find bars and convenience stores as much like those in Chapel Hill as possible, and the way to do that was to find some in the same market but not in the same police jurisdiction.

If the complete design had been followed, the analysis could have taken the following form:

$$X_2 - X_1 = D(X)$$
$$Y_2 - Y_1 = D(Y)$$

where D stands for "difference." If the police crackdown is effective, then $D(X)$ should be significantly larger than $D(Y)$. If both change, then some external force in the environment is acting on the entire community, not just on that portion covered by the Chapel Hill police department.

In fact, the design that was used was

$$X_2$$
$$Y_2$$

And the fact that carding was more frequent within the police jurisdiction than without was taken as evidence that the crackdown was real. Another possible abbreviated design would have been

$$X_1 \quad X_2$$

where the situation in Chapel Hill after the crackdown could have been compared with the situation before. In that case, Chapel Hill would have acted as its own control.

Notice that in this case the experimental manipulation is not something controlled by the researcher. This is a *natural experiment,* in that the manipulation would have taken place whether or not an interested researcher was around. The researcher's job is one of measurement and analysis. Sometimes you can introduce the experimental manipulation as well, and that gives you greater control in the randomization of potentially confounding variables.

For example, journalism students in Chapel Hill were interested in testing the proposition that folks in their town are more polite than people elsewhere. The town's reputation for civility is well known, but is it myth or fact? And, can it be objectively measured? One way to operationalize civility is by observing driver behavior. People are less inhibited in their social interactions when they are protected from each other by 2,000-pound shells of steel and fabric. We designed this simple test: Students in teams of two got into automobiles and drove to randomly chosen traffic lights, looping around until they were first in line at a red light. When the light turned to green, the driver held the car's position and waited for the car behind to honk. The passenger meanwhile used a stopwatch to clock the time from the green light to the first honk from behind. Hypothesis: Pre-honking time in Chapel Hill would be significantly longer than pre-honking time in other cities. When spring break came, the students scattered to their various homes and vacation spots and repeated the experiment at random intersections there. The outcome: Chapel Hill's reputation was justified. Its mean pre-honking time, more than eight seconds, was more than double that for other cities. In fact, some Chapel Hill motorists never honked at all, but waited patiently through another traffic light cycle.

Another famous experiment where the manipulation was introduced involved a militant civil rights group in southern California in the 1960s. A professor at California State College at Los Angeles recruited five blacks, five whites, and five Mexican Americans to attach "Black Panther" bumper stickers to their cars. All drove routinely to and from campus along Los Angeles freeway routes. All had had perfect driving records for the previous twelve months. All signed statements promising not to drive in unfamiliar parts of the city or in a manner to attract police attention.

The experiment was halted after seventeen days. The $500 set aside to pay traffic fines had been used up. The first arrest, for an incorrect lane change, was made two hours after the experiment began. One subject got three tickets in three days and dropped out. In total, the fifteen previously perfect drivers collected thirty-three citations for moving violations in the seventeen days that they displayed the bumper stickers.[8]

As journalism, the honking and bumper-sticker studies may have been sound enough, but even journalists need to know about the hazards of such research. When experiments are inadequately controlled, the expectations of both the experimenter and the subjects can yield spurious effects. There is some evidence that teacher expectancies have a lot to do with how a child performs in school. Robert Rosenthal demonstrated the effect by giving teachers lists of pupils whose psychological test results indicated superior performance. The pupils did in fact perform better than their classmates, even though Rosenthal had compiled his list by random selection. He called it "Pygmalion effect."[9]

HAWTHORNE EFFECT

A better-known problem occurs when the subjects in an experiment realize that something special is happening to them. Just the feeling of being special can make them perform differently. Surely, knowing that a Black Panther bumper sticker is on one's car could make one feel special.

This phenomenon is called Hawthorne effect, after a series of experiments at Western Electric Company's Hawthorne Plant in Chicago in 1927. Six women were taken from a large shop department that made telephone relays and placed in a test room where their job conditions could be varied and their output measured. Their task was fairly simple: assemble a coil, armature, contact springs, and insulators by fastening them to a fixture with four screws. It was about a minute's worth of work. Each time a worker completed one, she dropped it into a chute where an electric tape-punching device added it to the total for computing the hourly production rate.

To establish the base for a pretest-posttest design, the normal production rate was measured without the assemblers being aware of the measurement. Then the experiment was explained to them: how it was to test the effect of different working conditions, such as rest periods, lunch hours, or working hours. They were cautioned not to make any special efforts but to work only at a comfortable pace.

What happened next has achieved the status of myth in the separate literature of both social science and business administration. In the former, it is regarded as a horror story. For the latter, it is considered inspirational.

The second variable in the experiment (*Time 2*) was the production rate for five weeks in the test room while the subjects got used to the new surroundings. *Time 3* changed the piece rate rules slightly. *Times 4, 5,* and *6* changed the rest periods around. And so it went for eleven separate observations. And for each observation, production went up—not up and down as the conditions were varied. Just up.

Nonplussed, the experimenters threw the test into reverse. They took away all the special work breaks, piece rates, and rest periods. Production still went up. They put back some of the special conditions. More improvement. No matter what they did, production got better.

Something was going on. It was "testing effect." The six women knew they were in an experiment, felt good about it, enjoyed the special attention, and were anxious to please. They formed a separate social set within the plant, had frequent contact with management, and took part in the decisions over how the experimental conditions were to be manipulated. Their participation and the sense of being special overrode the effect of the initial admonition to make no special effort and work only at a comfortable pace. The study never found out what combination of rest periods, lunch hours, or payment methods has the most effect on productivity. But it was not wasted. The company learned that production improves when management shows concern for workers and management and workers are "organized in cooperation with management in the pursuit of a common purpose."[10] American management theorists took that idea to Japan after World War II, where it flourished, and it was eventually reintroduced to our shores in the 1980s. Those Hawthorne plant women were the first quality circle.

One of the flaws in the Hawthorne research design was that it tried to do too much. Expressed diagrammatically, it would look like this:

$$X_1 \quad X_2 \quad X_3 \quad X_4 \quad X_5 \quad X_6 \ldots$$

Following the notation system of Samuel Stouffer, we see many observations at different points in time. An experimental manipulation is inserted between each of the adjoining pairs of observations. A better design would have had a row of Ys parallel to the Xs to represent a control group with a similar special room and the same amount of special attention but no changes in working conditions. Better yet, get a different group (randomly selected, of course) for each experimental condition. Make repeated measurements and insert the change somewhere in the middle—say, between the third and fourth observations. In that way you can verify that the control group and the experimental group might be different to start with, but are still responding in the same way to the passage of time and to the effects of being measured.

Factors that correlate with the passage of time are an ongoing problem with field experiments. Your subjects get older and wiser, public policy makers change their ways, record-keeping methods change, the people making the observations, maybe even you, too, all change. The traditional way of coping with differences that correlate with time is with imagination. Stouffer noted that the basic research design, with all the controls and safeguards taken away, looks like this:

$$X_2$$

One measurement of one thing at one point in time. He was complaining about 1940s social science, but what he said is still relevant to twenty-first-century journalism. With such a research design, one phenomenon looked at once and not compared to anything, we "do not know much of anything," he said. "But we can still fill pages . . . with 'brilliant analysis' if we use plausible conjecture in supplying missing cells from our imagination. Thus we may find that the adolescent today has wild ideas and conclude that society is going to the dogs." The result is a kind of pretest-posttest comparison:

$$X_1 \quad X_2$$

The nonitalic cell is not an observation, but "our own yesterdays with hypothetical data, where X_1 represents us and X_2 our offspring. The tragicomic part is that most of the public, including, I fear, many social scientists, are so acculturated that they ask for no better data."

Since Stouffer's time, social scientists have become more careful. There is a tendency to add more control groups. The Black Panther bumper sticker experiment, for example, could have profited from this design:

$$X_1 \quad X_2$$
$$Y_2$$

The Y_2 represents a control group that drives without bumper stickers as a test of the possibility that police are cracking down at *Time 2*. The control group would be even better if both X and Y drivers had either a Black Panther sticker or a neutral sticker applied before each trip, and if the application were performed at random after each driver was already in the car and had no way of knowing which sticker was being displayed.

An even more thorough design could look like this:

$$X_1 \quad X_2$$
$$Y_2$$
$$Y_1 \quad X'_2$$
$$Y'_2$$

Here the nonstickered or neutral-stickered Y group is present at *Time 1* to verify its initial comparability. X' and Y' are present as a test of the possibility that the experiment made the original two groups of drivers too aware of their roles as subjects and made them behave differently, like the women in the Hawthorne experiment. Such an effect would be indicated by a difference between X_2 and X'_2, as well as between Y_2 and Y'_2.

Donald T. Campbell, with Julian Stanley, in an early evaluation of designs for experimental and quasi-experimental social research, pointed out that the previous design includes four separate tests of the hypothesis.[11] If the police are really prejudiced against the Black Panthers, then there should be the following differences in the quantity of arrests:

$$X_2 > X_1$$
$$X_2 > Y_2$$
$$X'_2 > Y'_2$$
$$X'_2 > Y_1$$

Tacking on control groups can be a good idea in survey research when you return to the same respondents to get a pretest-posttest measure. The *Miami Herald* did that when Martin Luther King was assassinated, just after it had completed a survey of its black population. The hypothesis was that King's nonviolent ideology was weakened by his death and the advocates of violence had gained. Fortunately, the earlier survey had asked questions about both kinds of behavior, and records of who had been interviewed had been retained. At the suggestion of Thomas Pettigrew, the *Herald* added a control group of fresh respondents to the second wave of interviews. The original respondents had had time to think about their responses, might have been changed by the interview experience, might even have read about themselves in the *Miami Herald*. Any differences at *Time 2* might simply be the effect of the research process, rather than of any external event. The second-wave control group provided a check against that.

As it turned out, the control group's attitudes were indistinguishable from those of the panel, providing evidence that the experience of being interviewed had not altered the *Herald's* subjects. Knowing that was important, because there was a big change between *Time 1* and *Time 2*. Miami blacks, after King's death, were more committed than ever to his nonviolent philosophy. The proportion interested in violence did not change.[12]

REGRESSION-DISCONTINUITY DESIGN

A design suggested by Donald Campbell could be a good fit for natural experiments. He calls it the regression-discontinuity design. It could be used for evaluating the effectiveness of awards or educational programs if the right kinds of records are kept. Consider the problem of evaluating the effectiveness of the Nieman fellowships. The program could create its own built-in control group without having to resort to random selection of fellows. Out of some 30 finalists chosen for interviews, a committee selects the dozen or so winners. It would be easy enough to order all 30 finalists on a continuous scale, according to the number of votes each received on the first ballot. If it were a 6-member committee, the number of possible votes would range from 0 to 6, creating a 7-point scale.

The next step takes a lot longer. Follow all 30, both winners and near-winners, for a period of years and rank their achievements by some objective method to see how well they met Agnes Nieman's injunction to improve the standards of journalism. You could give them points for staying in journalism, for winning prizes, for building national reputations, for rising in the ranks of management, for service in professional organizations, for getting stories on page one, and the like. If the selection committee's judgments had predictive power, there would be correlation between career achievement and the number of first-round votes.

That much is rather obvious. Campbell's contribution was to realize that if a program works—in this case, a mid-career year at Harvard—there should be a discontinuity along the regression line. The no-effect hypothesis predicts a smooth, straight line. If Nieman fellowships do have an effect, there should be a break in the trend between the data point representing the highest-ranking loser and the lowest-ranking winner. Figure 9.1 shows what it would look like.

Once you start looking for spurious effects, it is difficult to know where to stop. Donald T. Campbell, first with Julian Stanley and later with Thomas D. Cook, has made an intensive effort to figure out how to do things right. To do that, he first had to list the things that can go wrong. At Harvard, they

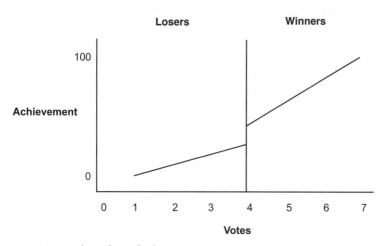

Figure 9.1   Regression-Discontinuity

used to call his sources of lurking variables "Campbell's demons." Here is a partial listing:

CAMPBELL'S DEMONS

1. *History.* If you measure something at two different times and get a difference, it could be because of any number of historical events that took place in the intervening period.
2. *Maturation.* Subjects and experimenters alike get older, tired, bored, and otherwise different in the course of an experiment.
3. *Testing.* Measuring the way a person responds to a stimulus can change the way he or she responds the next time there is a measurement. School achievement tests are notorious because teachers learn what is in the tests and start teaching their content. Pretty soon all the children are above average, just as in Lake Wobegon.
4. *Statistical regression.* Journalists have been easy prey to this one. A school board announces a program to focus on its worst-performing schools and improve them. It picks the two or three schools with the worst test scores in the previous year and lavishes attention and new teaching methods on them. Sure enough, the next year those schools have better test scores. The problem is that they would have done better even if there had been no special attention or new technique.

   The reason is that there is a certain amount of random error in all tests and rankings. The schools at the bottom of the list got there partly by chance. Give them a new roll of the dice with next year's testing, and chance alone will move them closer to average. The phenomenon is also called *regression toward the mean,* because it almost always moves the extreme performers, top and bottom, closer to the mean on the second test. It is a danger any time that you select the extremes of a distribution for treatment. Most educators know about it, but knowing about it doesn't stop them from taking the credit for it.
5. *Selection.* If comparison groups are not chosen strictly at random, then hidden biases can destroy their comparability. Self-selection is the worst kind. If you were doing the Black Panther experiment, and you let students volunteer to display the bumper stickers, you might get the risk takers and therefore the most reckless drivers.
6. *Mortality.* Not all of the subjects remain available during an experiment that lasts over a period of time. Those who drop out or get lost may be different in some systematic way. In the evaluation of Head Start programs for preschool children, for example, the children with the most-motivated parents were more likely to finish the treatment.

The selective dropping out of the less motivated took away children who had poorer family situations and maybe other strikes against them. Their absence for the final comparisons made Head Start look better than it really was.

7. *Instrumentation.* The measuring scale may have more flexibility in the middle than at the extremes. Audiences rating different moments of a presidential debate on a seven-point scale can make wider swings from the midpoint than when the comparison is made from an extremely high or low point.

8. *The John Henry effect.* Members of a control group might know they are in a control group and try harder just out of rivalry. Students in some educational experiments have been suspected of doing this. John Henry, you may remember, was the steel-driving man who "wouldn't let a steam drill beat him down" in the traditional folk ballad.

9. *Resentful demoralization.* This is just the reverse of the John Henry effect. Control groups see the experimental group as being more favored, and they stop trying.

See Cook and Campbell[13] for the full list of threats to experimental validity. But don't be discouraged by them. As Campbell noted many years ago, "all measures are complex and all include irrelevant components that may produce apparent effects."[14] It is not necessary to become so frightened of those irrelevant components that one avoids field experiments. It is only necessary to be aware of the things that can go wrong and treat your own work with the appropriate skepticism.

ODDBALL MEASURES

One way to foil many of Campbell's demons is to look for *nonreactive measures* of newsworthy phenomena. Such measures sometimes occur in nature. For example, you can estimate the age of viewers of a museum exhibit by locating the nose prints on the glass case and measuring their height from the floor. This example and many others comes from a wonderful book by Eugene J. Webb, Donald Campbell, and others that was written under the working title *Oddball Measures.* ("It is only a fear of librarians that has caused us to drop it," the authors reported.[15]) Their nonreactive measures include the simple observation of behavior where the observer does not intrude on the scene. For example, one study that they cite examined the social distance of whites and blacks in a college setting by observing the degree of racial clustering when whites and blacks chose their seats in classrooms. The effects of ghost stories told to a seated circle of children were observed by noting the shrinking diameter of the circle.

Content analysis is a nonreactive measure. You can trace the increased incidence of words that used to be taboo, like *ass* and *damn,* by establishing their relative frequency in different newspapers and at different times. Archival records normally are not changed by the act of measuring. With modern computer archives, however, one cannot be so certain. Publication of a paper evaluating a newspaper's editorial skill by measuring the rate of certain misspelled words might conceivably induce the paper's editors to correct the misspellings in the electronic database. Records kept over time are subject to changes in the efficiency of record keeping. Thus archival data can show an increase in criminal activity after a period of police reform, if one of the reforms is better record keeping.

Webb and colleagues also cite the case of a Chicago automobile dealer who had his mechanics check the radio of every car brought in for service to see what station it was tuned to. The dealership then placed its advertising with the most popular stations. And then there is the classic story of the measurement of attention to a football game by monitoring pressure gauges at the city water department. The greater the audience, the greater the pressure drop during commercials, as toilets are flushed across the viewing area.

EVALUATION RESEARCH

Government agencies often use evaluation research to test the effectiveness of their programs. Knowing about Campbell's demons can help you evaluate the evaluators.

A classic example is the great Connecticut crackdown on drunken drivers when Abraham Ribicoff was governor in 1955. He imposed a program of intensified law enforcement, and the annual rate of traffic deaths dropped by 12.3 percent in 1956. If you just look at the two years, you have a simple pretest-posttest design, and the governor's program seems to have worked. But if you check out the longer time series, you see that there was wide year-to-year variation, and 1955 happened to be a peak year. Reforms are often instituted when a problem is at its peak. Since chance alone may account for the peak, a measurement in the following year, thanks to statistical regression, will likely be closer to the long-run average. That may be all that happened in Connecticut.

The effect of reforms is easiest to measure if they are introduced abruptly. You then can look for their effect against the background of a longer time trend.

In educational reforms, look for Hawthorne effect and selective retention as factors that will make just about any school administration look good. Schools get a lot attention when they try a new technique, and their pretest-posttest studies show that it works. Journalists give it big play. Then you stop hearing about it, and after a few years the technique is forgotten. That's because the Hawthorne effect wears off, and the new technique proves no better than the old in the long run. However, nobody calls a press conference to tell you that.

Selective retention (Campbell's "mortality") occurs when only the most motivated students continue to show up for a special program. To prove that the program works, administrators compare those who finished with those who dropped out. Sure enough, they perform better. But chances are they would have done so in the absence of the new program, because they were more energetic, aggressive, and better motivated to start with. Indeed, even much of the beneficial effect of a college education has been shown to disappear when family background is held constant. Going to college identifies you as a person with above-average earning power. It does not necessarily give you that power. Your genes, and possibly your family connections, did that.

One of the frustrating aspects of evaluation research is that political realities tend to work against sound research designs. A true experiment requires randomization of the experimental treatment. That is the best way to assure that the experimental and control groups are equal to start with. But if there is some reason to believe that the experimental treatment really does confer an advantage, then the most politically astute are more likely to get it.

An experimental plan to eliminate poverty through the simple expedient of giving poor people money was devised by the federal government in the administration of Lyndon Johnson. It was to take place in New Jersey and would use entire communities as units of analysis. That way, there could be controls without people living next door to each other in similar circumstances and getting different treatment from the government. But nobody could figure out a way to decide what communities would get the treatment and which ones would have to settle for being controls.

The federal government's most ambitious attempt to distribute benefits and costs equally through randomization was the draft lottery during the war in Vietnam. In theory, the men in the armed forces should have been a representative sample of the population. They weren't even close, because the more affluent men of draft age were more clever at figuring out ways to beat the system by staying in school, joining the National Guard, feigning illness, or leaving the country. Actually, more than cleverness was involved, because staying in school cost money and getting into the Guard sometimes took political connections.

Where the government is not involved, randomization is easier. Clinical drug trials use the double-blind method, where treatment and control groups are randomly assigned a test drug or a placebo, and neither the person getting the drug nor the person administering it knows which is which.

Even that procedure sometimes is given a political justification: The new drug is scarce, and random selection is a fair way to decide who should get it. However, the tradition of using the marketplace to allocate scarce resources is strong, and opportunities for true experiments in education and social policy will probably always be rare. That makes the need for skeptical journalistic attention to policy-related quasi experiments all the more important.

NOTES

1. Phil Meyer, "Even Boors Get Break in Miami," *Miami Herald,* July 27, 1958, 26A.

2. Melinda Stubbee, "Survey: Pharmacists Lack Knowledge of Safest Condom Types," *Durham Morning Herald,* December 7, 1988, 1B.

3. Shawn McIntosh, "Wary Journalist Braves Good Ol' Boys' Hang-Out for Class Grade," *UNC Journalist* (December 1982): 10.

4. Sissela Bok, *Lying: Moral Choice in Public and Private Life* (New York: Vintage Books, 1979, 212.

5. Ernest Nagel, ed., *John Stuart Mill's Philosophy of Scientific Method* (New York: Hafner, 1950).

6. Thomas D. Cook and Donald T. Campbell, *Quasi-Experimentation: Design and Analysis Issues for Field Settings* (Boston: Houghton-Mifflin, 1979), 3.

7. Samuel Stouffer, "Some Observations on Study Design," *American Journal of Sociology* (January 1950).

8. Frances K. Heussenstamm, "Bumper Stickers and the Cops," *Transaction* (February 1971).

9. Cited in Cook and Campbell, *Quasi-Experimentation,* 67.

10. George Caspar Homans, "Group Factors in Worker Productivity," reprinted in *Sociological Research,* Matilda White Riley, ed. (New York: Harcourt, Brace & World, 1963).

11. Donald T. Campbell and Julian Stanley, *Experimental and Quasi-Experimental Designs for Research* (Chicago: Rand-McNally, 1966).

12. Philip Meyer, Juanita Greene, and George Kennedy, "Miami Negroes: A Study in Depth," a *Miami Herald* reprint, 1968.

13. *Quasi-Experimentation,* chapter 2.

14. Donald T. Campbell, "Reforms as Experiments," *American Psychologist* (April 1969).

15. Eugene J. Webb, Donald T. Campbell, Richard D. Schwartz, and Lee Sechrest, *Unobtrusive Measures: Nonreactive Research in the Social Sciences* (New York: Rand McNally, 1966).

10

+

Databases

There are two kinds of databases: those that you create yourself and those that were created by somebody else, usually without your convenience in mind.

In the early days of precision journalism, most databases useful to journalists fell into the first category. The pioneer database maker was Clarence Jones of the *Miami Herald,* who in 1968 led an investigation of the Dade County criminal justice system by analyzing 3,000 criminal cases. He hired University of Miami law students to code the information from court house records. It took four IBM cards to hold the data from a single case.

Jones's main analytical tool was cross-tabulation. Software was available to make it fairly easy. The University of Michigan had a crosstab routine for the IBM 360 called Filter Tau, and Harvard was already in the second release of its pioneering Data-Text software for the IBM 7090. But Jones and his computer guru, Clark Lambert, the *Herald*'s information systems manager, were unaware of these developments, so Lambert wrote a program from scratch in COBOL, a business-oriented language, for each table.[1]

As always happens, many tables raised new questions that required more tables. Computer time was scarce on the *Herald*'s busy 360, and Jones frequently resorted to a counter-sorter, the machine of nineteenth-century origin, to do his crosstabs. But that, of course, wasn't possible when the independent and dependent variables were not on the same card in the four-card set.

The project was abandoned when Jones was offered a Washington assignment and headed north. Then it was discovered that a *Herald* publicist had already bought a full-page ad in *Editor and Publisher* promoting the project. "Meet our newest reporting team," said the ad, along with a picture of Jones staring grimly at a continuous sheet of output, with an inset of a central processing unit bearing a cartoon smile.[2] Jones was recalled to Miami and finished the project three weeks after the ad ran.

Although Jones's original goal of documenting corruption in the system was not met, the series did show a surprising rate of youth crime, accounting for more than a third of arrests. And it revealed that most arrests for major crimes never resulted in prison time. Perhaps the most important finding was the inefficiency in the county's record-keeping system. At one point, the county sheriff asked for, and received from the *Herald,* a custom report on arrests by certain deputies who were under investigation. Searching by hand would have taken hundreds of hours, but the Herald's computer produced this information in minutes.

Government agencies keep their own computer records today, and many are in the public domain. But the need to create our own databases is still with us. The efforts by news media to recount contested Florida votes cast in the 2000 presidential election is an example.

In social science, there is a long tradition of content analysis that covers the problems encountered in both Jones's early effort and the more recent ballot study. As in any other research effort, the first tasks are conceptualization and operationalization. You must answer two questions: How do you define what you are looking for, and how will you know when you see it? If you start a content analysis project expecting to make these decisions on the fly, you will get frustration and much needless reworking of data.

The key to content analysis is taking care that your work is replicable. You need to write definitions and decision rules that are so clear that another investigator could follow your path and, working from the same rules and definitions, analyze the same data and get the same answers. The technical name for this condition is *reliability.*

Another chore that should be performed at the very start is to design the record layout for your computer analysis. Then you can create coding forms that match that layout. This will not leave to chance your ability to easily enter the data in a form that can be analyzed. When the *Miami Herald's* reporters and its accounting team rushed to get started collecting data in the 2000 Florida election recount, nobody bothered to make certain that the reporters and the accountants were using the same forms or data structure. That created later programming headaches and, in at least one large and important county, made intercoder reliability impossible to check.

The standard way to demonstrate reliability is to have more than one coder evaluate a sample of the cases being classified and then check their rate of agreement. If they agree, you have evidence of replicability. If they disagree, you need to retrain them, revise your categories, change their definitions, replace the loopy coders, or all four.

How much agreement is necessary? One rule of thumb is to shoot for 80 percent agreement.[3] But in cases where you are measuring something that does not occur very often, you could easily get that by chance alone. Suppose you are looking at 1,000 old-fashioned punchcard ballots and want to determine how many have dimples, indicating an attempt to vote for a particular candidate. If 90 percent of them are undimpled, you can expect 81 percent agreement just by chance.

This problem was anticipated in the 1950s by W. R. Scott of the University of Michigan, who proposed a measure that compares observed with expected agreement. The formula for Scott's pi, as it is known, measures the degree of improvement over chance in the agreement between a pair of coders.[4]

HOW TO CALCULATE THE RELIABILITY COEFFICIENT (SCOTT'S PI)

Two coders classified 868 Florida punchcard ballots to judge whether a punch in a given location was blank, clean, a hanging chad, a dimple, or a pinprick. (These data are fictitious but illustrative of what *USA Today* and the *Miami Herald* were working with in the 2001 recount of the previous year's election.) Cases where the two coders agreed are highlighted in boldface.

		Coder A					
		Blank	Clean	Chad	Dimple	Pinprick	Total
	Blank	**562**	6	1	3	43	615
	Clean	3	**89**	0	0	0	92
Coder B	Chad	7	3	**12**	0	0	22
	Dimple	0	0	0	**17**	27	44
	Pinprick	24	0	2	46	**23**	95
	Total	596	98	15	66	93	868

The first step is to see how often they agreed. Sum the values in the diagonal. They agreed in 703 out of 868 comparisons = 80.99 percent.

Now find how much they would have been expected to agree by chance alone. The formula for the expected agreement in each cell is $(R * C) / N$.

$$Blank = 596 * 615 / 868 = 422.28$$
$$Clean = 98 * 92 / 868 = 10.39$$
$$Chad = 98 * 92 / 868 = 0.38$$
$$Dimple = 66 * 44 / 868 = 3.35$$
$$Pinprick = 93 * 95 / 868 = 10.18$$
$$Total\ expected\ agreement = 446.58 = 51.45\%$$

The difference between expected and observed is $80.99 - 51.45$ or 29.54.

What's the maximum improvement over chance the coders could have achieved? The best they could have done is 100 percent agreement, and that would have been 48.55 percentage points better than chance.

They actually did 29.54 points better than chance. And 29.54 / 48.55 is equal to .608 percent of the potential. That .608 is Scott's pi. The general formula:

$$\text{Scott's pi} = \frac{PO - PE}{100 - PE}$$

where *PO* is the observed agreement and *PE* is the expected agreement. There is no firm rule for a minimum Scott's pi, but most of the literature in mass communications research cites values of .75 or higher. The important thing is to check all your pairs of coders early in your content analysis project so that you can take action in the cases where you need to revise your procedures or retrain coders.

It is not necessary to use multiple coders for all cases. But each coder should be paired with another in a large enough sample so that you can verify his or her consistency.

Reliability is not a problem when you are analyzing text and have an operational definition based on the frequency of certain words or strings of words. The computer will always get the same answer if it looks at the same data.

In chapter 4, you saw how a database search was used to discover the frequency of certain misspelled words in newspapers. Other kinds of content analysis are possible. You can track a social trend, for example, by counting the frequency of words associated with the trend, and watch its movement over time and from one part of the country to another. Public concern with the drug problem, for example, might be tracked just by counting the frequency of the word *drugs* in newspapers over time. By performing the same analysis for presidential speeches, you could see whether the president's concern preceded or followed the media concern. You could then track public opinion polls, archived in an electronic database by the Roper Center of the University of Connecticut, to see if officials and the media were responding to public concern or whether the public concern was created by the media. For a nice finishing touch, you could look at medical examiner records showing the number of drug-related deaths and determine how far public, media, and official responses all lagged behind the reality of the problem.

Standard search engines will give you the frequency of stories in which the search text appears without the need to print out each story. Using that capability, I was able to track a usage of an old word to form a relatively new cliché—the use of the word *arguably* to modify a superlative. It took only a small expenditure of connect time. I found that newspaper writers in the

East were the first popularizers of the expression, but that it gradually spread west, and that by 1989, the *Los Angeles Times* had become the heaviest user in the database. First recorded use in the system was in a record review by Rich Aregood of the *Philadelphia Daily News* in 1978.[5] "If you find that I'm also responsible for 'hopefully,'" said Aregood, "please don't tell me."

If the data whose content you wish to analyze are available only in print form or must be aggregated from a number of different online archives, you can patch together your own database with relative ease. My students created a computer-readable database of CEO messages to shareholders in the annual reports of public newspaper companies. Some of the more recent reports were downloaded from company Web sites. Older ones were found in the library or private collections and scanned with an optical character reader and cleaned for analysis with a word processor.

Instead of counting the incidence of single words, we created two dictionaries, one composed of words whose use often denotes a concern for community service and others that more often are associated with a concern for profitability. By comparing the frequency of words from the two groups, we could identify persistent differences in corporate culture that made some companies manifestly more concerned with social responsibility than others.[6]

GOVERNMENT DATABASES

The Government Printing Office is no longer the primary supplier of the most current government information. Data that have time value are now routinely loaded into computers for use by anybody with Internet access. So are the most frequently requested tables from the *Statistical Abstract of the United States*. Go to www.census.gov, and you can even get such tables as national health expenditures, broken down by source and object of payment in spreadsheet format, ready for further analysis. In addition, huge volumes of data are supplied on compact disks by various levels of government. For example, I have on my desk a compact disk containing the name, address, demographic, and voting participation history of every registered voter in the state of North Carolina. I use it for survey sampling and to test hypotheses about voting behavior. The tax assessor of Orange County, N.C., kindly supplied me with the ownership and tax valuation of every piece of real property in the county on a Zip disk for analysis by my students. There are also private organizations that compile and reformat government reports for easy analysis, including political campaign contributions. As recently as the 1980s, data sets of this size needed mainframe computers for analysis. No longer. And so reporters are becoming less dependent on information systems experts to decode the data.

Even so, there is nothing wrong with calling for help when a dataset presents an unfamiliar problem. One of the best known early uses of the computer to analyze public records was a study of the Philadelphia criminal justice system by Donald L. Barlett and James B. Steele of the *Philadelphia Inquirer* in 1972. They worked from a sample of paper records and hired clerks to transcribe the information into coding forms that could then be converted to a computer medium. I helped them design a coding system and wrote a program for the IBM 7090, a wonderful and busy-looking old mainframe that used ten refrigerator-size tape drives instead of disk storage. The program was in Data-Text, the higher-level language developed at Harvard in the previous decade. My goal was to teach the programming technique to one or more members of the *Inquirer* news staff as we conducted the analysis, so that they could do their own programming for the next project. I failed. *Inquirer* reporters won many prizes after that, but they did it with shoe leather. The inaccessibility of mainframes at the time—both physically and conceptually—was part of the problem. Today, an entry-level personal computer can do everything that the ancient mainframe could do, and a major barrier has been removed.

My first involvement with reporters using a high-powered statistical program to analyze public records that had been compiled by a government agency in computer form came in 1978. The reporters were Rich Morin and Fred Tasker of the *Miami Herald*. By then, I was on the corporate staff at Knight Ridder in Miami, and Louise McReynolds, my research assistant (who later became a history professor at the University of Hawaii), was the teacher. Morin, Tasker, and McReynolds acquired the tape of tax assessment records from the Dade County assessor's office, mounted it on the *Herald*'s IBM 360, and analyzed it with SPSS. In cases where property had been sold within the previous year, they were able to compare the sale price with the assessed valuation and calculate the degree to which assessed valuation equaled fair market value as required by Florida law. They found that expensive properties were assessed at a much lower ratio to market value than cheaper properties and that business property got a better break than residential property. The tax assessor resigned. When the analysis was repeated the following year, the disparities had been significantly reduced.

McReynolds's training mission in Miami, unlike mine in Philadelphia, was a success. Morin went on to study criminal justice records in Monroe County, Florida, and reported that drug-related crimes were dealt with much more leniently than those that were not drug related. He built a polling operation at the *Herald* and later went to the *Washington Post* to direct its polling and database investigations.

For sheer intensity in the 1980s, no journalistic database investigator matched Elliot Jaspin of the *Providence Journal*. He built a library of data tapes that included all the state's driver's license records, all the state's corporation records, all the state's criminal court records, all the state's civil court records going back for 10 years. We have all the state's financial records for the last three years. We have all real estate transactions for the last two years. We have all voter registration records. We have all traffic violations for the last three years. So, in other words, if you were picked up for speeding in Rhode Island, we have a record of it.[7]

At Providence, Jaspin's work was based on three fairly simple analytical tools: simple searches, frequency counts, and list matching. Examples:

Search: The Rhode Island Housing and Mortgage Finance Corporation was created to subsidize home mortgages for low- and middle-income buyers. Jaspin obtained a computer tape with records of 35,000 such mortgages, sorted them by interest rate, and found that loans at the lowest rates, exceptionally low for the time—8.5 percent when the market price was 13 to 19 percent—had been awarded to the sons and daughters of high-ranking state officials. Further investigation revealed that a participating bank ignored rules covering price limits, closing deadlines, and other procedures to aid those well-connected borrowers.[8]

Frequency count: The state attorney general gave a speech reporting on her two years in office and boasted of a high rate of conviction in cases of murder and welfare fraud. Jaspin used the computer to examine every indictment and to count the convictions and reported that the real conviction rate was much less than she had claimed. In the case of welfare fraud, her conviction rate was "unprecedentedly low."[9]

Record matching: Jaspin merged two files, the list of traffic violations in Rhode Island and the roster of names of school bus drivers. He discovered that more than one driver in four had at least one motor vehicle violation and that several had felony records, ranging from drug dealing to racketeering.[10]

Each of these three kinds of computer manipulation is easily within the range of a personal computer database program such as Access. While a great deal can be done with these programs, they are not the most convenient for statistical analysis of the sort done in the Philadelphia criminal justice study or the Dade County tax comparisons. For those databases, the story lay in comparisons of subgroups, which is most conveniently done by:

Cross-tabulation: Barlett and Steele, for example, reported that 64 percent of black murder convicts got sentences of more than five years when their victims where white, but only 14 percent got such long sentences if the victims were black.

Comparison of means: Property tax fairness can be evaluated by calculating a ratio of sales price to tax valuation and then finding the mean ratio for different classes of property.

For that kind of number crunching, SAS and SPSS are the software tools of choice. Both can also do the more elementary things, such as sort and rank-order cases on given variables and print out lists of the rankings. They also make it easy to create new variables out of old ones. The ratio of sales price to tax valuation, for example, is a computer-generated number that can then be used as input for the next stage of analysis. Even though SPSS and SAS are conceptually more difficult than the simpler database packages, they can do more complicated tasks. So, once learned, they are easier to use for most analytical chores and well worth the effort.

COMPLEX DATA STRUCTURES

The easiest database to use is one with a simple rectangular file format. A rectangular file, as explained in chapter 5, is one where each case has the same number of records and all the records are the same length. Telling the computer where to look for each record is fairly straightforward.

The gradebook for my course on ethics and professional problems is an example of a simple rectangular file. There is one record for each student. Each record contains the student's name, ID number, group identification, project grade, midterm grade, book report grade, final examination grade, and course grade. A typical record would look like this:

GRIMES 4534 86 102 76 85 90 85

I built the file using a spreadsheet program and then imported it into SAS. The following input statement told SAS how to interpret the numbers from the spreadsheet:

INPUT NAME SSN GROUP PROJECT PEER MIDTERM BOOKRPT
    FINAL COURSE;

Because the values are separated by spaces in the raw data, it was not necessary to tell SAS exactly where to look for them. I just had to give the correct order. Once the data were in SAS, it was easy to run validity checks, compare subgroups, test for a normal distribution, and look for natural cutting points for assignment of the letter grades.

Even large and complicated files can be rectangular. The Bureau of the Census issues a county statistics file that has hundreds of variables for more than three thousand counties and county equivalents in the United States. But it has the same variables for every county, and their relative locations are the same. Here is a portion of the SAS input statement to read that record:

INPUT #1 FIPS 1–5 SEG 6 TYPE 7 NAME $ 16–45 MEDAGE 53–62 .1

This statement tells SAS to look in positions 1 through 5 of the first record in each case to find the county's five-digit Federal Information Processing Standard code. SEG and TYPE are variables that help identify this particular record. The county's name is in letters instead of numbers (indicated by the $ sign) and it is in positions 16 through 45. Median age is in positions 53 through 62, and the computer is told to impute one decimal place—that is, divide whatever number it finds there by 10. Thus a 345 encoded there would mean the median age was 34.5.

NONRECTANGULAR FILES

A rectangular file is straightforward: a place for everything and everything in its place. Tell the computer where to find things for one case, and it knows where to find them in all.

The most common reason for departing from the rectangular form is an unequal number of attributes for each case. For example, in public records of criminal proceedings, a single indictment might cover a number of criminal violations or counts. The number will be different from case to case. You could handle this situation with a rectangular file only by making each record long enough to hold all the information for the longest case. Indictments with fewer counts than the maximum would have blank spaces in the record. We organized the Barlett-Steel criminal justice data in that way in order to maintain the simplicity of a rectangular file.

Another way to organize such a file would be to put all the identifying information—name of defendant, arresting officer, date, location of crime, and so forth—on the first record, along with the first count of the indictment. The second record would repeat the identifying information and then give the data on the second count. Each case would have as many records as there are counts in the indictment.

With such a file, you would be free either to make the indictment the unit of analysis or you could treat each count as a separate unit. Either SAS or SPSS can easily handle the problem of unequal record lengths or unequal number of records per case.

HIERARCHICAL OR NESTED FILES

The problem with the arrangement just described is that it wastes space. The key information about each indictment has to be repeated for each count of the indictment.

How much simpler it would be if the basic information about the defendant and the indictment could be given only once and the counts for that indictment then listed one after another. That kind of nesting is handled easily by either SAS or SPSS. Either system allows you to spread that basic information at the top of the hierarchy to all of the elements at the level below.

An SPSS manual gives the clearest illustration of a nested file that I have ever seen in print.[11] Imagine a file that records motor vehicle accidents. The basic unit of analysis (or observation) is an accident. Each accident can involve any number of vehicles, and each vehicle can contain any number of persons. You want to be able to generalize to accidents, to vehicles involved in accidents, or to people in vehicles involved in accidents.

Each case would have one record with general information about the accident, one record for each vehicle, and one record for each person. The total number of records for each case will vary, depending on how many vehicles were involved and how many persons were in those vehicles. The organization scheme for the first case might look like this:

Accident record	(Type 1)
Vehicle record	(Type 2)
Person record	(Type 3)
Vehicle record	(Type 2)
Person record	(Type 3)
Person record	(Type 3)

This would be a two-vehicle accident, with one person in the first vehicle and two persons in the second vehicle. There would be a different format for each record type. Record type 1, for example, would give the time, place, weather conditions, nature of the accident, and the name of the investigating officer. Record type 2 would give the make and model of the car and extent of the damage. Record type 3 would give the age and gender of each person, tell whether or not he or she was driving, and describe any injuries and what criminal charges were filed, if any.

In analyzing such a data set, you can use persons, vehicles, or accidents as the unit of analysis and spread information from one level of hierarchy to another. SAS or SPSS are the easiest programs to use for such complex data sets.

AGGREGATE VERSUS INDIVIDUAL DATA

In the examples just cited, the data provided information down to the individual person or incident. In many large government databases, the volume of information is so great that only aggregates of information are generally made available.

The United States Census, for example, releases data in which various geographical divisions are the observations or units of analysis. The data further divide those geographical units into various demographic categories—age, race, and gender, for example—and tell you the number of people in various categories and combinations of variables, but they never let you see all the way down to one person. For that reason, you can't do cross-tabulation in the sense that was described in the previous chapter. But you can produce original analysis by aggregating the small cells into bigger ones that make more sense in testing some hypothesis.

When dealing with aggregate data, watch out for the ecological fallacy. Generalizations about populations do not always apply to individual members of those populations. For example, when George Wallace was running for president on a segregationist platform, there were parts of the South where the Wallace vote was higher in counties with higher percentages of blacks in the population. This correlation did not mean that blacks were voting for Wallace. Voting rights reforms had not yet fully kicked in, and the areas with large black populations had the most frightened whites who turned out for Wallace, while blacks were still intimidated from full participation.

THE DIRTY-DATA PROBLEM

The larger and more complex a database becomes, the greater the chances of incomplete or bad data. The 1988 Uniform Crime Reports showed a big drop in all types of crime in the southeastern region. A second look revealed that Florida was missing from the database. The state was changing its reporting methods and just dropped out of the FBI reports for that year. A database reporter needs to check and double-check and not be awed by what the computer provides just because it comes from a computer.

In evaluating the information in a database, you always need to ask who supplied the original data and when and how they did it. Many government databases, like the Uniform Crime Reports, are compilations of material gathered from a very large number of individuals, whose reliability and punctuality are not uniform.

USA Today found a story in a database supplied by the Environmental Protection Agency about the high level of damage done to the earth's ozone layer by industries that the public perceives as relatively clean: electronics, computers, and telecommunications. They were the source of a large share of the Freon 113, carbon tetrachloride, and methyl chloroform dumped into the environment.

The computer made it relatively easy to add up the total pounds of each of the three ozone-destroying chemicals emitted by each of more than 75,000 factories that reported. Then they were ranked so that *USA Today* could print its list of the ten worse ozone destroyers.

What happened next is instructive. Instead of taking the computerized public record at face value, *USA Today* checked. Carol Knopes, of the special projects staff, called each installation on the dirtiest-ten list and asked about the three chemicals. Eight of the ten factories verified the amount in the computer record.

One of the companies, Rheem Manufacturing Co. of Fort Smith, Arkansas, a maker of heating and air conditioning equipment, did release some Freon 113, but the company had gotten its units of measurement mixed up, reporting volume instead of weight. It had filed an amended report with the EPA showing a much lower number, and so it came off the list.[12] A similar clerical error was claimed by another company, Allsteel Inc. of Aurora, Illinois, but it had not filed a correction with EPA. Because *USA Today*'s report was based on what the government record showed, the newspaper kept Allsteel on the list, ranking it fifth with 1,337,579 pounds, but added this footnote: "Company says it erred in EPA filing and actual number is 142,800 pounds."[13]

As a general rule, the larger the database and the more diverse and distant the individuals or institutions that supply the raw information, the greater the likelihood of error or incomplete reporting. Therefore, database investigations should follow this rule:

Never treat what the computer tells you as gospel. Always go behind the database to the paper documents or the human data gatherers to check.

Naturally, you can't check every fact that the computer gives you. But you can check enough of a representative sampling to assure yourself that both the data and your manipulation of them are sound. And where portions of the data are singled out for special emphasis, as in the dirty-ten list, you can and should check every key fact.

THE UNITED STATES CENSUS

One government database that is both extremely large and reasonably clean is the report of the U.S. Census. The census is the only data collection operation mandated by the Constitution of the United States: "enumeration shall be made within three years after the first meeting of the Congress of the United States, and within every subsequent term of ten years, in such manner as they shall by law direct."[14]

The first census was in 1790, and its data, like those of later censuses, are still readily available in printed form.[15]

In 1965, for the first time, the Bureau of the Census began selling data from the 1960 census on computer tape. That proved a popular move, and the tapes were replaced by compact disks and downloadable online datasets as technology improved.

Most of the census data are in summary form. Like the Uniform Crime Report tapes described earlier in this chapter, they give no data on individuals, just the total number of individuals in each of a great number of geographic and demographic cells. The analytical tools available, therefore, are generally limited to the following:

1. *Search and retrieval.* For example, a crime occurs in your town that appears to be racially motivated. If you have the right census file at hand, you can isolate the blocks that define the neighborhood in which the crime occurred and examine their racial composition and other demographic characteristics.
2. *Aggregating cells to create relevant cross-tabulations.* You are limited in this endeavor to whatever categories the census gives you. They are, however, fairly fine-grained and a great deal can be learned by collapsing cells to create larger categories that illuminate your story. For example, you could build tables that would compare the rate of home ownership among different racial and ethnic groups in different sections of your city.
3. *Aggregate-level analysis.* The census divides the entire United States into city blocks and their equivalents, so that even the remotest sheepherder's cabin is in a census-defined block. That gives the analyst the opportunity to classify each block along a great variety of dimensions and to look for comparisons. For example, you could compare the percentage of female-headed households with the percentage of families with incomes below a certain level. That could tell you that areas with a lot of poor people also have a lot of female-headed families. Because this analysis only looks at the aggregates, it is not in itself proof that it is the female-headed households that are poor. But it is at least a clue.

   Aggregate analysis is most useful when the aggregate itself—that is, the block or other small geographic division—is as interesting as the individuals that compose that aggregate. Example: Congressional redistricting has carved a new district in your area. By first matching blocks to voting precincts, you can use aggregate analysis to see what demographic characteristics of a precinct correlate with certain voting outcomes.

THE PUBLIC-USE SAMPLE

There is one glorious exception to all of these constraints involving aggregate data. The decennial census publishes files that contain data on individuals, so that you can do individual-level correlations and cross-tabulations to your heart's content. These files each contain a sample of individual records, with names and addresses eliminated and the geographical identifiers made so general that there is no possibility of recognizing any person. These are sample data, so they can be analyzed just like survey data, as described in the previous chapter. The potential for scooping the census on its own data is very rich here, especially when breaking news suggests some new way of looking at the data that no one had thought of before.

The bad news about the public-use sample is that it is close to the last data file to be published. Typically, it shows up about two years after the year in which the census was taken. By that time, journalists covering the census are tired of it and may have prematurely convinced themselves that they have squeezed all the good data out already. And if that is not the case, the two-year lag makes it hard to convince oneself that the data are still fresh enough to be interesting. But they are. Many opportunities to test conventional wisdom about population characteristics are available in the public use samples.

ONLINE TOOLS

The Bureau of the Census is one government agency that wants you to use its data. To encourage its use, the bureau is continually developing interactive retrieval and analysis tools that you can use online. Among the most useful are data extraction tools that will get you useful subsets of very large files that would be a lot of trouble to download and manage in their entirety.

There is also a growing list of downloadable software for displaying data and performing certain statistical tasks. And, in case you want to know the boundaries of the census tract where you live, a convenient mapping program is online. Finally, the bureau keeps faith with its buyers of CD-ROM products by offering updates and corrections online.

Geographic Structure of the Census

Some census files are flat, others are nested. This is the general hierarchy of the census:

United States
Regions
Divisions
States
Counties
County subdivisions
Places (or parts)
Census tracts (or parts)
Block groups (or parts)
Blocks

In older parts of the United States, a block is easily defined as an area surrounded by four streets. The blocks of my youth were all rectangular, and they all had alleys. Today, many people live in housing clusters, on culs-de-sac, on dead-end roads, and at other places where a block would be hard to define. The census folks have defined one where you and everyone else lives anyway. A block is now "an area bounded on all sides by visible features such as streets, roads, streams, and railroad tracks, and occasionally by non-visible boundaries such as city, town, or county limits, property lines, and short imaginary extensions of streets." And, since 1990, the entire United States and Puerto Rico have been divided into blocks.

Blocks fit snugly into block groups without crossing block group lines. And block groups are nested with equal neatness and consistency into census tracts. At the tract level, you have a good chance of making comparisons with earlier census counts, because these divisions are designed to be relatively permanent. They have been designed to hold established neighborhoods or relatively similar populations of 2,500 to 8,000 persons each. Now all of the United States has been tracted. You will find census tracts in all of the metropolitan statistical areas and in nonmetropolitan counties. In the 1990 census, areas that did not have tracts had block numbering areas (BNA) instead, and you can treat them as the equivalent of tracts for the sake of comparison with 2000. Neither tracts nor BNAs ever cross county lines, and a single county never crosses a state boundary.

Census regions and regional divisions are designed to conform to state lines. So here you have a hierarchy where the categories are clear and consistent. From block to block group to tract or BNA to county to state to division to region, the divisions are direct and uncomplicated. Each block is in only one block group, each block group is completely contained within only one tract or BNA. But the true geography of the United States is a little more complex, and the remaining census divisions were created to allow for that.

For one thing, cities in many states are allowed to cross county lines. Other kinds of divisions, such as townships or boroughs, can sometimes overlap with one another. Because such places are familiar, have legal status, and are intuitively more important than collections of blocks that statisticians make up for their own convenience, the census also recognizes these kinds of places. A "place," in the census geographical hierarchy, can be an incorporated town or city or it can be a statistical area that deserves its own statistics simply because it is densely populated and has a local identity and a name that people recognize.

What happens when a census "place" crosses a county line or another of the more neatly nested categories? The data sets give counts for the part of one level of the hierarchy that lies within another. The data use numerical summary-level codes to enable the user to link these patchwork places into wholes. For stories of local interest you will want to do that. It will also be necessary when there is a need to compare places that are commonly recognized and in the news. But for statewide summaries, the work will be much easier if you stick to geographic categories that are cleanly nested without overlap: counties, tracts, block groups, and blocks.

Timing of the Census

Computer readable materials are easier to compile than printed reports. So the online data generally appears first. The very first release is the constitutionally mandated counts for the apportionment of the House of Representatives. The president gets the state population counts by the end of the census year. Those counts determine how many representatives each state will have in the next Congress.

Next, under Public Law 94-171, each state gets detailed counts for small geographic areas to use in setting the boundary lines for congressional districts. These districts are supposed to be compact, contiguous, and reasonably close in population size. So that state legislatures can take race and ethnicity into account, these reports include breakdowns by racial category, Hispanic origin, and age grouping. Deadline for these materials is the first of April in the year after the census. When all goes well, it arrives earlier. As soon as the Bureau of the Census has fulfilled its legal obligation to the states with the delivery of these data, the PL 94-171 data sets become available to the public.

Although the PL 94-171 data are the sketchiest in terms of solid information, their timeliness makes them newsworthy. The obvious story is in the possibilities for redistricting, and in the ethnic and age composition of the voting-age population within the district boundaries being considered.

Another obvious story opportunity is the growth of the Hispanic population. Although Hispanics have been an important part of the U.S. population since the 1848 cession of the Mexican territory, the census has been slow to develop a consistent method of enumerating it. The 1970 census was the first to base Hispanic classification on a person's self-definition. Before that, it relied on secondary indictors such as a Spanish surname or foreign language spoken. But the growth and movement of the Hispanic population since 1970 is an ongoing story.

County boundaries seldom change from one census to another, so a comparison from ten years previously can show the relative magnitude of Hispanic gains in different parts of the country. For local stories, the availability of the counts at the block level allows precise identification of the Hispanic neighborhoods. Growth or decline of different racial groups will also be newsworthy in some areas.

The census data get better and better as time goes by. The problem is that they also get older. By the time the really interesting material is available, the census is several years old, and readers and editors alike may be tired of reading about it. The trick in covering it is to plan ahead so that the minute a new data set becomes available, you can attack it with a pre-written program and a well-thought-out strategy for analysis.

ANALYSIS OF DATA FROM MULTIPLE SOURCES

Information from the census is seldom as interesting in isolation as it is when compared with information from other sources. Election returns offer one obvious source, but there are many others, depending on how the news breaks.

For example, a reporter could combine census data with real estate tax records to test the conventional belief that real estate values drop when a neighborhood changes from white to black. Juanita Greene of the *Miami Herald* looked at the history of real estate transactions in her town and found that prices in the long run tended to rise as much in changing neighborhoods as in those that remained all white.[16] It was not a surprising finding to social scientists, who had done research on the same subject in the same way.[17] But it was surprising to Miami newspaper readers. And these readers would not have been convinced that their intuitive beliefs were wrong by reading a social science treatise. To convince Miami readers, you have to give them Miami addresses, Miami dates, and Miami prices, as Greene did.

One of the issues during the war in Vietnam was the fairness of the draft. President Johnson, in order to minimize public opposition to the war, oversaw a selection system that was biased toward the powerless. The educational deferment was the chief mechanism, but not the only one. The smart and the well-connected knew how to get into a reserve unit, how to qualify for conscientious objector status, or, as a last resort, how to get out of the country. This state of affairs reached public awareness only dimly. The *Washington Post* shed some light in 1970 when it correlated socioeconomic status of neighborhoods with their contributions of military manpower. The inner-city black neighborhoods sent far more of their young men off to war than did the upscale neighborhoods of Georgetown and Cleveland Park. Such a situation is more believable when you can put a number to it.

Bill Dedman of the *Atlanta Constitution* won the 1989 Pulitzer Prize for investigative reporting with an overlay of census figures on race and federally mandated bank reports on home loans. The guts of his series were in a single quantitative comparison: The rate of loans was five times as high for middle-income white neighborhoods as it was for carefully matched middle-income black neighborhoods.

One number does not a story make, and Dedman backed up the finding with plenty of old-fashioned leg work. His stories provided a good mix of general data and specific examples, such as the affluent black educator who had to try three banks and endure insulting remarks about his neighbor-hood before getting his home improvement loan. One of the most telling il-lustrations was a pair of maps of the Atlanta metropolitan area. One showed the areas that were 50 percent black or more in the census. The other showed the areas where fewer than 10 percent of owner-occupied homes were financed with loans from banks or savings and loan associations. The two patterns were a near perfect match.[18]

Dedman had help. In evaluating the evidence of racial prejudice on the part of banks, he followed a methodological trail that had been established by university researchers. Dwight Morris, the assistant managing editor for special projects, supervised the computer analysis. No complicated main-frame or sophisticated statistical analysis package was needed. The job was done with basic word processing, database management, spreadsheet, com-munication, and graphics software.

There are a lot of good, complicated stories behind simple numbers. The trick is to identify the number that will tell the story and then go find it. The new tools for manipulating data in public records should make it easier for journalists to find and reveal such light-giving numbers.

NOTES

1. Scott R. Maier, "The Digital Watchdog's First Byte: Journalism's First Com-puter Analysis of Public Records," *American Journalism* (Fall 2000): 75–91.

2. *Editor & Publisher* (November 26, 1968): 1.

3. Ole R. Holsti, *Content Analysis for the Social Sciences and Humanities* (Read-ing, Mass., Addison-Wesley, 1969).

4. William A. Scott, "Reliability of Content Analysis: The Case of Nominal Scale Coding," *Public Opinion Quarterly* 19, no. 3 (1955): 321–25.

5. Philip Meyer, "Trailing a Weasel Word," *Columbia Journalism Review* (Jan.–Feb. 1990): 10.

6. See, for example, David Loomis and Philip Meyer, "Opinion without Polls: Finding a Link between Corporate Culture and Public Journalism," *International Journal of Public Opinion Research* (Autumn 2000).

7. Elliot Jaspin, "Computer = Reporting Tool," in *The Computer Connection: A Report on Using the Computer to Teach Mass Communications* (Syracuse, N.Y.: Syra-cuse University, 1989), 21.

8. "Sons, Daughters of State Leaders Got 8 Percent RIHMFC Loans," *Provi-dence Journal*, June 2, 1985, 2.

9. Jaspin, "Computer = Reporting Tool," 19.

10. "R.I. System Fails to Fully Check Driving Records of Bus Applicants," *Provi-dence Sunday Journal*, March 1, 1987, 1.

11. *SPSS X User's Guide* (New York: McGraw-Hill, Inc., 1983), 171.

12. Interview with Carol Knopes, November 21, 1989.

13. "Plants Sending Out Most CFCs," *USA Today,* July 13, 1989.

14. The Constitution, Article I, Section II, Paragraph 3.

15. U.S. Bureau of the Census, *Historical Statistics of the United States, Colonial Times to 1970, Bi-Centennial Edition* (Washington, D.C.: U.S. Government Printing Office, 1975), two volumes.

16. *Miami Herald,* November 22, 1964.

17. Davis McEntire, *Residence and Race* (Berkeley: University of California Press, 1960).

18. Bill Dedman, "Atlanta Blacks Losing in Home Loans Scramble," *Atlanta Journal-Constitution,* May 1, 1988, 1. The series has been reprinted under the title "The Color of Money" by the *Journal-Constitution* Marketing Department.

11

+

How to Analyze an Election

The following statement is true, even though almost everyone involved in election polling denies it.

The purpose of an election survey is to predict the outcome of the election.

Editors, pollsters, and pundits will curse, evade, or ignore the truth of that statement, sometimes with great heat. But it is still true. And if you are going to do election surveys, you might as well get used to this simple fact: Your success or failure will be judged by how well your poll predicts the outcome. It is a reasonable test and a fair one.

In polling, there are not many opportunities to test the validity of a poll against the real-world values that the poll is supposed to approximate. The reason is as obvious as it is simple: If we could measure the real-world values, we wouldn't need a poll in the first place.

There are two exceptions to this general rule. One is the United States Census, which does a valiant job of attempting to reach everybody and collect some basic information about each person. But even the census has found that it can get a more accurate measurement of the population if it combines sampling techniques with the effort to find every citizen. One way to check on the validity of a standard poll is to compare the demographics of the poll's sample with the census demographics of the population from which the sample is drawn. This method works best in years close to the census.

The other opportunity for such an external test of validity comes with every election. If 56 percent of a sample says it is going to vote for Crockett for mayor, and if the sampling error is 4 percentage points, and if Crockett gets between 52 and 60 percent of the vote, the poll has passed the test. Such a test separates the wimps from the stout-hearted in a way that a comparison with the census does not. If the census says that a population is 22 percent black and the poll only finds 15 percent, the pollster will merely shrug and crank in a statistical weight bringing blacks up to their quota. (An ethical pollster will report that procedure.) But the pressures of election reporting compel the poll to be published before the validity check, which is poetic justice indeed. There is no way to hide from it or cover it up with cosmetic weighting procedures.

Watch the newspapers in the last two weeks of any national election. You will find that the weaker polls suddenly become silent. Ask why, and you get a variety of reasons: The polling budget ran out, polling distracts attention from the issues, it might affect the outcome of the election, and so forth. Don't believe any of them. The real reason is that the pollster doesn't want the poll to be compared to the election. By stopping two weeks in advance, he or she can claim that the poll was accurate as of the time it was taken, no matter how the election turns out. If the election results differ from the poll results, the voters must have changed their minds. As, indeed, voters sometimes do.

An election poll is, of course, good for other things than predicting the outcome of elections. It can show what issues are motivating the voters. It can measure familiarity with the issues and the candidates. It can show what coalitions are being formed or renewed. It can provide insights into candidate strategy that are in turn derived from the candidate's own polls.

But to do any of these good things, the poll must be a valid representation of the participating electorate. And the election is the check on whether it succeeds at that. This chapter is about the things you can do to make certain that your own poll matches the election outcome.

SAMPLING

Very few organizations are content with single preelection polls. If one poll is newsworthy, a lot of polls are a lot more newsworthy. To pay for more polls, there is a strong temptation to cut costs in procedure, and sampling is a frequent target for cutting. Because personal, in-home interviews are too slow for the competitive needs of modern media, virtually all election polls are done now by telephone or Internet.

Drawing a representative sample of telephone households is easy, using the random-digit methods discussed in chapter 6. The issue is how far down in the respondent selection process randomness needs to be preserved. Many polls still use quota selection to choose a respondent within the random household. This practice had theoretical justification in the 1970s because members of the same household tended to have similar political views and to vote alike. Ronald Reagan changed that. Two trends, the growth of the women's movement and the rightward movement of the Republican Party, combined to make voting behavior correlate with gender in a way that it had not done before. Journalists called the phenomenon the "gender gap" when women were suddenly more likely to be Democrats than men.

Although the gender difference could be controlled to some extent by setting quotas for males and females, the breakup of homogeneous households raises the possibility that household members might vary in other ways not controlled by the quotas. Probability sampling down to the individual level is therefore the safest procedure, but it comes at a cost. It requires taking the time to list the household members, to choose one at random, and to call back later if that person is not at home. Irving Crespi, in his excellent roundup of current wisdom on election polls, reported that failure to conduct callbacks leads to underrepresentation of Democrats—Republicans evidently being more likely to be found at home on a typical evening.[1]

Polls using callbacks generally set a fixed number of attempts, usually one, two, or three, and dedicate the last night or two of a poll to finishing up the callbacks. That procedure necessarily extends the polling period, which is another cost when you are under deadline pressure.

There is another way to sample. Some states—North Carolina is an example—keep a central database of registered voters. It makes an excellent sampling frame because you don't waste time talking to persons who are not registered and who refuse to admit it. The problem is that the records are not uniformly clean and up to date. For the 2000 presidential election in North Carolina, I drew a sample of persons that I operationally defined as "active voters." An active voter was one who had some contact with his or her county election board within the previous four years, either by voting, registering for the first time, or reporting a change of address. I tested it by sending out a questionnaire by first class mail and only 18 percent came back as undeliverable. That is a very clean list, compared to a random-digit telephone number list.

REFUSALS

The nerd boxes—those little clumps of agate type that newspapers use to disclose the methods and limitations of their polls—rarely talk about refusals. But refusals are one of the main sources of error in all polls. Their effect is far more serious than sampling error because you can't estimate their effect the way you can specify the probability of different ranges of sampling error. In fact, the maddening thing about this source of error is that it is often totally unpredictable. Often it will cause no visible error at all. This is true because of the following general rule:

A bias in a sample will be both invisible and harmless so long as the bias is not correlated with anything that you are trying to measure.

To make the harmless bias rule intuitively clear, think about a barrel of apples. You want to estimate the ratio of green apples to ripe apples in the barrel. The apples were thoroughly mixed before they were packed. Therefore, you can draw your sample from the apples in the top of the barrel, which are the easiest to get, and make a good estimate. Position in the barrel does not correlate with greenness.

Now suppose that the barrel was packed by some sinister force. It did not want you to know about the green apples, and so it put them all in the bottom of the barrel. Take a sample from the top, generalize to the barrel as a whole, and you will be wrong. This time, the bias in your selection is correlated with the thing you are measuring.

The harmless bias rule sounds like a gift to pollsters. It is not. The only way to be sure that a bias is harmless is to compare the biased sample with an unbiased one—or, as in the case of an election or a census, with the total population. A bias that is harmless in one poll can give you an unjustified sense of confidence and set you up for a disaster in the next poll. That happened to the *Literary Digest* in 1936. Its sample was based on telephone and motor vehicle registration lists, both indicators of relative affluence. Affluence was not correlated with voter choice in 1932, and its poll was right on the mark. Then President Roosevelt built his New Deal coalition of farmers, workers, and minorities and caused a historic party realignment that left voter choice very much correlated with economic status. The *Literary Digest* confidently repeated its biased sampling in 1936, was horribly wrong, and did not live to poll again. George Gallup used an unbiased sample, got it right, and became the dominant pollster of his time.

This history is worth remembering when we think about refusals. The polling industry doesn't like to talk about this, but the proportion in telephone samples who refuse—once fairly constant at about one-third—has been growing over time. Refusal to participate has been shown to correlate with age (older people are less likely to consent to an interview), with education (the less educated are the most reluctant), and with urban residence (city dwellers are less likely to cooperate). Place of residence is more of a problem with face-to-face interviews than with telephone interviews.[2]

These factors give a Republican bias to telephone interviews. As luck would have it, they also provide some correction for another problem faced by election polls: weeding the nonvoters out of the sample. The people who don't like to take part in telephone interviews tend to be the same people who don't like to vote. This is good luck for pollsters, but it is the same kind of luck that the *Literary Digest* enjoyed in 1932. A benign correlation pattern could turn nasty in some future election campaign. And there is not much a pollster can do about it except watch out for issues that involve old folks, the less educated, and city dwellers. Some day they will do important things that the conventional polls will not detect. Think about that if you are a young person hoping to make a name in this business. If you can anticipate that inevitable day and avoid the bias that sends the conventional pollsters running for the hills, you could be the Gallup of the twenty-first century.

IDENTIFYING THE LIKELY VOTERS

The low election participation rates in the United States make life hard for pollsters. It is now common for less than 50 percent of the voting age population to show up at the polls. The low turnout creates two obvious problems:

1. You need a bigger sample. To get the 3 percent error margin provided by a sample of 1,000, you have to interview more than 2,000 people in order to end up with 1,000 voters.
2. You have to figure out which of the people in your oversized sample will belong to the voting minority.

The second problem is by far the most difficult. Of course, you can just ask people if they plan to vote or not. The trouble with that tactic is that voting is perceived as a socially useful activity, and so respondents do not like to admit not participating. About 80 percent say they are registered, but only about 65 percent actually are. And those who are registered greatly overestimate their likelihood of voting.

Over the years, pollsters have developed a number of stratagems for weeding out the nonvoters. At one point, the Gallup Poll used nine questions to predict turnout likelihood, built them into a scale, and then went back to the public records after the election to see who really did vote. From that information, a statistical weighting procedure was devised, based on the predictive power of each of the nine items. Some of the nine items were direct and some were oblique. Samples:

> Generally speaking, how much interest would you say you have in politics—a great deal, a fair amount, only a little, or no interest at all?
>
> How often would you say you vote—always, nearly always, part of the time, or seldom?

Here is a picture of a ladder. Suppose we say the top of the ladder, marked 10, represents a person who definitely will vote in the election this November, and the bottom of the ladder, marked zero, represents a person who definitely will not vote in the election. How far up or down the ladder would you place yourself?[3]

The best predictors were a registration question, a direct question about the respondent's plans to vote in the upcoming election, the ladder scale, and the question on frequency of voting.[4] All nine questions were used to form a cumulative scale. At the top of the scale, where people gave all the pro-voting answers, turnout averaged 87 percent. At the bottom of the scale, it was only 8 percent.

The straightforward way to apply this scale, and the method used for many years by the Gallup Poll, was to array all of the respondents along the scale according to the likelihood of their voting and then estimate the turnout. If a turnout of 50 percent was expected, then the people who formed the bottom half of the sample in voting likelihood would be dropped and the prediction would be based on those who were left. The Gallup folks, leaving as little as possible to chance, also used their turnout scale to estimate the turnout itself.

This bootstrapping is effective, but a hardworking pollster who goes to all of the trouble to interview hundreds or even thousands of people hates to throw half of those interviews away. The Election and Survey Unit at *CBS News* found a way to avoid that. Using the same kind of public-record data to find which survey respondents really vote, they constructed a voting-rate scale using the same principles as Gallup's but with fewer questions. Then they used these probabilities as weights across the entire sample. A person with an 89 percent probability of voting gets a statistical weight of .89. The respondent with only a 3 percent chance is weighted at .03. Every interview is used, and the probability model should, in theory, project to the election with at least as much accuracy as the model that drops the least likely voters. However, Crespi reports that polling organizations that use such weighting schemes are less likely to be successful predictors of election outcomes than those that kick the low-likelihood voters all the way out of the sample. Paul Perry, the quiet statistician who guided the Gallup Poll in its years of methodological improvement after 1948, tried using a weighting model with his data and found that the results were almost identical. So he stuck to the cut-off model because of its simplicity—a virtue when you are under deadline pressure.[5]

One reason for the success of the CBS method is the use of an internal check to catch voters who are lying about being registered. The following three questions are asked:

What was the most recent election of any kind you voted in? (PROBE) What year was that?

When was the last time you registered to vote? What year was that?
Did you live in the same community two years ago that you live in now?

It used to be possible to screen out voters who could not be legally registered because some states had length-of-residence requirements. Motor
voter laws changed that. But CBS creates an effective purge by giving a zero
weight to people who have not voted or registered since they last moved.

For the 2000 election, the remaining voters were divided into nine categories, depending on their past voting frequency and their interest in the campaign. A different probability was assigned to each category. The range is 88
percent to 11 percent. After October 30, 2000, CBS added a tenth category,
people who had already voted by mail or in-person absentee voting. These got
a 100 percent probability of voting, even if they had moved since last registering. CBS was closest of all the media polls to the final result in 2000.[6]

A CHEAPER METHOD

The CBS method is effective but complicated. Simpler methods are
cheaper. Many election pollsters try to identify the likely nonvoters at the
very front of the interview, so that they can get rid of them immediately.
Why spend twenty minutes on the telephone with someone whose interview
you are going to throw out at the analysis stage? If a person's responses indicate that he or she will not vote, the interviewer can politely end the conversation and go on to the next number.

But watch out! If the procedure calls for the interviewer to hang up without collecting the basic demographic data, the means for checking the sample against the known census characteristics is lost. So some low-budget
pollsters design the survey to collect at least that much information from
the likely nonvoters so that they will have a sample of the entire population
to compare to census information. Weighting can be performed on the total sample to make it conform to the census, and then the nonvoters can be
dropped out.

Here's another way. The need to collect demographic data from folks who
are not likely to vote can be avoided without forgoing demographic weighting altogether. The Bureau of the Census asks about voting participation in
its Current Population Survey. From that survey, one can derive estimates
of the demographic characteristics of the voting population. Weight your
sample of likely voters to conform to those demographic estimates, and you
have bypassed the need to deal with nonvoters at all.

But there are a couple of problems. One is that the census survey is notoriously inaccurate. Far more people claim to have voted than actually
turned out. Another potential problem is that the turnout patterns of past

elections may not be the same as the pattern for the current election. And the census survey is national in scope. The turnout demographics in the city or state you are surveying might be quite different.

The old Gallup method of throwing away the unlikely voters still looks pretty good. That system was based on personal, in-home interviews. Telephone interviewing adds a complication, because the telephone itself is a kind of nonvoter screen, due to its bias against the less educated. This bias, you will recall, stems from higher refusal rates among the less educated, as well as the unevenness of telephone penetration. Therefore, if you expect a turnout of 50 percent and drop 50 percent from your sample, you will have dropped too many. If one-third of those called refused the interview, and if they are all nonvoters, you have already eliminated a substantial portion of the nonvoting problem.

It is somewhere around here that polling ceases to be a science and becomes an art. You need to build some experience in your state or city to find out what kind of nonvoter correction works best. Some pollsters get by with a short, sweet method: Ask one screening question about registration and one about likelihood of voting, and count only those who say they are registered and certain to vote. This method generally eliminates far fewer unlikely voters than are theoretically necessary, but the remainder tend to eliminate themselves by not having telephones or by refusing the interview. Such a shortcut is quick, it is easy, and it is cheap. Crespi, however, reports that polls that use this method do not enjoy the accuracy of those that use a tighter screen—that is, with more questions. It did not appear to make much difference in the polls that Crespi looked at whether the questions were used as up-front screeners or applied after the fact to dump the unlikely voters.[7] The after-the-fact method is more theoretically sound, however, because it gives you a full-population sample to evaluate against the census.

ASKING THE QUESTION

Most polls stick pretty close to the Gallup language, with only minor variations:

> If the presidential election were being held today, which would you vote for—the Republican candidates, Bush and Quayle, or the Democratic candidates, Dukakis and Bentsen? (If undecided) As of today, do you lean more toward Bush and Quayle or to Dukakis and Bentsen?

Giving the party identification is essential, because party label remains one of the basic tools used by voters in arriving at a decision. The order in which the candidates are named can also make a difference. Unfortunately, there is a big gap in the literature about the nature of that difference. In an experiment with the Carolina Poll in the 1988 presidential election in North Carolina, we found a recency effect. We programmed our CATI system so that the interviewers named the Democratic candidates first for a random half of the sample and the GOP contenders were first in the other half. Bush and Quayle did better when they were named last. As it happened, they were listed last on the North Carolina ballot, and that version proved to be the most accurate in predicting the election. This outcome is at least consistent with theory. The form of the survey question should be as much like the form of the election question as possible, down to the relative positioning of the candidates. Since the vice-presidential candidate is listed on the ballot along with the presidential candidate, both names should be in the survey question.

One reason the internal order effect has never received much attention may be that it is fairly well randomized nationally. However, when the Gallup Poll used a paper ballot in personal interviews, care was taken to match the candidate order with the actual ballot in each state. That order varies because the party in power in each state generally tries to rig the ballot to its own benefit. Political folklore expects a *primacy* effect, meaning that the candidates mentioned first should be favored. But if the single experiment in North Carolina is indicative, they have it all wrong and are actually hurting their candidates by putting them first on the ballot.

Folklore is often well grounded, and it should not be lightly dismissed on the basis of a single experiment. Perhaps primacy effect was dominant in an earlier period, when people had more time to look at things and ponder them. Recency effect, on the other hand, could be the product of the information overload of our age. With so much data streaming through our heads, there may be less chance of any given particle staying put there for very long. If so, the most recently processed quanta could have the best chance of remaining salient. Or perhaps primacy effect dominates in written communication and recency effect in oral communication. If that is true, matching the ballot order is not important, and you should probably neutralize the effect by rotating candidate order.

DEALING WITH THE UNDECIDED

One difference between an election and a poll is that in the privacy of the voting booth, all but a very few can make up their minds. In a poll a significant minority is still undecided. If the election is to be the standard by which the poll is judged, some procedure needs to be found to deal with the undecided.

As the election gets closer, the percentage of undecided begins to drop, but levels of 10 to 15 percent in the final days are not uncommon. Some media pollsters are perfectly happy with that. The cushion of undecided makes a nice explainer if the poll turns sour. If a poll shows a 40-40 tie with 20 percent undecided, the election results can be as lopsided as 60-40 in either direction, and a pollster can claim that his or her results were right on the money and those pesky undecided voters all went the same way. (Pollsters do make outlandish excuses. I once read about a pollster caught with a bad prediction, who claimed that it was the respondents' fault for lying to his interviewers.)

Paul Perry of the Gallup Organization struggled for years with the problem of allocating the undecided and concluded that reducing their number is a lot easier than figuring out what they are going to do. The "leaning" question, the second part of the two-part Gallup question cited previously, will cut the undecided by about half. Using it is simple. Just add the leaners to the decided group and report both totals, but make it clear that you are basing your election prediction on the sums with the leaners included. The procedure clearly improves predictive power.[8]

In personal interviews, the undecided can be reduced still more by using a secret ballot. Instead of asking the respondent how he or she plans to vote, the interviewer offers a printed ballot and displays a box with a padlock and a big label, SECRET BALLOT BOX. The paper ballot also makes it possible to replicate the physical layout of the real ballot so that any positional biases in the actual election are built into the poll as well. This can be an important advantage in a state that allows straight-ticket voting. It is easier to simulate the straight-ticket option on paper than it is in a telephone interview. The straight-ticket choice can be offered in a telephone survey, however, and you should consider it if you are polling in a state that uses straight-ticket voting and if there are state and local candidates who might receive some coattail effect from better-known national candidates.

ALLOCATING THE REMAINING UNDECIDED

Even after the leaning question, a hard core of undecided voters remains. What to do about them? Paul Perry found that many of them are unlikely to vote at all. In the 1976 Gallup Poll, for example, the leaning question reduced the undecided to 5 percent. Kicking out the unlikely voters dropped it to 3.7 percent.[9]

Lots of different ways have been tried for getting rid of that last remnant of undecided respondents. There are complicated ways and simple ways. An example of a complicated way would be to use logistic regression to predict candidate choice from demographic and issue preference variables. These are regression-like models that deal with categorical variables. Some pollsters have tried splitting the undecided by party preference. Nick Panagakis of Market Shares Corporation believes that in state and local elections, the undecided tend to go against the incumbent. My own work with the Carolina Poll suggests that it is hard to beat the procedure of dropping the undecided from the percentage base in making the final prediction. It has the virtue of simplicity. And it is based on a reasonable theory: That many of the hard-core undecided will not vote, and those who do will tend to divide in the same way as those who have decided. Crespi, after looking at the records of a number of pollsters, endorsed this practice, although he also believes there may be something to be said for basing the division on party affiliation.[10]

WEIGHTING

In considering whether to weight your data, it is important to keep this distinction in mind: Some weights are *design weights* built into the sampling procedure. Others are *corrective weights* employed after the fact to fix (or cover up) flaws in the sample. Use of the latter is controversial. Employment of the former is not.

The obvious example of a design weight in a telephone survey is household size. Most phone surveys are designed to obtain only one interview from a household that was selected with a probability of being chosen equal to that of all other households. That means that people from large households get less of a chance to be interviewed than people from small households. The inequity is easily corrected by weighting for household size. A person in a household with four adults gets counted with four times the weight of a person who lives alone.

In the old days before computers, weighting was done by replicating cards. An interview from a four-person household would have its card copied three times. SAS and SPSS make weighting easier. It is all done mathematically inside the computer. To keep the weighting from inflating sample size and throwing off your statistical tests, you can divide each person's household size by the average household size to arrive at the final weight. For example, if the average household size is two, the four-person household will have a weight of two, and the one-person household will have a weight of one-half.

Corrective weights are another matter. The theory behind them is less sound. In the Carolina Poll we typically get 15 percent black respondents, even though the true proportion of blacks in the voting-age population is closer to 22. Weighting the 15 percent up to 22 is based on a theoretical assumption that we know is wrong: That the blacks who cannot be reached by telephone are just like those whom we do reach. In fact, they are poorer, younger, more alienated, and more likely to be male. But we do the weighting anyway. Why? It helps the election prediction. Unrepresentative blacks are better than no blacks at all.

The only other weight we use in the Carolina Poll is for age category. In some elections it makes a difference, as when social security is an issue. Our poll usually needs adjustment of no more than a point or two in each category.

The source for the weighting data is a biennial publication of the Bureau of the Census. Early in each election year, it produces a report for each state on the characteristics of the voting-age population. The report is based on estimates and projections from the most recent census, but it is the best estimate of what's really out there that you can get.[11]

Some pollsters go much more heavily into weighting. There are basically three ways to do it.

1. *Sequential weighting.* Put the weights in one at a time. After each weighting, run a new frequency count and check the next variable that you intend to weight, so that you can calculate how much adjustment it needs. Proceed in this manner until all of the weights are in.

    Problem: One weight affects another. For example, if your first weight is to bring up the proportion of blacks, you will throw off the sex balance because black respondents are disproportionately female. Fix the gender balance, and race goes back out of line.

2. *Cell weighting.* Find out from census data what proportion of the population is in every possible combination of your weighting categories. If you are weighting by age, sex, race, and education, find out what the population has in each combination, cell by cell.

    Problem: There can be a lot of cells. Figure 4 categories of age, 2 of sex, 3 of race, and 5 of education. That's 120 cells. Some will be very small. A few might even be empty. A few wildly deviant cases might get blown up to create some large and strange effect.

3. *Rim weighting.* A computer program applies weights in sequential fashion, varying the order, and checking the marginals to find the optimum solution. It stops when it finds a simple combination of weights that yields good approximations for the marginals (total frequencies) of the weight variables.

    Problem: It takes a special computer program. When I last looked, neither SAS nor SPSS offered rim weighting, although they well might by the time you read this.

The experience of the Carolina Poll suggests that it is good to be conservative about weighting. In North Carolina, at least, the telephone itself is a crude nonvoter screen. When we try to weight for education, we destroy that feature by boosting the influence of low-educated unlikely voters. Our best election predictions are produced when we weight by race and age and, when necessary, gender. Crespi reports that those are the most popular weighting variables among the polls that he examined, and that those who weight get better predictions than those who do not.[12]

WHAT TO DO WHEN

It used to be so simple. Pollsters took their time, collected results from interviewers by mail, and reserved the more complicated procedures, including adjustments for undecided and nonvoters, for the last poll before the election. That tended to give the national polls a Democratic bias in the early going. Unlikely voters are disproportionately Democrats, and so dropping them out gave the Republicans an apparent last-minute boost.

Competition has made the national polls more honest. The nonvoter screens now kick in much earlier. When national polls give sharply different results in late summer, the differences can sometimes be traced to differences in timing for the nonvoter screen.

Older polls differed from today's in another important way. They assumed a voter decision model that was relatively static. It assumed that once you had the voters pegged, they would not change very much. That assumption was one of the causes of the great debacle of 1948, when all the major polls predicted that Thomas E. Dewey would defeat President Harry S Truman. The pollsters quit too soon, and a lot of disaffected Democrats who had earlier vowed not to vote for Truman came back to the fold near the end of the campaign.

Today's media-driven campaigns and the related decline of party loyalties produce elections that are even more volatile. Polling data suggest that Jimmy Carter lost the 1980 election in the last forty-eight hours of the campaign.

Such instability makes election predictions more difficult, but the track records of the serious pollsters are still quite good. Timing is now considered critical. All of the careful methodological details discussed previously take time. When do you stop and make your prediction? Can you base it on a poll taken the night before the election?

One-night polls are notoriously inaccurate. They don't allow time for the callbacks needed to get the folks who are not always at home. But you can plan a poll for three or four nights that will end in time for publication the Sunday or even the Monday before the election. By tracking the results of each night, you might pick up on gross last-minute shifts, although you can't be sure because of sampling variability and unequal completion rates

for each day. Finishing up on a weekend is convenient because you can interview in the daytime to call back people who could not be reached at
night. A popular schedule is to finish callbacks on Sunday afternoon, use
the early evening hours to do the final weighting and screening, and produce the final prediction in time for Monday morning newspapers.

MAIL AND INTERNET SURVEYS

As cooperation rates fall, mail and Internet surveys are starting to look more
attractive for predicting elections. A mail poll done regularly by the *Colum-
bus Dispatch* has established a good track record against the more conventional Buckeye Poll at Ohio State University. Jon Krosnick, a social scientist
who was puzzled by the newspaper's success, looked into it and suggested
several explanations. One is that the minority that responds to a mail survey is probably the most likely to vote. Another is that a voter filling out a
questionnaire in the privacy of his or her home is in a situation more like
that of the voting booth. There is time to reflect and no social pressure to
come up with a top-of-the-head answer in an unwanted phone conversation.

But what about the well-known volatility of the voters? A mail poll needs
a turnaround time of days or even weeks, and that gives the voters too much
time to change their minds. Maybe, suggests Krosnick, the voters don't
change their minds as much as conventional polls lead us to believe. Maybe
there is a firm choice in their minds all the time, but telephone interviewers aren't getting to it. The self-administered survey bypasses the interviewer as a source of error.

The idea of self-administered surveys is attractive enough to make commercial pollsters want to spend large sums of money getting survey data
through the Internet. Two firms, Harris Interactive and Knowledge Networks, tried that in 2000 with results that were comparable to those of conventional polls. As Internet penetration increases, that will be the methodology to watch.

Self-administered formats are especially valuable when the questions are
complicated. In the fall 2000 Carolina Poll, voters were asked this question:
"Do you support or oppose the plan to improve public university and college
facilities by issuing about $3 billion worth of long-term bonds?"

In the telephone poll, 83 percent responded to this question by saying
they would support the bond issue. But a mail survey asked the question exactly as it would appear on the ballot:

Vote for or against: The issuance of State of North Carolina Higher Education
Improvement Bonds, constituting general obligation bonds of the State se-

cured by a pledge of the faith and credit and taxing power of the State for the purpose of providing funds, with any other available funds, to pay all or part of the cost of (i) renovating laboratories, classrooms, academic buildings, and worker training facilities and providing other capital improvements at the 59 institutions of the North Carolina Community College System and (ii) renovating and replacing classrooms, laboratories, and academic buildings and providing other capital improvements at the 16 campuses of the constituent institutions, and affiliated institutions, and the Center for Public Television (UNC-TV) of the University of North Carolina system; in the amount of three billion one hundred million dollars ($3,100,000,000)

When it was put that way, only 75 percent said they would vote for the bonds. The actual vote: 73 percent.

WHAT TO REPORT

A good reporter will give the numbers for each stage of the process: the response to the straight voting intention question, the response with leaners added, and the response with leaners added and the undecided allocated. But which should be emphasized?

The honest thing to do is to emphasize the numbers that can be compared most directly to the election outcome—that is, the ones with leaners added and undecided allocated, the ones that add to 100 percent. It is the only way to ensure full credit for being accurate or full blame for getting it wrong. The Gallup Organization found that out years ago. But some others don't. The next chapter will explore their reasons and the consequences for precision journalism.

ELECTION-NIGHT PROJECTIONS

Election day opens a whole new world of data collection possibilities. Newspapers and broadcasters alike have an interest in detecting the outcome ahead of the official vote count. The television networks try the hardest to do the most in this area, but newspapers with early deadlines also have an interest in early detection. There are two basic methods:

1. Projection from the early-reporting precincts.
2. Exit polls.

The first attempts of the networks to do early projections on election night were primitive. In 1960, CBS used a model based on the timing of the returns. At given intervals on election night, the computer looked at the number of Republican and Democratic votes for president and compared them to the votes at the same time in 1956. On that basis, an early prediction was produced. It said Richard M. Nixon would defeat John F. Kennedy.

What the computer couldn't know was where those votes were coming from. Kansas had introduced a faster method of vote counting between 1956 and 1960, and so the votes from Republican Kansas hit the wires at about the same time that Connecticut had come in four years before. The error was corrected when more votes came in.[13]

A better way is to base the model on geography. Pick either a random sample of precincts, which is the safest way, or pick a sample that you know will report early. If the sample is random, you can simply generalize from it to the whole electorate. If it is purposeful, you will have to assume that it will deviate from the whole in the same way that it did in the previous election.

The method works. On election night in 1976, I hung out at the ABC studio in New York City, looking over the shoulder of David Neft, an associate of Louis Harris. Neft had prepared a model based on early-reporting precincts. When the first returns came in, I noticed that the turnout was less than in 1972 across a great variety of locations. Because 1972 had had the lowest voting participation since 1948, I filed a story that said turnout in this election was "the lowest in a generation."

My bureau chief was upset. All the wires were writing stories about what they perceived to be a high turnout. Some even talked about a record turnout. This is a common election-day phenomenon. After covering the campaign for months, wire service reporters have nothing to write about for the p.m. cycle on election day, so they call up precinct officials and ask about the turnout. The officials look out their windows, notice a long line, and say something like, "Wow, we've got a really great turnout." What they forget to allow for is that the previous election, with which they are making the mental comparison, was not a presidential election. Also, the population has grown, so it takes more bodies to equal the same percentage turnout. And, perhaps most important, a high turnout makes their jobs seem more significant. I explained all this, and my story was put on the wire. Most gratifying of all, the next issue of *Columbia Journalism Review* reproduced two sets of headlines side by side. One set was from a Knight Ridder paper with my low turnout story. The other was from some bigger papers that went with the wire accounts of the imagined heavy turnout. The final figure was 53.5 percent, compared to 55.2 percent in 1972 and 60.9 percent in 1968. Not since the Truman–Dewey contest of 1948 had it been so low.

Newspapers sometimes need the benefit of election-night projections if they are in slow-reporting areas and have early deadlines. Election night was a constant source of frustration for the *Detroit Free Press* until Mike Maidenberg introduced an early-projection system in 1969. Maidenberg, who later became a publisher, used a probability sample of 20 out of Detroit's 1,111 precincts. That is not very many, but he reduced the risk by stratifying on two dimensions.

Race was a factor in that election. Richard Austin, a black candidate, was running against Sheriff Roman Gribbs. Detroit had never had a black mayor before. To get good representation of racial attitudes, Maidenberg drew the sample from a list that had been divided into two groups, according to percentage of vote cast for George Wallace in the 1968 presidential election. One group was above average in Wallace support and the other was below.

Within each group, precincts were ordered according to their historic Democratic strength. Maidenberg then used a random start and a constant skip interval to draw the 20 precincts. As a check, he compared the twenty precincts to the total for the 1968 election. They were close, but not perfect. Abandoning science for art, he added two black precincts to improve the model and used it in the 1969 primary election for a toe-in-the-water, carefully hedged projection for use in early editions. The highest error in any race was less than 2 percent.

Emboldened, Maidenberg revised the model for the general election, using the primary as the benchmark. He added three more precincts for a total of twenty-five. It proved to be accurate within a percentage point. Some clerical errors made the lead of the winner, Sheriff Roman Gribbs, seem larger than it was, so the *Free Press* was bolder than it should have been that night. But the system quickly became routinized. When the first black mayor was finally elected in Detroit—it was Coleman Young—the fact that black precincts were the slowest to report made the evening especially suspenseful. Kurt Luedtke was the executive editor and Neal Shine was managing editor. The projections indicated Young would win. Here is Shine's version of what happened next:

> So Page One of the late editions carried a headline declaring Young the winner, the story explaining that, although the raw vote still had Nichols in the lead, the uncounted precincts would sweep Young into office.
>
> Then we repaired to the London Chop House, where we took a series of calls from an increasingly edgy news editor who told us that since it was well after midnight and Young was still losing by large numbers, we might want to soften the "Young Elected City's 1st Black Mayor" headline.
>
> We decided that if we were wrong, it was too late to save our jobs, so we ordered more scrambled eggs and a bottle of champagne to enhance the stories future *Free Press* generations would tell about the night the careers of Luedtke and Shine came crashing down while they nibbled eggs and drank champagne at the Chop. But Young won, we kept our jobs.[14]

Mike Maidenberg was not drinking champagne that night. He took copies of the *Free Press* down to city hall and passed them around. The election returns were being posted on a blackboard. They showed Young losing. The members of the city hall crowd looked at the blackboard, looked at the *Free Press* headline, and scratched their heads. Then, as they held those papers in their hands, the numbers on the board began to change. The black precincts came in, Coleman won, and it almost looked like the *Free Press* had caused it. "It was like magic," Maidenberg recalled.

When Maidenberg left the *Free Press,* he was succeeded in his election night role by Tim Kiska. Kiska developed the habit of buying a new suit to wear on each election day. It made him seem more authoritative, he explained, when he had to convince editors and writers of the right way to interpret his numbers. And if his projection should turn out wrong, he would have a new suit to wear when he went out hunting for another job.

EXIT POLLS

The networks now use a combination of sample precincts and exit polls to do their early calls. Exit polls have a nobler purpose, of course. They are excellent tools for assessing the hidden forces in an election. By comparing issue preferences with candidate choice, you can find out what campaign themes made the most difference. If new coalitions are forming, you can identify them. And, since you already know who won by the time you finish the analysis, you are not distracted by the horse-race aspect.

The methodology of an exit poll is straightforward. Draw a random sample of precincts. Interview every *n*th voter coming out of those precincts, using a one-page (both sides), self-administered questionnaire. Make sure the questionnaire has the words SECRET BALLOT in 24-point type or larger at the top. Have each interviewer carry a box with a slot in the top to hold the ballots. This kind of survey has the following obvious advantages:

1. You know that your respondents are voters, because you intercept them at the polling place.
2. Nobody is undecided at that time.
3. Sampling does not depend on households or telephones. Your sample will therefore be the best evidence of the demographic characteristics of the voters.

And you have instant reassurance that your sample is representative, because you can compare its election decision to the election itself. In all of survey research, there is no better external test of validity.

There is, however, still the problem of refusals. Exit polls are refused by about a third of those approached. Those who refuse generally do so because they are in a hurry. Evidently, being in a hurry does not correlate with voter choice, because well-administered exit polls are quite accurate.

Of course, like anything else, they can be administered in a sloppy manner. Some exit pollsters sample day parts as well as precincts. For example, Precinct A might be sampled from 8:00 to 10:00 and the interviewers then move to Precinct B for sampling from 11:00 to 1:00. That increases the number of precincts in the sample, but it adds some administrative confusion. My own preference is to go with as few as twenty-five precincts, but keep the interviewers there all day to ensure a good sample from each one.

Be sure to establish a procedure that prevents the interviewers from selecting the respondents. Station at least two interviewers at each place so that one can count off the voters while another solicits the interviews. That way, the every *n*th rule can be enforced. If you let the interviewers choose the respondents, they will pick people who look nice, friendly, or sexy. Looking grubby or menacing could well correlate with voter preference. That might explain why the *New York Times*'s earliest attempts at exit polling in 1972 presidential primaries turned up undercounts of voters for George Wallace, who was then running on a segregation platform that appealed to poor whites.

Short and simple questions work best in the exit polls. An agree-disagree list can help sort respondents into categories on a number of key issues in a hurry. Very simple multiple-choice questions work well. A question on when the respondent made up his or her mind on the main contest is a staple of most exit polls and helps explain the dynamics of the campaign.

Some state legislatures have tried to stop exit polls by banning interviews within some minimum distance from the polling place. Such laws were found to be a violation of the First Amendment. The attempt represents the surfacing of an uneasiness with precision journalism and its fruits that will likely be seen again. The sources of that uneasiness will be explored in the next chapter.

NOTES

1. Irving Crespi, *Pre-Election Polling: Sources of Accuracy and Error* (New York: Russell Sage Foundation, 1988), 44.

2. Robert M. Groves and Lars E. Lyberg, "An Overview of Non-Response Issues in Telephone Surveys," in Robert Groves et al., eds., *Telephone Survey Methodology* (New York: John Wiley & Sons, 1988), 203–205.

3. Paul Perry, "Certain Problems in Election Survey Methodology," *Public Opinion Quarterly* 43, no. 3 (Fall 1979): 320–21.

4. Paul Perry, "Certain Problems in Election Survey Methodology," 322.

5. Crespi, *Pre-Election Polling*, 93.

6. Kathleen Frankovic, personal communication, August 2, 2001.

7. Crespi, *Pre-Election Polling*, 82.

8. Crespi, *Pre-Election Polling*, 115.

9. Perry, "Certain Problems in Election Survey Methodology," 317.

10. Crespi, *Pre-Election Polling*, 116.

11. The report for the 2000 election was available online at http://www.census .gov/population/www/socdemo/voting/tabs00.html. For an earlier example in print, see "Projections of the Population of Voting Age, for States: November 1988," *Current Population Reports*, Series P-25, No. 1019, Bureau of the Census (January 1988).

12. Crespi, *Pre-Election Polling*, 39–40.

13. Nelson Polsby and Aaron Wildavsky, *Presidential Elections*, Third Edition (New York: Charles Scribner's Sons, 1971), 209.

14. Neal Shine, "The Story behind the Receding Hairline," *Detroit Free Press Magazine*, April 9, 1989.

12

✛

The Politics
of Precision Journalism

Technological advances and the social systems for dealing with them do not develop at the same pace. When old social and cultural systems are applied to new ways of doing things, the fit is sometimes awkward and even painful. The reaction to that pain is a common theme in history. In England, early in the nineteenth century, the Luddites tried to stop the economic dislocations resulting from labor-saving machinery by destroying the machinery. At about the same time, the Erie Canal Commission passed up a chance to build a railroad, for which the technology was then available, to construct a waterway, whose concept was more comfortably familiar.[1] It should be no surprise to find that the same cultural lag that afflicted the Industrial Revolution is also present in the Information Age. Precision journalism will take some getting used to—both by the practitioners of journalism and by its customers.

In its early applications to coverage of the political and social movements of the 1960s and 1970s—civil rights, the anti–Vietnam war movement, and the youth counterculture—no paradigm shift seemed called for. The application of social and behavioral science research methods was simply the extension of journalism by other means. "The ground rules are no different from those on which we've always operated," I admonished my fellow journalists in the first edition of this book in 1973. "Find the facts, tell what they mean, and do it without wasting time. If there are new tools to enable us to perform this task with greater power, accuracy, and insight, then we should make the most of them."[2]

That description suggested that precision journalism involves little more than the maintenance of the journalist's traditional role, with only a modest quantitative improvement in speed and accuracy. When a quantitative change reaches a certain magnitude, however, it becomes a qualitative change. Some current objections to precision journalism are based on the assumption that such a change in magnitude is taking place or is likely to take place in the future. These objections are beginning to lead to proposals to regulate the practice of precision journalism—either directly by law, or indirectly by pressuring the media to adopt voluntary self-restraint. The efforts by some otherwise democratic nations to ban preelection polls are one example. Another is found in the voluntary withholding of exit-poll information by the networks in the United States until the voting is finished in the jurisdiction in which the poll was taken. Pressure for other forms of restraint may be building.

PRIVACY CONCERNS

The notion that a journalist should be concerned with a possible invasion of privacy may seem surprising and self-contradictory. Invasion of privacy is almost part of the journalist's job description. However, there are precedents for observing self-restraint in some circumstances. The codes of some of the major professional associations in journalism recognize a duty to provide protection of privacy. In the utilitarian ethical systems used, consciously or not, by most journalists, the right to privacy is easily overridden by a more pressing concern for the public's right to know. The question for precision journalism is whether the power of its methods adds a moral burden that did not exist for less powerful methods.

Elliot Jaspin and Maria Miro Johnson's exposure of the criminal pasts of Rhode Island school bus drivers is an example.[3] That the named individuals were school bus drivers and that they had criminal records were both matters of public information. At the *Milwaukee Journal,* James Rowen linked public records of drunk driving convictions with pilots' licenses for a story on aviation safety.[4] Without the computer, neither reporter would ever have made the connection. The quantitative change in the amount of time and effort to search and link such records has led to a qualitative shift in the things that journalists can discover.

Is this extension of journalism by other means still journalism, or is it something new and different that ought to be regulated? The regulators have their eye on us. Although the exercise of freedom of the press cannot be regulated directly, barriers can be placed between the journalist and the sources of information. A current theory of regulation that has yet to be fully tested holds that a public document is public only if it is on a piece of paper that can be read by a person. If the same information is in a medium that can be read by a machine, it is not, this theory holds, a public document—or at least not the same kind of public document and not subject to the same kinds of rules.

The theory is novel and not generally accepted. Lawyers and judges like to reason by analogy, and the analogy between a paper record and an electronic database is easy to understand. But some government agencies have begun to claim a substantive difference between the two kinds of records. When the *Boston Globe* asked for computerized Treasury Department records for a story on money laundering, the department coughed up the records, but laid down some ground rules. It asked for a detailed statement of the information sought and how it would be used. It demanded an agreement that the computer programs for analyzing the information would not produce the identities of individuals or businesses.

"In the event that a search of the database results in the inadvertent disclosure of personal identifiers," the Treasury regulations say, the user must "terminate the search until appropriate security measures can be implemented; relinquish all records of personal identifiers to Treasury officials; and make no further disclosure of the information."[5]

Democratic theory holds that the public's information ought to be available equally to all members of the public. That is fairly easy to do with paper records that anyone can walk in and inspect. But complicated computer records take special equipment and special skills that are not generally available to the ordinary citizen. The issue of who should pay the cost of access is still open. Some government agencies charge special fees for the use or copying of computerized public records, and these fees could easily be manipulated to create barriers to the freedom of information. Time, however, is on our side. Agencies are discovering the convenience of putting reports and raw data online to avoid the hassle of responding to endless requests for copies.

Retrieving information is easier when a reporter or an inquisitive citizen wants a specific piece of information and can describe it in some detail: a real estate transaction, a birth certificate, or a list of campaign contributors, for example. It is usually pretty clear that the government has a duty to provide the information and pay the expenses of providing it or charge a nominal copying fee. But should the government support a fishing expedition? Is merging two databases and browsing through them to see what turns up an activity that should be subject to the same rules of access? The Privacy Act of 1974, one of the last projects of the late Senator Sam Ervin, puts barriers in the way of government agencies that would like to swap and match data. A Reagan administration proposal to move the Bureau of the Census from the Commerce Department to the Treasury Department was defeated on the ground that the agency that controls income tax records should not also keep census records. On the other hand, a resourceful journalist can sometimes get government record keepers to provide active assistance in matching records. The *Milwaukee Journal*, for example, asked the Wisconsin Department of Transportation to match its computerized driving records against a list of licensed pilots supplied by the Federal Aviation Administration. The state officials obligingly supplied reporter James Rowen with the names of 302 Wisconsin airplane pilots who had been convicted of driving motor vehicles under the influence of alcohol. Seventeen of them were licensed to fly passenger airliners.[6]

Washington Post publisher Katharine Graham, shortly before her death in 2001, warned the Reporters Committee for Freedom of the Press of a possible overreaction by "well-meaning legislators" fearful of potential invasions of privacy made possible by the power of computers and the Internet.

"Federal and state officials are now considering whether to change the rules and deny public access to court documents that have always been open to the public—simply because they are now available in electronic form," she said.[7]

What future barriers are erected against such searches may very well depend on the self-imposed restraint of journalists who know how to deal with computerized public records. Identifying drunks who fly airliners or drive school buses serves a clear public purpose, and few are likely to argue that the right of privacy of the pilots or bus drivers overrides the welfare of the passengers they serve. But if journalists use the computer to reveal embarrassing private facts just to show off their technical virtuosity and without any clear public benefit, a regulatory backlash could result. As a minimum, journalists should impose on themselves the same moral standards and the same restraints that would be observed for information gathered by other means. If we are to argue that an electronic record has the same legal standing as a paper record, we should treat that record with at least the same sensitivity.

DEFINING PUBLIC OPINION

Precision journalism is at its best when it is sorting out the conflicts among special interest groups, measuring their support, and estimating their potential for having an effect. When it does this, it departs from the referendum model of public opinion, whose only virtue is that it is easy to understand.

By the referendum model, I mean a view of public opinion that holds that policy makers ought to be guided by whatever the majority thinks on any given issue. In the referendum model, every citizen's vote counts exactly the same.

In the real world, that is not so, not even for those few issues that are actually decided by referendums. Even in those cases, decisions are made by those who pay the cost—in time and energy consumed—of voting. Nothing in this country is decided by a representative sample of the public.

Why, then, do we go to so much trouble to acquire and interview a representative sample of the public? Because it is there, perhaps. And because we are intuitively comfortable with the fairness of the referendum, majority-decides model. George Gallup, the pioneer American pollster, is also partly to blame, because he promoted the habit of thinking of a poll as a continuous referendum by which majority will could be made known.[8]

But observers of American politics since Alexis de Tocqueville have known that pure majority rule is neither possible nor perhaps even desirable. Tocqueville worried that pure popular control would prevent the wisest and best from using their gifts for the public good. He welcomed the formation of interest groups as ways of concentrating the power of minorities to create "a necessary guarantee against the tyranny of the majority."[9]

As originally conceived during the social protest movements of the 1960s, precision journalism was a way to expand the tool kit of the reporter to make topics that were previously inaccessible, or only crudely accessible, subject to journalistic scrutiny. It was especially useful in giving a hearing to minority and dissident groups that were struggling for representation.

Representative government in the United States has always involved tension among competing factions, as James Madison, the fourth president and one of the authors of the Constitution of 1787, had foreseen.[10] But the referendum model is much too simple for the complexities of representative government in a large and conflict-ridden society. The majority wants conflicting things. The composition of the majority shifts from one issue to the next.[11] Some voters feel so strongly about single issues that they will yield on almost everything else to get their way on that one issue. Such trading is called logrolling, and it takes place quite visibly among elected representatives, but you can see its origins in the work of single-issue pressure groups. Like most modern democracies, we are governed by temporary coalitions. The process of forming those coalitions, always less formal and more difficult to follow than in European parliamentary democracies, is worth following, but it demands a special kind of public opinion polling, including a recognition that not all opinions are equal. We might serve democracy better by spending less effort finding out what the majority thinks and more in probing the attitudes of specialized subgroups to help them learn about one another.

ELECTIONS

People who vote are an interesting and deviant subset of the general population. Of late, they are usually a minority. Measuring their attitudes and behavior is especially relevant and especially challenging. This effort has been one of the most popular applications of precision journalism.

For many journalists, the effort to measure and even predict electoral behavior has been motivated by simple competitiveness. The most interesting fact about an election is who wins. If you can find out ahead of time, it is news by definition. The *Literary Digest* demonstrated the news value of election predictions in a series of surveys from 1916 through 1936. At just the moment that their technology failed, George Gallup demonstrated that it could be perfected. He performed a polling hat trick. Not only did he predict that Franklin Roosevelt would win the 1936 election in a landslide, he also predicted that the *Literary Digest* poll would show the opposite. He even had an accurate estimate of the percentage that the *Digest* poll would give Alf Landon. (He did it by checking a small sample from the same lists of telephone and automobile users that the *Digest* used to recruit its two million respondents.) That established Gallup's reputation and made polling credible. Since then, the technology has improved to the point where a national poll is considered a failure if it misses the election outcome by more than two percentage points. In the 1988 presidential election, none did.[12]

When I was a Washington correspondent in the 1960s, poll watchers focused chiefly on the two nationally syndicated newspaper polls, those of George Gallup and of Louis Harris. Interviewers talked to citizens in person in their homes and mailed the results to the home office, and the results of each poll were analyzed and reported in leisurely fashion over the course of several weeks.

Competition, technology, and a faster-paced presidential selection process changed that. Now there are many national polling organizations in the field, with a new poll reported every day in the final weeks of the campaign. Neither the public nor the press corps has adjusted comfortably to this density of polling data. Because the presidential selection process has itself been changing, some associated the undesirable and worrisome aspects of change with the polls and began to blame the polls.

A LIST OF COMPLAINTS

There have been five basic complaints about election polls:

1. *There are too many polls.* "Every newspaper and television station thinks it has to have its own poll," complained columnist Jack Germond. "So we keep quantifying the obvious."[13] That, at least, is a self-limiting problem. Polls are produced in response to a free-market demand for information. When they merely restate the obvious, demand will decline.

2. *The polls are not accurate enough.* This complaint is typically heard in the early part of a presidential campaign, when different polls published

within a few days of one another give seemingly different results. Surely, it is assumed, they could not all be accurate.

Much of this problem, if not all, is due to the fact that polling organizations reserve their best and most expensive methodology for their later measurements, the ones that will be compared to the election results to provide an evaluation of the poll. Early polls leave more room for error for a variety of methodological reasons, including smaller samples and less rigorous methods for identifying likely voters. In a nation where only about half the voting-age population participates in a presidential election, identifying those who will vote is both important and difficult.

Differences among polls are also exaggerated by the journalistic convention of reporting the point spread between two candidates, rather than the size of the leader's majority. For example, back in 1988, the final Gallup poll in the presidential election reported a twelve-point lead for George Bush, while the final Harris survey gave Bush a four-point lead. Surely, it seemed, one poll or both had to be seriously in error. They were not. Gallup gave Bush 56 percent of the two-party vote, and Harris gave him 52. Bush actually got 54 percent, so both polls were accurate to 2 percentage points, well within normal sampling error. The other national polls that reported in the week of the election were even closer.

Another complaint is related to the one of inaccuracy:

3. *The polls are often wrongly interpreted.* This, too, seems to be a self-solving problem. Three decades ago, I wrote an article on misinterpretations of polls by journalists for *Columbia Journalism Review,* and a rereading shows that the media have made considerable progress in understanding and interpreting election polls.[14] Some common assumptions then, that a poll in one city or county is generalizable to the entire nation, or that a poll in August predicts voter decisions in November, are no longer so widely held. Errors are still made today, but they are more subtle: for example, the failure to distinguish between a poll of voting age adults and one of likely voters. The proliferation of polls will, of course, force journalists to become more proficient at interpreting them. The information marketplace will demand it. But that will only aggravate the next complaint on the list:

4. *Polls are too accurate.* The logic behind this complaint is that polls were relatively harmless when they were wrong much of the time, because nobody took them seriously. But when they are right, the public believes them and responds to them, and this possibly affects voting behavior. The logic parallels that of seventeenth-century English libel law, where it was held that the greater the truth in a defamatory statement, the greater the tort.

This complaint is related to the one that is probably discussed the most:

5. *The polls affect the outcome of the election.* Until recently, the polling fraternity tended to dismiss polling effects on the election process itself as either nonexistent or negligible.[15] As recently as 1980, Albert E. Gollin was

able to write that such concerns "have faded away for lack of supporting evidence."[16] No more. As research has become more sophisticated, that position has become difficult to sustain, particularly as researchers look at in-
direct effects through political contributors, campaign volunteers, and
endorsers.[17] Early polls are a special problem. Such polls are name-recognition tests rather than predictors of who will win. Unsophisticated consumers of polling data do not always recognize this limitation, and that can
make it difficult for a little-known challenger to attract the backing needed
to mount a serious challenge against a well-known incumbent. Potential
backers, mistaking the name-recognition data for an election prediction, are
frightened off. That error contributed to the defeat of Hubert H. Humphrey
by Richard M. Nixon in 1968. Humphrey lagged in the early polls and failed
to get the financial backing that he needed to get an advance commitment
of late-campaign television time. Because that election was so close, a late
media push could have made the difference.

Campaign contributors still make that kind of mistake. "A poll of 47 percent to 30 percent looks good for the incumbent and makes it hard for the
challenger to raise money," says pollster Gordon S. Black. "In truth, we
know from research that an incumbent with less than 50 percent of the vote
is in deep trouble."[18] The democratic solution, of course, is not to curtail
the polls but to teach those who use them to make decisions to do so rationally.

Where direct effects on voters are concerned, the effects are often so
slight as to lack statistical significance, but that does not mean they lack
substantive importance. In a close election, there is no such thing as a negligible effect. The presidential elections of 1960, 1968, and 2000 could
have been tipped the other way by any number of normally inconsequential
factors.

The complaint of election effects begs the question of whether such effects are good or bad for democracy. Even the pollsters trying to defend
themselves often start with the assumption that such effects are bad. But
another argument needs to be considered. In today's media-driven elections, the information provided by polls—from the primary polls to the early
calls on election night—may actually help the process.

That this sounds like a radical notion is a measure of how much we have
forgotten the roots of democratic theory.

The sanctity of the ballot has an emotional, almost mystical, quality in the
United States, as though democracy were a religion rather than a practical
way of letting the people govern. We are a nation of immigrants, and for
those who came from nondemocratic or less democratic countries, the right
to vote symbolizes the difference between tyranny and popular control. We
tend to forget that the secret ballot is an import from Australia and a fairly
recent development in our history, and that its original purpose was not to

protect the privacy of the citizen but to make it more difficult for corrupt politicians to bribe him. A citizen whose vote is unknown is less likely to be paid for voting a certain way, because he has no way of proving that he carried out his side of the contract. The earliest postcolonial elections in the United States were carried out in full public view. In Virginia, for example, the voter entered the courtroom, stood before the sheriff, and announced his vote. The candidates were even present to thank him personally in some cases. If not, their representatives were there to record the vote.[19]

Voting in the New England town meeting, the archetypal model of democracy in America, was done in full public view. And voting on the record is standard practice in legislative bodies. Tactical voting, where one withholds one's vote until one sees how other members are voting and makes a decision based on that information, is an accepted practice in legislative bodies, and it makes perfect sense.

THE BUILDING OF CONSENSUS

A representative democracy in a large and complex nation faces the problem of forming a working majority from many small and diverse segments of interests. There are never enough resources for everyone to get everything he or she wants. The problem of pulling together enough of the conflicting goals to make the best and most coherent policy is one that has haunted philosophers from the dawn of recorded human thought. Economists call it optimization. Moral philosophers who worry about it are called utilitarians. Political scientists call it consensus formation. In every field where the problem is considered, information is crucial to a solution. This need for information is especially important in politics, where the main tool of consensus formation is coalition building. To build a coalition, you have to know what each group wants and how badly the group wants it—in other words, what the group will give up to get it.

In European parliamentary democracies the process of coalition building comes mainly after the election, as members of specialized parties representing minorities of various sizes strike their bargains with one another to form a government. In the United States, with its two-party, winner-take-all system, the coalition building has to take place before the election. This structural difference accounts at least in part for the historically lighter voting participation in the United States than in Europe. If the two major political parties have done their job properly, the process of consensus formation will have brought them so close together by election time that the voters will be relatively indifferent to the final choice.

But the major parties in America have not been doing that job as deftly as in the past. The brokering that took place at national party nominating conventions, through a series of ballots edging ever closer to a working majority, was a fairly efficient method of coalition building. But the last multiballot convention was in 1952, when the Democrats nominated Adlai Stevenson on the third try. The flow of information through the mass media has become so efficient that all the players know who has what bargaining chips and what the outcome will be before they arrive in the convention city.

The role of the media became even greater after the party reforms of 1970 took power away from the party professionals and gave it to the rank and file. This change was effected mainly through rules that encouraged the states to select their delegates through primary elections. One effect of this so-called reform was that candidate selection fell to nonprofessionals who were more interested in promoting their narrow ideological goals than in finding a candidate who could capture the broad center of the spectrum, where the likelihood of winning was greatest. George McGovern (who headed the commission that wrote the new rules for the Democratic party) in 1972 and George W. Bush in 2000 were examples of the new noncentrist candidates.

Coalition building was never as easy in the American system as it is in parliamentary systems, and the weakening of the political parties has made it more difficult still. And it places a heavy burden on the mass media of communication, which must now provide rank-and-file voters with information that previously only the party professionals needed. Isn't it reasonable to suppose that giving the voters accurate information about each other, about the relative voting strength and the preferences of different groups in the electorate, might help, not hurt?

TACTICAL VOTING

Take the case of the early primaries, for example. Assume that you are a Democrat, and your first choice is Ralph Nader, your second choice is Bill Bradley, and your least favored choice is Al Gore. You need poll information to make a rational choice. If the polls show that Gore is ahead, that Bradley has a chance of beating him, and Nader is dead last in a field of six, your vote will count the most if you go for your second choice. Why should you not have the benefit of that information?

Here is another kind of example. In 1980, the candidates were Ronald Reagan, Jimmy Carter, and a dissident moderate, break-away Republican, John Anderson. A centrist voter might prefer Carter, as long as he seemed to have a chance of winning. Given information that Carter would lose, this voter might want to cast a ballot for Anderson to protest the capture of the Republican Party by the right-wing Reaganites.

Consider yet another possibility. The American system works most efficiently when the president and Congress are in the hands of the same party. A rational voter who was aware of this fact, and considered it important, might reasonably use polling information about the probable winner of the presidency to decide how to vote for a congressional candidate.

Finally, there is the matter of turnout. A voter can make rational use of information about whether or not an election will be close to decide whether or not the possibility of affecting the outcome is enough to justify the effort to vote. Not everyone wants to be rational about this. My California cousins express resentment when the networks tell them the election is over before they have had a chance to vote. They say it makes them feel powerless. I, on the other hand, think they should be grateful because they have more information on which to act than do I, who must vote blindly from the East Coast. Some day, I tell them, there will be an election so close that the network anchor will look them in the eye and tell them that the outcome depends on the voters on the western seaboard. My western cousins can then go charging out of their hot tubs and proceed to the polls feeling powerful indeed.[20]

Can polls really be used to provide tactical guidance to voters in this way, or is this just empty theory? Let's look at the extreme case, early calls by the networks on election night. The best opportunity for studying the results comes in the extreme cases because they leave less room for subtlety. The extreme case is an early call of a landslide in an election that was expected to be close. And the best example is the 1980 election, when President Jimmy Carter was defending his office against challenger Ronald Reagan. Using exit poll and sample precinct data, NBC announced shortly after 8 p.m. that Reagan had won. President Carter promptly conceded, even though polls in many states, from New York to California, were still open.

Among the most thorough studies of the effects of that early call on voter behavior were investigations by political scientists. John E. Jackson of the University of Michigan[21] used data from panel surveys, and Michael X. Delli Carpini of Rutgers University[22] looked at aggregate voting data at the congressional district level. Both found evidence that participation declined among voters potentially affected by the knowledge that Carter had conceded. In other words, the response was rational.

In addition, Delli Carpini found intriguing evidence that the voters were using the information rationally along the more subtle lines that I have just mentioned. In districts where polls were open after NBC's call, there was a decline in the Democratic vote and a 2 percent surge in the vote for John Anderson. And there was nearly a 5-percent swing toward the Republican candidates for Congress. Is there a measurable segment of voters really sophisticated enough to cast a protest vote for Anderson when they know that Carter will lose—or to vote for a Republican congressman because they expect a Republican to be in the White House? The Republican congressional boost, Delli Carpini found, came from the districts with higher levels of income and education—exactly from the people whom one would expect to make such calculations. Jackson's individual-level data contained a consistent, though statistically insignificant, relationship: Republicans were more likely to be deterred from voting by hearing about the early call or Carter's concessions than were Democrats. Republicans tend to be higher in socioeconomic status than Democrats.

WHEN FORECASTS ARE WRONG

All of these benefits are moot, of course, if the early calls are wrong, as they were in 2000 when the outcome of the presidential election turned on the vote in Florida. But exit polls were not to blame for that fiasco. Election night projections start with exit polls in states where the vote is not close, then gradually shift to reliance on models built from selected precincts. The Florida model in 2000 had several problems, not the least of which was a defective memory card from Precinct 216 in Volusia County. Precinct results were supposed to be sent to county headquarters by modem, but a communications glitch forced a worker to carry the memory card by hand. Somewhere along the way, the card got corrupted, and when it was fed into the main computer it registered a negative 16,022 votes for Al Gore and a positive 2,813 votes for George W. Bush. This from a precinct where only 412 had voted![23] That was enough to tip the statewide model to a strong forecast for Bush. By the time the error was detected and fixed, the networks had announced a Bush victory and Gore had prematurely conceded. In fact, the statewide vote was a virtual tie, and it took the Supreme Court of the United States to eventually decide that Bush was the winner.

It is hard to argue for the rational use of election data by voters if the media can't get it right. Some diversity in data sources would help. But to save money, the major news organizations pool their data collection efforts so that if one gets it wrong, they all get it wrong. The lone exception in 2000 was the Associated Press, which relied on its own network of reporters and avoided the premature Bush call.

Even the most accurate election forecasts are resented by politicians, who believe they are damaged by them. Candidates for state and local office, hoping for a coattail effect or a high turnout, can justly say that early release of results is harmful to them. But these effects are situation-dependent. They are not amenable to being turned into ideological issues. And complaints tend to ignore the question of whether the harm is unjust. Nothing in democratic theory says that elections should be decided by voters who care so little about the outcome that they need some external motivation to get to the polls.

On the whole, a case can be made that the rational use of information about what other voters are doing or may do helps the democratic process. Voters have always had this kind of information to act on. What is new is that polling makes the information less often wrong. When the early forecasts show an election to be close, they can stimulate turnout. Richard Nixon had been expected to beat Hubert Humphrey in a landslide in 1968, but the election turned out to be extremely close. If good early projections had been in place then, turnout could have gotten a boost from voters motivated by the knowledge that they had an extraordinary opportunity to make a difference.

This rational-voter theory does not take care of all the problems. There may still be voters who will use the information irrationally. But that's not against the law in a democracy. No doubt there were voters who opposed Michael Dukakis because of his Greek ancestry or who voted against George W. Bush because he came from Texas. I have not heard anyone argue that information about a candidate's origins should be suppressed because voters might use it irrationally or unfairly. A democracy that tries to protect its voters from information that they might use irrationally ceases to be a democracy. The voting decision cannot be forced into a sterile, information-free environment, nor should it be.[24]

UNEASINESS IN THE MEDIA

The mass media organizations that sponsor the polls are uneasy in their new role, but they have no choice except to fulfill it, just as the rank-and-file voters must accept new and heavier responsibility. When the *Miami Herald* reported the details of Gary Hart's sexual escapades, it was responding to this new need. Voters were given a view of a candidate that in a previous era would have been confined to the smoke-filled rooms where the power brokers negotiated. Because the primary election system has shifted the decision out of those rooms and placed it directly in the hands of the voters, the media have a greatly increased duty to give those voters the information with which to exercise that power.

The "bandwagon effect" is a term that originally was applied to delegates in a national nominating convention, where the goal of a delegate was to get on the winning side in time to make a difference and place the winner under some obligation to the delegate. It is a useful phenomenon, helpful in coalition building, and no less useful when the arena becomes the nation at large instead of the convention hall. And yet the media persist in feeling guilty about contributing to a bandwagon effect, even when the contribution is in the form of accurate information.

This guilt is especially intense where quantitative data are involved. The election process demands information, and the media cannot and should not avoid supplying information that has the potential to affect the outcome. But when the information is about the voters themselves, a certain circularity is introduced into the process that makes media people uneasy. The additional fact that polling involves numbers gives it some special mystique, making it seem more like a "pseudo-event" than would be the case if the investigation had been initiated by a news medium using purely qualitative methods.[25] Moreover, the use of numbers and scientific method gives polling information more credibility than information from conventional reporting modes. This enhanced credibility, paradoxically, increases the cost to society when the information is wrong. And so, in what amounts to intellectual self-mutilation, some organizations go out of their way to cloak their numbers in ambiguity. They do this by ignoring pollsters' attempts to produce a number that can be compared directly with the election outcome (and thereby sacrificing the one direct test of the poll's validity) and by clinging to undecided and leaning voters as if their existence denoted a major uncertainty over the outcome.

When the *New York Times* reported the final Gallup poll result in November of 1988, for example, it deleted the Gallup Organization's basic prediction of a Bush win with 56 percent of the two-party vote and reported only the less refined numbers, suppressing Gallup's allocation of the undecided portion.[26] The *Times* evidently did not think its readers were up to handling that knowledge. *USA Today* used Gordon Black's straightforward prediction of 55 percent for Bush in a page-one graphic display, but failed to mention it in the accompanying story, which emphasized leaners and the undecided.[27] The three network polls attempted no allocation of the undecided. Anyone wanting to compare their polls to the election outcome had to do so after the fact by dropping the undecided from the percentage base. And some newspapers have even become leery of incorporating leaners into their final figures. (Leaners, as you will recall from the previous chapter, are persons who give a choice only when asked a follow-up question—for example, "As of today, which way are you leaning?") One explanation of this bizarre behavior is that the media want to avoid the obvious validity test and leave the leaners and undecided voters positioned as a cover for their polls' possible mistakes. A more subtle explanation is also plausible: The complaints against polls have made the media managers feel guilty about their own precision, and so they seek to conceal that precision.

This guilt may in turn be based on the violation of one of journalism's norms: that the media should observe and report with detachment and not participate. Publishing polls may seem too dangerously close to participation. This stance bespeaks a certain ignorance of how democracy works in the United States. Every decision on what to print and what not to print is, after all, a form of participation.

Democracy was never meant to operate in a sterile, information-free environment. And yet one media pollster wrote in an article published just after the November 1988 election that consensus formation is "the real danger in media polling."[28] This view is widely held, and it shows how poorly some of us Americans appreciate the subtleties of our own system and the theory behind it. Consensus formation is the aim of the election process. If precision journalism, in the form of preelection and exit polls, helps the electorate to communicate with itself and bring about consensus, then there is hope for the brave new world of direct democracy that mass communication technology is trying to bring us. Precision journalism is part of that technology.

If precision journalism can wholeheartedly embrace the openness of scientific method, its potential dangers and abuses will be self-correcting. A journalism based on scientific method leaves a trail where error can be detected and truth verified. Nowhere is that as true as in the case of election polls. The public will trust polls as much as they deserve to be trusted, no more and no less. The comparison of polls with election results is a wonderful way for the public to judge, and journalists should not create barriers to inhibit or cloud that judgment. If the accuracy of other forms of journalism could be put to such a test, the marketplace of ideas would reward the purveyors of truth relentlessly and efficiently. Journalists should welcome the chance to be put to such a test.

NOTES

1. Roger Burlingame, *March of the Iron Men* (New York: Grosset & Dunlap, 1938), 239.

2. Philip Meyer, *Precision Journalism* (Bloomington: Indiana University Press, 1973), 15.

3. Elliot G. Jaspin and Maria Miro Johnson, "R.I., System Fails to Fully Check Driving Records of Bus Applicants," *Providence Sunday Journal*, March 1, 1987, 1.

4. James Rowen, "3% of Pilots Have Record of Driving while Drunk," *Milwaukee Journal*, February 12, 1989, 1.

5. Cory Dean, "Computer Use for News Raises Legal Questions," *New York Times*, September 29, 1986, A12.

6. Rowen, "3% of Pilots Have Record of Driving while Drunk."

7. Katharine Graham, speech on court records and privacy concerns, on the occasion of her Lifetime Achievement Award from the Reporters Committee for Freedom of the Press, New York, N.Y., May 22, 2001.

8. George Gallup, *The Sophisticated Poll Watcher's Guide* (Princeton, N.J.: Princeton Opinion Press, 1972).

9. Alexis de Tocqueville, *Democracy in America* (New York: Schocken Books, 1961), 192. (Originally published 1835.)

10. James Madison, Federalist No. 10, *The Federalist* (New York: Putnam, 1888).

11. For an excellent discussion of the difficulties of the majoritarian model, see James M. Buchanan and Gordon Tullock, *The Calculus of Consent: Logical Foundations of Constitutional Democracy* (Ann Arbor: University of Michigan Press, 1962).

12. George Bush won the election with 54 percent of the two-party vote. The percentages given him by the various polls (based on decided voters in the network polls, plus allocated undecided voters in the rest) were: *USA Today* (Gordon Black) 55; CBS, 55; ABC, 55; NBC, 53; Harris, 52; Gallup, 56.

13. Quoted in Michael Traugott, "Marketing the Presidency: Is There a Tyranny of Media Polls?" *Gannett Center Journal* (Fall 1988): 60.

14. Philip Meyer, "Truth in Polling," *Columbia Journalism Review* (Summer 1968).

15. See, for example, the chapter on bandwagon effects in Gallup's 1972 book *The Sophisticated Poll Watcher's Guide.*

16. Albert E. Gollin, "Exploring the Liaison between Polling and the Press," *Public Opinion Quarterly* 44, no. 4 (Winter 1980): 445–61.

17. Richard L. Henshel and William Johnston, "The Emergence of Bandwagon Effects: A Theory," *Sociological Quarterly* 28, no. 4 (1987): 493–511.

18. Gordon S. Black, personal communication, January 16, 1989.

19. Neil Spitzer, "The First Election," *The Atlantic* (November 1988): 20.

20. There are such voters. My cousin Marillyn Cozine of Danville, California, advises me that she cast a tactical vote for John Anderson in 1980 on the basis of the network projections.

21. John E. Jackson, "Election Night Reporting and Voter Turnout," *American Journal of Political Science* 27 (1983): 615–35.

22. Michael X. Delli Carpini, "Scooping the Voters? The Consequences of the Networks' Early Call of the 1980 Presidential Race," *Journal of Politics* 7 (February/March 1984): 48–50.

23. Philip Meyer, "Glitch Led to 'Bush Wins' Call," *USA Today,* November 29, 2000, 15A.

24. For an excellent exposition of this argument in a Spanish context, see Jose Ignacio Wert, "Uses and Misuses of Survey Polls in the Media," paper presented at the IAMCR-WAPOR joint session on Mass Media and Public Opinion, Barcelona, July 1988.

25. Identification of the poll as pseudo-event was popularized by Daniel Boorstin in 1961, when both polls and their use by news media were less sophisticated than they are today. For a useful discussion of the concept, see Gollin, "Exploring the Liaison between Polling and the Press," 449.

26. "Bush and Dukakis Travel to West for Final Jousts of Campaign," *New York Times,* November 7, 1988, B14.

27. *USA Today,* November 7, 1988, 1. The editor who supervised production of the graphic and the editor who had final review of the story had different views on what should be reported.

28. Michael Traugott, "Marketing the Presidency," 64.

Appendix: Three Things to Measure with Census Data

ETHNIC DIVERSITY

When the first results of the 1990 census were released, Shawn McIntosh, who was then with *USA Today*, and I realized that the nation's increasing diversity was a good story. Because a national newspaper has a lot of geography to cover, we needed a way to capture the concept of racial and ethnic diversity in a single number.

We did it with a simple probability-based index.[1] A decade later, the 2000 census complicated matters by creating multiracial categories and dividing the Asian/Pacific Islander category into two. Paul Overberg, who had by then replaced McIntosh on the census story at *USA Today*, worked with me to adapt the old index to the new system. It turned out to be easier than we expected.

To explain it, let's start with the simpler 1990 census. It had two categories of national ethnicity, Hispanic and non-Hispanic, and four categories of race: white, black, Native American, and Asian or Pacific Islander. (Since 1970, the census has treated Hispanic status as a separate dimension from race. Thus Hispanics can be classified into any of the racial categories.)

The diversity index is simply the probability that two persons drawn at random from a given population will differ on at least one category of race or ethnicity. As is the case with any probability, it can be expressed as either a decimal or a percentage.

In all of the following calculations, the proportions used are based on the population that listed one of the specific categories. "Other" is dropped from the base.

247

Step 1: Calculate the probability that the two persons will be members of the same racial group:

$$P_R = (A^2 + B^2 + C^2 + D^2)$$

where *A, B, C,* and *D* are the proportions in the population of whites, blacks, Native Americans, and Asians or Pacific Islanders. For example, if a population is .5 white, the probability of choosing two whites at random is .25. Probabilities of getting a like pair of each of the four possible groups are added.

Step 2: Calculate the probability that two persons chosen from a population at random will be either both Hispanic or both non-Hispanic:

$$P_H = (H^2 + N^2)$$

Where *H* is proportion Hispanic and *N* is the non-Hispanic proportion.

Step 3: Calculate the probability that your two randomly chosen persons are the same in both race and Hispanic/non-Hispanic status.

$$P_R * P_H$$

We multiplied in this case because the two dimensions, race and ethnicity, are independent events. It's an "or" question, not an "and" question as in Step 2.

Step 4: Subtract the result from 1.

$$1 - (P_R * P_H)$$

The result is the probability that the two persons are different on at least one of the two dimensions.

Adaptation for the 2000 Census

The most important step for the 2000 census is to add a term recognizing the splitting of the Asian-Pacific Islander category into two: Asians and Native Hawaiian/Other Pacific. We'll let *D* stand for Asians and *E* for the Native Hawaiians and other Pacific Islanders.

So, putting it all together to create the formula for 2000, we have:

$$DI = 1 - ((A^2 + B^2 + C^2 + D^2 + E^2) * (H^2 + N^2))$$

What about the multiracial people? We leave them in the percentage base for calculating inputs to the equation, but do not include them in the equation. By default, that leaves them representing diversity. The logic behind this decision is that each person in a multiracial pair has at least one racial characteristic that is different from at least one characteristic in the other. Because both their number and the number of Hawaiians and Pacific Islanders is small, the effect of the changes is very small, and comparisons with earlier censuses (1970 through 1990) are good approximations. If you are dealing with a population with an unusually large proportion of Asians and Hawaiians/Pacific Islanders, you can collapse them into a single category for better comparison with previous censuses.

INCOME INEQUALITY

One social indicator worth tracking is the inequality of income. It can be done for small areas with numbers from the decennial census or for the United States as a whole with the Current Population Survey.

News media usually report on income inequality by comparing quintiles: the proportion of income received by the wealthiest fifth against that received by the poorest fifth. That method is intuitive enough, but it loses information in the middle three categories. The Gini coefficient captures it all in one number.

It is based on the following model:

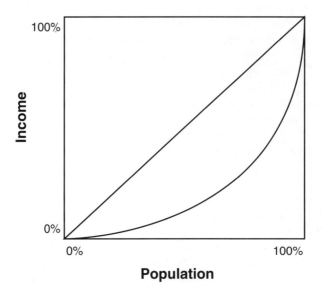

The income and population scales are cumulative. The horizontal axis is the cumulative percentage of population, and the vertical axis is the cumulative percentage of income.

The straight diagonal line is the *line of equality*. It is called that because it represents a hypothetical situation where 10 percent of the population gets 10 percent of the income and so on. If that were true, the Gini coefficient would be zero.

The curve shows what really happens. At the beginning, income accumulates at a slower rate than population and at a faster rate than population at the end. The more the curve sags below the straight line, the greater the inequality. If it sagged all the way to the bottom and right borders of the graph, it would mean that one person had all the income, and Gini would equal 1.

Gini's coefficient simply calculates the area between the diagonal and the curve as a proportion of the area of the half square. The formula for calculating it takes into account the fact that income data are reported in categories: For census data, it makes more sense to use households as the income unit, rather than the individual.

$$\text{Gini} = 1 - \text{SUM} (X_i - X_j) * (Y_i + Y_j)$$

where X is the cumulative proportion of households, Y is the cumulative proportion of income, i is a given income category, and j is the preceding income category. Figuring out the width of the top category takes some estimation.[2]

Try this on the back of an old envelope; you will see that it approximates the area under the curve if you build a series of rectangles under it, one for each income category, and add up their areas. The more fine-grained your income categories, the more accurate it will be.

A spreadsheet works much better than pencil and paper, and the steps have been spelled out for you by J. J. Thompson in "A Tool for Measuring Income Inequality," *Nieman Reports* (Spring 1997).

A number like the Gini makes more sense with a historical or geographic comparison, so here are a few. The Gini in the United States hit an all-time low in 1968 (when Lyndon Johnson was president) of .388. It has been moving upward ever since (with a few zigs and zags), and in 1998 it stood at .456.

Contrast that with figures listed by the World Bank for countries with different histories and forms of government. Income inequality tends to be greater in South America—for example, Brazil with .601 (1995) or Chile at .565 (1994).[3]

Income inequality is much less in some countries with which we often compare ourselves, like Sweden with .250 (1992) or Canada with .315 (1994). Because extreme income inequality is often associated with political instability, the number is worth following, no matter what country you are in.

SEGREGATION

Segregation is a relative term, and so you have to establish a basis of comparison. One logical base is the larger population within which the unit being evaluated is nested: a school within a county, for example. That's the logic behind the Dissimilarity Index, often used by sociologists to produce a single number that measures the amount of segregation in a population.

It yields a number between 0 and 1 that represents the proportion of all students of either race who would have to change schools in order for each school to have the same racial mix as the district as a whole. In other words, the higher the number, the greater the segregation.

The formula:[4]

$$D = S \, t_i |\, p_i - P\,| / 2TP \, (1 - P)$$

t is the number of students in the individual school.
p is the percentage white in the same school.
P is the percentage white in the entire district.
T is the total school population in the district.

The S and the subscripts $(_i)$ mean that the calculation has to be done for each school and the results summed.

The vertical bars $|.|$ mean that the difference inside them is absolute (no negative values allowed).

Here is a hypothetical example of a district of 1,800 pupils in four schools:

School	White	Black	Total
A	300	100	400
B	250	250	500
C	100	300	400
D	250	250	500
Total	900	900	1,800

The easiest way to deal with the formula is to create a spreadsheet with each school in its own row. The sum in the lower right-hand corner yields the numerator of the formula.

School	Size (t)	School % White (p)	District % White (P)	|p − P|	t(p − P)
A	400	.75	.50	.25	100
B	500	.50	.50	.00	0
C	400	.25	.50	.25	100
D	500	.50	.50	.00	0
					Sum: 200

The denominator is straightforward. In this example:

$$2TP\ (1 - P) = 2\ *\ 1800\ *\ .5\ *\ (1 - .5) = 900$$

And so $D = 200\ /\ 900 = .222$

To verify this, go back to the previous table and figure out who has to move to make all the schools 50-50 black and white. It can be done by moving 200 white students from A to C (or 200 black students from C to A).

Either way, it is 22.2 percent of one race or the other that would have to move to give all schools the same racial balance as the district as a whole.

Another way to interpret D is as the weighted mean deviation of every school's white proportion from the overall white proportion expressed as a fraction of its theoretical maximum.

The use of white proportions in these calculations is arbitrary. Black proportions would work just as well. The formula is limited to the two-category case. If you have more races, you'll need to collapse them into two categories—for example, Asian and non-Asian.

Spreadsheet tip: For $|p - P|$ with Excel, use the ABS( ) function. Put the subtraction inside the parenthesis, and you'll get no minus sign.

NOTES

1. We reported our efforts in "The *USA Today* Index of Ethnic Diversity," *International Journal of Public Opinion Research* (Spring 1992).

2. My source is J. J. Thompson, *The Journalist and the Gini Coefficient: A Statistical Approach to Covering Income Inequality.* M.A. thesis, University of North Carolina at Chapel Hill, 1995. She credits the estimation formula for grouped data to Mike Fuller, *Economic Letters* 3 (1989), 189.

3. These figures were found at www.worldbank.org.

4. David R. James and Karl E. Taeuber, "Measures of Segregation" in Nancy Tuma, ed., *Sociological Methodology 1985*, published by Jossey-Bass.

Index

About the Author

Philip Meyer grew up in Clay Center, Kansas, and was a newspaper reporter in Topeka, Miami, and Washington, D.C., before joining the faculty at the University of North Carolina at Chapel Hill. He holds the Knight Chair in Journalism and pursues research on news media and social responsibility.